Managing the Factory

Warwick Studies in Industrial Relations
General Editors: G. S. Bain, R. Hyman and K. Sisson

Also available in this series

Dismissed: A Study of Unfair Dismissal and the Industrial Tribunal System
Linda Dickens, Michael Jones, Brian Weekes and Moira Hart

Consent and Efficiency
Eric Batstone, Anthony Ferner and Michael Terry

Unions on the Board
Eric Batstone, Anthony Ferner and Michael Terry

The Changing Contours of British Industrial Relations
William Brown (ed.)

Profiles of Union Growth
George Sayers Bain and Robert Price

The Social Organization of Strikes
Eric Batstone, Ian Boraston and Stephen Frenkel

Shop Stewards in Action
Eric Batstone, Ian Boraston and Stephen Frenkel

Trade Unionism under Collective Bargaining
Hugh Armstrong Clegg

Conflict at Work
P. K. Edwards

Managing the Factory

A Survey of General Managers

P. K. Edwards

Basil Blackwell

First published 1987

Basil Blackwell Ltd
108 Cowley Road, Oxford, OX4 1JF, UK

Basil Blackwell Inc,
432 Park Avenue South, Suite 1503
New York, NY 10016, USA

British Library Cataloguing in Publication Data
Edwards, P. K.
   Managing the factory: management organisation, labour relations and productivity in large manufacturing establishments. — (Warwick studies in industrial relations)
   1. Factory management——Great Britain
   I. Title II. Series
   658.5'00941   TS155

   ISBN 0-631-15599-6

Library of Congress Cataloging-in-Publication Data

Edwards, P. K. (Paul K.)
   Managing the factor.

   (Warwick series in industrial relations)
   Bibliography: p.
   Includes index.
   1. Supervisors, Industrial——Great Britain.
2. Industrial relations——Great Britain. I. Title.
II. Series.
TS155.4.E39 1987   670'.68   86–32049
ISBN 0–631–15599–6

Typeset in 10 on 11½ pt Times
by Photo·graphics, Honiton, Devon
Printed in Great Britain

Contents

Glossary of Terms and Conventions

Company	In divisionalized firms (q.v.), the subsidiary firm, operating company, division, or other level between the establishment and the ultimate owning body. In non-divisionalized firms, the top level of the organization.
Corporation/corporate level	Highest level of a divisionalized firm (q.v.) as distinct from the immediate operating company.
Division/divisionalized firm	A firm with separate operating divisions, each of which may have a considerable degree of autonomy and may even be a publicly quoted company in its own right. Different from a multi-plant firm without any internal differentiation between operating units.
Factory manager	Manager at the top of the organizational hierarchy on each site. In single-establishment enterprises, will be the managing director or chief executive. In multi-plant firms, will have a title such as factory manager, general manager, or plant director.
Conventions in tables	0 = zero, i.e. category applies but there were no answers in it. Blank = category not applicable. (...) = less than 0.5 per cent but not zero.

Numbers in a category are the result of weighting, and are rounded to the nearest whole number. Weighted $N = 235$, unweighted $N = 229$.

List of Tables

x   *List of Tables*

Editors' Foreword

The University of Warwick is the major centre in Britain for the study
of industrial relations. Its first undergraduates were admitted in 1965.
The teaching of industrial relations began a year later in the School of
Industrial and Business Studies, which now has one of the country's
largest graduate programmes in the subject. Warwick became a national
centre for research in industrial relations in 1970 when the Social
Science Research Council (now the Economic and Social Research
Council) located its industrial Relations Research Unit at the Univer-
sity. In 1984 the Unit was reconstituted as an ESRC Designated
Research Centre within the School of Industrial and Business Studies.

The series Warwick Studies in Industrial Relations was launched in
1972 as the main vehicle for the publication of the results of the Unit's
research projects. It is also intended to publish the research findings
of staff teaching industrial relations in the University as well as the work
of graduate students. The first six titles were published by Heinemann
Educational Books of London; subsequent volumes have been published by Basil Blackwell of Oxford.

This book reports the results of a survey of manufacturing plants
that was carried out in 1984. It builds on earlier survey work conducted
by the Unit, notably that reported in a previous volume in this series,
The Changing Contours of British Industrial Relations, edited by William Brown. That survey, like several others, focused on the manager
responsible for personnel and industrial relations in each plant. The
present study goes further by looking at 'factory managers', that is the
managers with overall responsibility for the operation of manufacturing
sites. It is the first survey of a representative sample of this stratum of
management. What do these managers think about labour relations,

how important are personnel considerations in their decision-making
and what changes have they been making recently? The book provides
detailed and sometimes surprising answers to these questions. But
it does not treat labour relations in isolation from other aspects of
management. Thus it looks closely at the managers' careers and at their
attitudes to the managerial task and considers the links between the
individual plants and the firms owning them. It also assesses the links
between many aspects of firms' operations and productivity. It con-
cludes by arguing that the role of factory managers, which has always
been considerable, is likely to increase if current policies of decentralization continue.

   The book thus forms part of the Unit's programme of research that
relates labour relations to other aspects of management. Its detailed
picture of a hitherto neglected group will be of interest not only to
students of industrial relations but also to specialists in management
studies as well as to managers and their companies.

George Bain
Richard Hyman
Keith Sisson

Preface

Conducting a survey involves the co-operation of a large number of people even though only one or two names may appear on the title page of a book. The idea of the present survey was first mooted towards the end of 1983. My colleagues in the Industrial Relations Research Unit, particularly the then Director William Brown, David Deaton, and Paul Marginson, provided valuable help and encouragement in defining its aims and scope and in designing the questionnaire. They, together with Peter Nolan, Stephen Frenkel, and the editors of this Series, also commented on previous presentations of the results. The survey was financed by a special grant from the Economic and Social Research Council, which also of course covered, through its support of the Industrial Relations Research Unit, the salary of the author and the overhead costs. The Chairman of the ESRC, Sir Douglas Hague, played an important role in providing the funding, and two members of the secretariat of the ESRC's Industry and Employment Committee, Chris Caswill and John Malin, provided valuable support as well as carrying out liaison work between the present survey and others being conducted. The fieldwork was carried out by IFF Research Ltd under the direction of David Spilsbury. I am very grateful to him and his staff. Working to very tight time constraints, they conducted the work with efficiency and attention to detail. The analysis was carried out in the Unit, and I am grateful to Margaret Morgan for her help here and in the collection of data on the companies whose plants were included in the survey. The secretarial burden of typing draft questionnaires, preliminary research reports, and the manuscript of this book fell on Connie Bussman, who bore it with her customary efficiency and cheerfulness. Finally, thanks are due to the 229 managers who gave up their time to answer the questions. I hope that they find the results worth while. The interpretations are, of course, my own and are not the responsibility of any of the people or organizations mentioned.

Paul Edwards

1

Introduction

The 1980s have seen a revolution in Britain's manufacturing industries. Foreign competition has increased, and the need to produce as efficiently as firms abroad has become an important theme not just within companies but also in political debate. There have been dramatic changes in work organization, as new technologies have been introduced, managerial hierarchies have been re-structured, and efforts have been made to deploy labour more flexibly by breaking down demarcation lines and broadening job descriptions. The decentralization of operations, making operating units responsible for their own decisions, has also been much discussed. Most obviously, there have been massive redundancies, together with the re-organization of work that often follows them.

This book is about a group of key actors in the process, the managers in charge of manufacturing establishments. It reports the results of a survey of a representative sample of such managers from large factories (defined as plants with at least 250 employees). Job titles included managing director, works manager, and factory director, but for convenience all these managers will be termed 'factory managers'.[1] They are an important group, for in addition to their recent role in the management of change they occupy a significant place in the management hierarchy between headquarters and first- and second-line supervision. They operate between the levels of general policy-making and detailed day-to-day supervision, and have to implement higher-level decisions while co-ordinating the running of their factories. Any trend towards decentralization, which on some arguments is quite substantial, will increase their role. Yet they have been little studied.

The survey focused on three aspects of the position of factory managers. Since factory managers have not been studied closely before, information on their careers and attitudes was sought. Second, most large plants belong to multi-plant enterprises, and the question arises of how much discretion company management gives to local managers. Third, the survey had a particular concern with the factories' industrial relations arrangements and with the degree of involvement of general managers in the management of labour. It has also proved possible to investigate the links between each of these three matters and an issue of considerable contemporary concern, namely productivity. In this introductory chapter the reasons for concentrating on these issues and the ways in which they are related to each other are first indicated. The design of the survey and the plan of the book are then outlined.

Studying Factory Management

The Management of Labour
When the management of British industry is discussed, problems of labour relations are almost always mentioned. The management of labour may thus be discussed first. There were some specific issues that the survey addressed, but before mentioning these the reasons for the particular focus on labour matters needs to be explained. Since this study was conducted in an industrial relations research body the answer, at one level, is obvious. But such an answer enables the question to be put the other way round: why, assuming the reasons for doing a survey of labour relations are valid, should industrial relations specialists concern themselves with managers and their careers?

Writers such as Purcell (1983) have argued that industrial relations needs to be seen in the context of managerial behaviour more generally: it is insufficient to concentrate on industrial relations institutions as though these are self-contained entities, and it is necessary to examine their place within firms as wholes. A key aspect of this broadening of scope has been something of a redefinition of the subject-matter of industrial relations. It has tended to be equated with trade unions and collective bargaining. This has always been a narrow definition, and one that has never adequately described the concerns of students of the subject. But its narrowness has become increasingly apparent. This is not a matter of industrial relations specialists redefining the subject so as to branch out into new areas but of their following through an approach that was always inherent in the definition of the subject to assess new substantive topics. If, as one authority states, industrial relations 'is the study of job regulation' (Clegg, 1979: 1), then informal as well as formal organizations, and processes as well as institutions, are valid objects of inquiry.[2] It is also as important to study employers' systems to recruit, motivate, and train employees as it is to examine the institutions of collective bargaining. There is thus nothing odd about a study which looks at labour relations along with other aspects of firms' activities or which sees them in the broad sense of all the ways in which employers and employees interact. Industrial relations is about the employment relationship as a whole and not just about institutional arrangements.

Even when the subject is defined in this broad way, there remains a gap between it and, say, investigation of the careers of factory managers. The gap is not, however, as wide as appears at first sight. There has always been a tradition of examining the backgrounds of work histories of actors on the industrial relations stage (for example Watson's, 1977, study of personnel managers). Broadening the scope of industrial relations implies the need to look at other managers who, although not personnel specialists, play a direct or indirect role in the management of labour. This is particularly so in the present case, for it turns out that factory managers have quite a high level of direct involvement in labour management, so that their attitudes and views are at least as important as those of personnel specialists. As noted above, moreover, factory managers are employees, and their relations with their firms are as much 'industrial relations' or 'employee relations' as are the links between manual workers and their employers. If it is relevant to inquire into how long such workers have been with their firms or what attitudes they hold on their wages, in order to establish the degree of attachment that they feel and thus to assess patterns of motivation and commitment, it is also important to carry out a similar exercise for more senior employees. A factory manager's job thus has its employee relations aspects, in regard both to his position as an employee and to his responsibility to manage the labour of his subordinates.

There are, then, several themes tying together the topics of this study. The central one is that of the motivation and control of employees. The interest in factory managers' careers is thus less for its own sake than for the contribution, albeit a preliminary one, that the study can make to the understanding of the managers' work roles. The interest is not in their general social attitudes but in their jobs and how they are motivated and controlled in carrying out their tasks. This concern is squarely within the remit of (an adequately defined) industrial relations.

What, then, are the specific matters concerning labour relations to which the study was addressed? A major point arises from the choice of respondent. As Purcell (1983) notes, studies of the managerial side of industrial relations have tended to concentrate on personnel specialists. This is exemplified by the two most recent major surveys of labour relations, in both of which the respondent was the manager responsible for industrial relations. These are the 'Warwick Survey' of manufacturing plants (Brown, 1981) and the Workplace Industrial Relations Survey of private industry (Daniel and Millward, 1983). In large manufacturing plants this person would generally be a personnel specialist, although in smaller plants he or she was more likely to be a general manager who had duties other than personnel.[3] This concentration is desirable when details of bargaining arrangements are sought, but it raises problems when respondents are asked to assess the importance of the personnel function in managerial decision-making or the degree of discretion granted to the plant. A personnel specialist will have a perspective on these things that need not be shared by other managers. The present survey thus tries to deal with this problem by investigating the views of general managers. It provides the first assessment of the views of non-specialists about the role of the personnel function within management and about labour management issues more generally to be based on a representative sample of senior plant-based managers.

A related consideration was the changing climate in which labour relations have been conducted. A widely held view could be described, with only a little caricature, as follows. During the 1970s companies were busy reforming their payments systems, introducing formal procedures for handling collective disputes as well as individual matters such as discipline, and formalizing their relationships with their shop stewards. The number of full-time stewards rose, and union organizations were made more secure with the spread of the closed shop and the 'check-off' of members' subscriptions. The law, as in the provisions for union recognition contained in the Employment Protection Act 1975 (Section 11), generally favoured unions. Since 1980, these trends have been reversed. The law has attempted to shift the balance of power in favour of employers. Firms themselves, faced with intensifying foreign competition and reaping the gains of the growth in their bargaining power consequent on the recession, have rationalized and restructured. The emphasis is no longer on formalization but on improving efficiency and removing those labour-related barriers to productivity, notably demarcation lines, 'excessive' manning levels, and 'restrictive practices', that they had hitherto been forced to tolerate. The power of shop stewards has been reduced, and in several significant cases, such as British Leyland and British Shipbuilders, steward organizations have been attacked head-on. One consequence has been a decline in the importance of the personnel function within management. When there were obvious problems of industrial relations such as strikes, and when firms were trying to reform their bargaining arrangements, the function gained in prestige. But, as the problems have receded, the reform has been completed, and the pressing through of improvements in productivity has become a dominant theme, the importance of the personnel function has waned. Purcell (1982) captured some of these arguments when he wrote of the rise of 'macho' management: shop stewards were being excluded from any effective influence over decisions, personnel specialists were being marginalized, and a tough and uncompromising style of leadership was emerging.

Factory managers in large plants are a particularly useful population with which to test these arguments. They might be expected to be tough-minded, production-oriented people with little time for 'soft' personnel managers. And, since it is well established that large plants are more likely to have full-time shop stewards and to have experienced strikes than are small ones, it is here that the problem of restrictive practices could be expected to be concentrated. The survey therefore asked about changes in methods of dealing with stewards and about experience of strikes, as well as about the managers' assessment of the importance of the personnel function. Unlike previous industrial relations surveys, it also asked directly about changes in working practices and the presence of labour-related constraints on efficiency. It thus concentrated not on the details of closed shop arrangements or the extent of disciplinary procedures but on the relationship between labour relations and productivity.

It did not, then, simply reproduce the interests of other surveys. Some assessment of changes between 1978, when the Warwick Survey was conducted, and 1984 was a useful by-product. But a second Workplace Industrial Relations Survey was carried out later in 1984, and this covered a much wider population (all establishments in manufacturing and private services with 25 or more employees) than the present survey. The present results would have some immediate interest, but little lasting value, if they reproduced the approach of other surveys.

A second, and broader, difference from such surveys was the way in which labour management was viewed. As well as asking directly about productivity, the survey asked in what ways labour matters were seen as important in running the business and what kind of policy or philosophy was applied to them. The aim was to assess managers' views not just about institutional change but about the way in which their firms sought the compliance and commitment of their workers. Did they simply adopt a tough, take-it-or-leave-it approach, or did they try to foster more positive feelings of involvement in the aims of the enterprise? There has been a good deal of speculation about the emerging style of labour relations. Information based on particular companies points to attempts to develop a spirit of commitment using such things as quality circles and briefing groups. The trend is allegedly away from collective bargaining through shop stewards and towards dealing with workers as individuals. The survey offered the chance of using broadly based and representative data to assess such arguments.

An attempt was also made to obtain managers' assessments of the success of their plants on criteria such as profitability and unit labour costs. As explained below, it was not felt practicable to ask for 'hard' financial data, and it was thus necessary to rely on rather broad assessments, backed up with data derived from published sources on the performance of the companies that owned the plants. The study thus took a step, albeit a small one, in the direction of relating labour management arrangements to plants' economic performance.

Managers and their Roles
The survey also sought to uncover something about the factory managers themselves. Numerous studies of managers have been carried out. Many have relied on postal questionnaire methods; examples include the well-known early study by D. Clark (1966) and the more recent survey of over 1,000 members of the British Institute of Management (BIM) by Poole *et al.* (1981). Others have involved more detailed investigation within a small number of organizations (for example, Sofer, 1970). The present study departs from the concerns of such studies in two main ways.

First, the focus is not managers in general but a particular level of, and functional specialism within, management. The problem of defining what constitutes 'a manager' is a long-standing one. A manager is plainly a white-collar employee, but, as Bain and Price (1972) point out, even this broadly-defined group has defied precise delimitation. Questions about the particular group of white-collar employees known as managers have included where the line dividing managerial from non-managerial duties can be drawn, whether it is possible to distinguish supervisors from managers proper, and how far it is possible to separate salaried managers from the directors of companies. As Melrose-Woodman (1978: 6) remarks, 'the term "manager" has defied definition ever since people first began to analyse its meaning'. Many studies adopt an essentially agnostic approach, treating as a manager anyone who is so called in the organization investigated; Clark is among those to take this route. Others, including Poole *et al.*, and Melrose-Woodman, have used members of the BIM as the population for study. The problem with the latter approach is, of course, that members of the BIM are unlikely to be representative of managers in general, for by their membership of the Institute they are adopting a distinct view of themselves as part of a profession. Both agnosticism and concentration on the BIM have the problem of including within the sample an extremely varied group of people, at many different levels within their organization and doing very different jobs. One solution is to look at fairly small numbers of 'managers', assessing the nature of their responsibilities and how they perform their tasks. The limitation here is a loss of generality, with any idea of presenting a broad picture being abandoned.

The present study starts from a different point. Instead of asking what management is, it identifies a group of managers carrying out a broadly similar job. For reasons indicated above, managers with production responsibilities are particularly interesting since they have recently been involved in significant changes. But it would not be sufficient to focus on production directors, for instance, for the duties of a group so identified may vary widely. The factory managers of large units perform basically similar tasks in taking overall responsibiity for manufacturing operations. They represent an important and yet homogeneous group whose characteristics may usefully be studied. The present approach may be seen as extending that adopted in studies of groups such as supervisors (for example, Child and Partridge, 1982): not trying to define the undefinable but identifying an important role in the social division of labour and investigating its occupants.

A 'factory' can range in size from a workshop with half a dozen or so employees to a massive enterprise employing thousands. As explained above, it was decided to concentrate on plants with at least 250 employees. This has the benefit of substantially increasing the homogeneity of the sample, as compared with the diversity that would arise if small plants were included. Each factory manager was in charge of a substantial production unit, and he occupied an important place in the managerial hierarchy for he was responsible for the overall running of the unit and for ensuring that policies developed at higher levels of a firm, be they on production scheduling, health and safety, manpower planning or a range of other matters, were in fact implemented at shopfloor level. The managers were not just 229 people with 'manager' in their job titles, or even 229 production specialists, but a group of senior employees responsible for large and complex manufacturing operations.

It is worth noting that conventional criteria for allocating occupations to social classes put the managers well within the top class, or Class I. The most thorough British investigation of the social grading of occupations is that by Goldthorpe and Hope (1974). This uses as one of its categories 'manager in a large establishment'. In later work (Goldthorpe, 1980), this category was included in Class I. This is in fact quite a broad definition of someone qualifying for the top class, for it includes all managers and not just factory managers and 'large' is taken to mean 'more than 25 employees'. A production manager in a 26-strong plant would be included in Class I, but such a person may well have life chances which are very different from those enjoyed by an executive in a larger organization, and his or her managerial duties may be rather limited. Thus Crockett and Elias (1984) show, in their analysis of respondents to the National Training Survey who could be classed as managers, that the size of firm (not establishment) was a significant influence on their earnings. It is plain, however, that respondents to the present sample, who were in charge of plants at least ten times larger than the size necessary to qualify as 'large', fell squarely within the top class.

Even a very large sample of people called managers will end up with small numbers sharing closely similar responsibilities. This study takes the opposite approach of identifying a distinct type of job and investigating the people filling the jobs in question. The only strata of management to receive such close attention to date are those of company director and supervisors. On the former, with the notable exception of the study by Fidler (1981), who interviewed the directors of large firms and who produced a valuable portrait of their social attitudes, however, most studies have been content to analyse the social class and educational backgrounds of the managerial elite using such sources as *Who's Who* (for example, Stanworth and Giddens, 1974b). Studies of supervisors (for example, Child and Partridge, 1982) are valuable, but plainly examine only the lower levels of management. A more specific focus on a stratum between these two extremes thus helps to advance knowledge about management in general.

A final benefit of the present approach, which is obvious once it is mentioned but which is not immediately apparent, should be mentioned. Studies of strata other than elite groups such as company directors who have fairly small numbers rely on some form of sampling. As indicated above, there is no adequate sampling frame of 'managers', and students have thus fallen back on BIM membership or on samples drawn from small numbers of organizations. The supervisors studied by Child and Partridge came from two firms in the Birmingham area, while an earlier study of managers was drawn from 78 firms from the service as well as the manufacturing sectors (Ellis and Child, 1973). The resulting problems of generalizability can be side-stepped here. There can by definition be only one factory manager in each plant. Since adequate sampling frames for plants exist, a sample can be drawn that is representative of the relevant population, in this case all factory managers of large manufacturing establishments. The results are thus generalizable as well as being based on a reasonably homogeneous population.

The second departure from past studies concerns the main issues that are addressed. The existing literature concentrates on managers' social and educational backgrounds, the times that they have spent with their firms, and other aspects of their careers. Some attention has also been given to such things as the alleged professionalization of management and managers' attitudes to broad social and political questions.[4] The present concern was not with the last of these. The managers' perceptions of social class and inequality, and information on their patterns of sociability, were not of interest. Some attention was paid to their careers and educational experience so that their position on these things could be compared with information on managers as a whole available from other surveys. That is, do factory managers stand out from the 'average', and if so in what ways? But this, too, was not a central concern. Instead, the interest was in specific aspects of the managers' jobs. Four of these indicate the focus. First, what role do factory managers play in managerial decision-making, that is, how far do they delegate decisions within their plants and how far are they free to take decisions without reference to management higher in the company? Second, how are they rewarded: are they paid in formal salary structures or is pay determination relatively informal? Third, what kind of careers have they had in their firms, and in particular how far have they had experience of general strategic management as against being limited to strictly routine operating management? Finally, what do they themselves make of this? As people with considerable responsibility for capital equipment and for large numbers of employees, do they feel that their firms give them due attention in planning company development or do they feel resentful that their contribution is not given adequate recognition?

The interest, then, is in the handling of the managerial task and some of the specific issues that arise in connection with it. This is not to deny the relevance of rather broader sociological investigations of class awareness. But since virtually nothing is known about factory managers it is advisable to concentrate on more immediate matters. Part of the aim is thus to provide information where none is available, either on such broad issues as those mentioned above or on some more specific matters of current interest, for example, to determine how widespread share ownership is among this stratum of management. But tying together these separate interests is a concern to see the factory managers as employees who control other employees while themselves being controlled by, and accountable to, others. Factory managers are being studied not as exemplars of management in general or as members of Social Class I but as employees occupying an important place in the hierarchy of management. The aim is to understand something about how they do their jobs and how they see their position in the firms that employ them. This might be called the employment relations aspect of factory management.

The Plant and the Company
One feature of a factory manager's job is the extent to which he is constrained by rules from above.[5] There is a massive literature on organizational design and on such things as the relative merits of tight centralized control of operation and the delegation of responsibility to subordinates. To cite but two examples, Williamson (1975) has argued that large firms suffer the problem of 'control loss': the head office cannot oversee all the operations of the subsidiaries, and communi-

cation both upwards and downwards becomes increasingly difficult. The response of many firms has been to create a multi-divisional structure, the M-form. Each division is self-contained, with its own production and marketing functions; the head office can concentrate on strategic planning. And Peters and Waterman (1982) include among their characteristics of excellently managed companies a 'loose–tight' relationship between the centre and the operating units: the firm has strong central direction in terms of its basic philosophy and has a strong corporate identity, but within this people are given a great deal of autonomy and are encouraged to develop their own ideas.

The present study does not pretend to deal with all the issues that arise in this literature, although, as noted below, a test of some of Peters and Waterman's arguments was possible. Instead, it concentrates on those aspects most connected to its overall concern of analysing the work situation of factory managers. These are the nature and extent of control and monitoring by higher company management. A factory manager's position is determined not just by his own personal character- istics but by the ways in which the unit for which he is responsible is managed from above. Analysis of these methods can help to throw light on general issues of organizational structure as well as on the careers of factory managers. Such a specific focus has some benefits. A debate about the strengths and weaknesses of decentralization can easily become a rather imprecise discussion of competing models of organizations. The aim here is to focus on one particular aspect, namely links between a manufacturing site and the rest of the company, and not the overall characteristics of organizations. Some light may be thrown on more general discussions, but these are not the primary focus.

Since one aim of this study was to investigate the management of industrial relations and the role of general managers in labour ques- tions, it will be convenient to discuss the links between plants and firms with reference to this area. Several recent discussions have pointed to the need to examine managerial organization above the level of the plant. Marsh (1982) conducted a survey of manufacturing firms and suggested that personnel managers at corporate level felt that the decision-making ability of plant managers was tightly constrained. Pur- cell (1983: 2) has criticized the concentration on the workplace that he finds in recent studies of labour relations, arguing that 'terms like "top management" or "senior managers" are used to describe the works director or personnel manager of the establishment in question ... but viewed from corporate headquarters such operational managers are in the middle of the management hierarchy and have little control over corporate policies or resources.'

Littler and Salaman (1982: 264) criticize writers adopting a 'labour process' perspective, suggesting that they give undue attention to the shopfloor, thus overlooking 'the possibility that control of work and work force can be achieved for the capitalist away from the point of production, indeed away from the organisation itself'; they cite the development of production facilities by multinational firms in Third World countries as an example of a managerial strategy formulated away from the factory level itself. And Kinnie (1985) has recently argued that local autonomy is largely a myth, which is sustained by senior company managers for purposes of their own.

These are powerful arguments, which will be considered in detail at the appropriate point (see chapter 4). Some general comments may also be made. First, there is what might be called the baby and the bathwater problem. It may be true that there has been an excessive concentration on the workplace, but there is a danger of denying that events at this level have any importance or autonomy. To put the matter at its crudest, it is at plant level that managements assemble the technical means of production and the labour that is applied to them, and it is here that corporate plans, policies, and strategies have to be put into effect. It is a commonplace of studies of organizations that plans do not work perfectly, for they exist in an uncertain environment and in a context in which those subject to them may resist or modify them. The conceptual belittling of the point of production is not well founded, and theoretical arguments (for which, see P. Edwards 1986a) can be developed to analyse the 'relative autonomy' of the point of production. In brief, these state that this level is governed by principles that pertain to the application of labour to the material means of production and that are peculiar to it. Forces from elsewhere in an organization, and from outside the organization, obviously affect it, but the effects are not immediate or direct, for there is necessarily an indeterminacy about them, and they are subject to processes of negotiation and definition within the factory.

Second, factory managements plainly have their own areas of responsibility. Operating decisions are likely to be left to them. Thus Hill and Pickering (1986) report a survey of 144 chairmen of large British firms. A majority of these top executives reported that 'operating subsidiaries' were normally responsible for marketing, production, and buying decisions, and for industrial relations. This level was also said by the majority of respondents to share responsibility with another level of the firm, or to have sole responsibility, for financial control, public relations, personnel decisions, and management development. The alleged trend towards decentralizing decision-making should also be borne in mind, for this is likely to increase the degree of discretion at plant level. A study of factory managers will not be a study of junior functionaries.

Third, even allowing for the importance of decisions taken higher in organizations, it is pertinent to investigate how plant-level managers view the controls to which they are subject. Do they, for example, think that these controls are excessively strict? A more difficult question concerns the accuracy of replies on matters of corporate decision-making. If factory managers say that they are dissatisfied about their lot, then this can be taken as a true statement of the position. If, however, they say that the right to decide on, say, investment plans lies with them, how do we know that they are not just exaggerating their own importance? Such exaggeration need not, of course, involve deliberate deception, for part of the argument about the illusion of plant autonomy is that plant-level managers are encouraged to believe that they have real discretion: a manager could genuinely believe that he was free to decide when higher managers had already constrained his area of choice or taken all but the minor operational decisions.

Within the confines of a study at factory level this issue cannot be dealt with thoroughly. In assessing the results it is necessary to bear in mind the possibility of 'establishment illusion'. It is also sensible to focus on those areas where factory managers might reasonably be expected to have some influence. Assuming that deliberate mis-reporting is rare, their replies on an area such as production scheduling can be taken as reasonably accurate. The concentration on factory managers, and not more junior functional specialists in the plant, is also of value in this regard. Such specialists might be unaware of financial control systems and other means of corporate control, whereas a factory manager is more likely to know about the framework of organizational controls within which his plant operates. It also seems sensible to ask directly about these controls, that is, to enquire how tightly the plant is monitored. There is no reason why a factory manager should not be able to provide a reasonable assessment of this issue. Indeed, if he cannot do so, one may ask what the point of corporate controls is. A final consideration is that, although it may be impossible to obtain an absolute measure of the amount of factory autonomy, there is no reason to suppose that there are systematic sources of bias in factory managers' answers. Variations in the replies may then be correlated with other aspects of organizational structure to see whether some types of firm monitor their plants more closely than do others.

There are, then, grounds for maintaining a focus on the establishment while also taking account of the firm of which it is part. This study therefore investigates the extent of corporate monitoring and control of plant performance. In the investigation of careers and attitudes, the factory managers are considered because they represent an important stratum of management. In the analysis of the plant and the company they are used in a rather different way, less as individuals and more as authoritative informants about the plants and links with their companies.

Productivity
The link between productivity and various other features of the plants, including both their organizational characteristics and their industrial relations arrangements, was the final issue investigated. The initial aim was to study the management of productivity in a way which showed how management organizes itself, what problems are felt to stand in the way of improving productivity, what efforts are being made to deal with these problems, and what, if anything, distinguishes those making most changes in the pursuit of higher productivity from the remainder. In short, the concern was the managerial process and not the explanation of differences in productivity. As noted above, however, some assessments by the factory managers of their plants' profitability and efficiency were sought.

In the context of a general survey it was not felt practicable to seek detailed data on the financial performance of the plants. Two considerations entered here. First, it was not known whether the information would be readily available on a basis suitable for comparison with other plants and, even if it was, there was some doubt as to respondents' willingness to disclose sensitive material. The risk of interfering with the other aims of the survey was felt to be too great to justify an attempt. Second, to obtain the necessary data would have required some careful questioning on a range of matters. In addition to information on performance (itself a difficult thing to measure) data would have been needed on a range of influences on productivity so that the effects of these could be controlled for when the separate effects of organizational structure were investigated. One obvious influence is the amount of capital employed per worker, but several others, such as the 'quality' of the work force, are discussed in the literature on productivity. It is, in principle, possible to design an appropriate questionnaire, but this would need to be a carefully developed special-purpose instrument. The present survey was not appropriate for such a questionnaire, although it is hoped that the results from its more limited approach will encourage further work on these lines.

It was, however, possible to analyse some 'hard' data in addition to managers' reports of productivity. These data were based on published information on the turnover and profitability of the firms owning the plants in the survey.[6] There is obviously a problem with linking information on an individual plant to data on the whole of a company, for the plant may not be typical of the firm as a whole. Some ways round this problem have, however, been devised.

Two main models of productivity are considered. The first may be derived from a growing body of literature on the characteristics of successful companies. This may be called the 'In Search of Excellence' school, after the title of one of its leading works (Peters and Waterman,

1982). Much of it is American, although it has some British epigones (for example, Goldsmith and Clutterbuck, 1984). It tries to identify the reasons why some firms perform better than others in similar circumstances. Among the reasons of importance here are the 'loose–tight' properties mentioned earlier and a strong 'people orientation' in the running of the business. Not all the hypotheses contained in the literature are open to quantitative tests. Indeed, one possible limitation is its informal methodology, wherein lessons are derived from particular companies but formal tests of relationships are absent. It therefore seemed useful to apply the approach to the present sample, to see whether its arguments work in a quantitative analysis of a fairly large cross-section of establishments.

The second model is that of the Harvard school of economists (see Freeman and Medoff, 1984a, for a summary of its approach). This takes formal econometric models of productivity and adds variables measuring trade union presence in an industry or plant. The major result is that unionization is found to exert a positive influence on productivity, which contradicts the 'obvious' expectation that unions interfere with efficiency. The reason for the result is said to be that the presence of a union forces management to manage better, for example, by developing grievance procedures, and also provides a channel of communication between workers and managers thus solving some problems of co-ordination. This school is also largely American. The one major British test of its models finds a negative association between unionization and productivity, although it is applied only to the coal industry for the period 1900–13 (Pencavel, 1977). The survey offered the opportunity of carrying out a rather broader study of the Harvard model in the British context. Although in some respects the present data are less precise than those used in tests of the Harvard model in America, they have some compensating advantages. In particular, they contain more detailed information on workplace union organization and industrial relations institutions than is employed in most of the Harvard studies.

Concluding Remarks
It proved possible, then, to move from the analysis of the management of productivity as defined above to assessment of the determinants of fairly 'hard' measures of productive performance. Since these assessments draw on information from each of the topics of inquiry discussed above they provide a useful way of linking together the apparently disparate themes arising from these topics. These themes are, in any event, less diverse than appears at first sight. They are pursued by focusing on factory managers as a fairly homogeneous stratum of management and not by trying to encapsulate the characteristics of management as a whole. And they are linked by the emphasis on the

Introduction 15

forms of motivation and control to which factory managers are subject and which they in turn employ in dealing with their subordinates.

Structure of the Survey

Design

The resources available permitted no more than 230 interviews, and analysis across the whole of industry was not feasible. The restriction to manufacturing requires some comment in view of the sector's declining importance as an employer and arguments that Britain is no longer primarily a manufacturing nation. There were some specific benefits of such a limitation. Good sampling frames are available so that it is possible to obtain a sample that is representative of the population in question; and much existing information, both on managerial careers and on labour relations, relates to manufacturing, so that several points of comparison with the present results exist.

More important, however, were two features of manufacturing. First, as noted above, the study aimed to relate information on company structure and labour relations to productivity. Concepts of productivity are more straightforward, and measurements of it are more readily available, in manufacturing than in the service sector. Second, the intensification of competition and the resulting pressure for change have probably been greater in manufacturing than elsewhere, and it is particularly interesting to examine how managers have been dealing with these pressures. If, for example, 'restrictive practices' are seen as a major problem, it should be here that their role is greatest. It may also be suggested that the devaluation of the importance of manufacturing has been exaggerated. The sector accounts for a large proportion of exports, many jobs in the service industries depend directly on it, and it continues to play a significant role in the economy.[7]

Similar considerations led to the limitation to plants each with at least 250 workers. It is here that alleged labour problems are likely to be the greatest. It is also in such plants that the distinct role of the factory manager can be investigated for, as noted above, there is generally a hierarchy within the plant such that personnel and other matters are the responsibilities of other managers, with the factory manager exercising overall directive authority. Such plants are also more likely than are smaller units to be parts of large companies, so that the relationship between the plant and the company owning it can usefully be investigated. One can be fairly confident that the factory managers of such large units exercise considerable responsibility and that the question of their relationship with their firms is of some significance.

Although plainly not representative of all manufacturing, large plants, apart from being those where change is most likely, account for a substantial proportion of total employment in the sector. A precise figure cannot be given, because the present threshold of 250 employees does not correspond to that of 200 used in most official publications, and because employment in establishments with fewer than 20 workers is not known exactly. A guess at the proportion of the official category of '200 to 499' employees accounted for by plants with between 200 and 249 workers leads to the estimate that those with 250 or more workers contained 65 per cent of all employees in plants with at least 20 workers each. When an estimate of employment in very small plants is included, the figure is 59 per cent of all manufacturing employment.[8] The practices and institutions of large plants affect a large part of the manufacturing work force.

Even the limitation to such plants would, if establishments were sampled from all manufacturing industries, lead to small numbers from any one sector. It was, however, desirable to try to assess whether there were any differences between industries in managerial careers or in changes in the management of industrial relations. In the assessment of productivity, it was also useful to have plants from fairly similar product market and technological environments, instead of having a collection of very diverse establishments. Five sectors were therefore chosen for special attention, with a target of 30 plants from each; the remainder of the sample was drawn from the rest of manufacturing so that, with appropriate weighting, the results can be generalized to the population as a whole.

The five sectors were chosen to give a range of market, technological, and institutional circumstances. They were chemicals; textiles; electrical engineering; paper, printing, and publishing; and food, drink, and tobacco. Chemicals is a capital-intensive industry with a reputation for innovation in organizational design. A reasonably straightforward response to change might be expected, particularly since shop steward organizations have grown only recently and since entrenched restrictive practice are generally felt to be rare. Textiles is a more traditional and less innovative sector in which recent competitive pressures have not reversed previous expansion but have accelerated a process of decline. Workplace trade union organization has remained much less developed than in other industries, and resistance to change would be expected to come not from institutionalized shopfloor controls but from a conservative dislike of new methods. Electrical engineering is likely to contain more developed steward organizations and to have more of the alleged problems of strikes and restrictive practices.

All three of these sectors operate in industries with considerable foreign competition. This is less marked in the other two industries, although they differ in other important respects. Paper, printing, and publishing is widely seen as the industry where unions' controls of the shopfloor are, or at least until recently have been, the most extensive. Food, drink, and tobacco is similar in being a domestically oriented industry, but different in that it has not been seen as having any substantial amount of union control on the shopfloor. It was thus hoped that industry-specific developments in some rather different environments could be charted while also keeping the sample representative of the population as a whole.

Structure of the Sample
In addition to stratification by industry, the sample was stratified into two size bands: 250 to 499 employees, and 500 or more employees. This was to ensure that there were adequate numbers of small and large plants for any size effects to be properly assessed. The sampling was carried out by the organization responsible for the survey's fieldwork, IFF Research Ltd. The sample is, when re-weighted, representative of all large manufacturing plants in Britain. The weighting factors used have been divided by a constant so that the number of cases in the weighted data is similar to the number actually studied. Further details on sampling and weighting are given in Appendix A.

Target numbers of interviews in each industry wre generally achieved. The main problem, on which some comment is needed here, was that we did not achieve our aim of interviewing the factory manager on each site in every case. Just over three-quarters of the 229 respondents (177 or 77 per cent) were factory managers. The remainder were deputy managing directors (6 per cent), production directors or managers (7 per cent), personnel managers (7 per cent) or some other functional group. Again, full details are given in Appendix A. The failure to interview the factory manager in every case can be attributed to two factors: first, some respondents may have felt that, given the survey's concern with labour issues, the personnel specialist was the appropriate person to be interviewed. Interviewers were instructed to explain why the factory manager was the target, but in some cases they were plainly unsuccessful in securing co-operation. Second, the survey faced some quite severe time constraints, stemming from the need to design the questionnaire, carry out pilot interviews, formulate the final questionnaire, and conduct the main fieldwork within the limited period covered by the available funding. This meant that it was not always possible to arrange an interview with a very busy factory manager within the specified time. Interviewers were instructed as a last resort to go instead to a deputy managing director or someone with similar general managerial responsibilities such as a production director. There were also plainly some *ad hoc* adjustments wherein a personnel manager was interviewed if there was no one else available.

In analysing the results a distinction may be drawn between a sample of plants and a sample of people. If the criterion of interviewing the factory manager had been made absolute, interviews would not have been carried out in a significant number of establishments. This might well have biased the results. Given the need to have a representative sample of plants in order to assess the pattern of current developments it was reasonable to speak to other managers. The rationale is that a manager who was in almost every case a senior and knowledgeable person is used to provide the information required. This approach works for the sample of plants but not for the sample of respondents, for what was sought was information about the role and attitudes of a particular stratum of managers. The solution adopted when analysing this material is to restrict discussion to the factory managers. It is possible that biases are introduced as a result. But, to the extent that a major reason for failing to interview a factory manager was simply lack of time, it is unlikely that any large or systematic biases were involved.

This leads to the question of response rates. The ratio of interviews achieved to interviews attempted was 53 per cent, a figure which IFF Research, which is an extremely experienced organization in the field of industrial and business research, considers to be generally acceptable for this kind of survey. Appendix A contains the detailed figures. The main reason for refusing an interview was that the respondent was too busy or that the firm did not participate in market research studies of any kind. As mentioned above, time constraints were important, and it is possible that more interviews would have been achieved had they been less pressing. In the light of these considerations, the response rate appears to have been adequate. In particular, there are no reasons to suspect that there are any systematic biases in the data. Response rates of less than 100 per cent become worrying only if it seems likely that there are systematic differences between those who co-operate and those who do not. In the present case, if non-respondents were more likely than respondents to adopt an aggressive policy towards their shop stewards, the results will underestimate the true extent of such a policy. There is no particular reason to suspect that this was the case. A more likely source of bias lies in the decision of factory managers on whether to be interviewed. Given the aim of the survey of looking at labour issues, it is possible that factory managers who take an interest in these matters agreed to be interviewed while those who found them uninteresting did not. The results would then exaggerate the involvement of factory managers in labour matters.

It is certainly possible that some form of self-selection of this type was taking place. One way to assess it is to compare the plants where the factory manager was interviewed with those where another manager was the respondent. (It is being assumed here that no bias was intro-duced at the stage of deciding whether the plant would co-operate in the survey. It is of course still possible that outright refusals were

6

concentrated among factory managers who took no interest in labour matters, but there is no way of assessing this possibility.) In general, there do not seem to have been any systematic sources of bias. On various key questions there were no statistically significant differences between factory managers and other respondents. To take but two examples, respondents were asked whether they had made any changes in working practices to increase the efficiency of labour utilization and whether they had altered the ways in which they dealt with their trade union representatives. These were questions 106 and 112 on the questionnaire. (The full wording is given in Appendix B; throughout this report, whenever a question is first mentioned the reader will be referred to its precise wording by indicating its number on the questionnaire.) On these two questions there were no significant differences between factory managers and others; on question 106, for example, 87 per cent of factory managers and 89 per cent of other managers said that changes had been introduced. Some further relevant similarities are discussed in Appendix A.

Some of the issues covered by the survey were the familiar ones of trade union organizaton at plant level and the importance assigned to industrial relations matters. Others, notably the assessment of managerial decision-making structures, were, however, novel. And the method of approaching factory managers was also largely untried. A small pilot survey was therefore undertaken, and as a result some modifications were introduced in the final design. Interviewing for the main stage of the fieldwork was conducted by members of IFF's trained and experienced fieldwork staff. Interviews took place during February and March 1984. The mean length was just over one hour, with the shortest being 45 minutes and the longest 105 minutes.

Plan of the Book

Several references have already been made to the organizational structures of firms owning large manufacturing plants, and to the competitive environment facing these plants. Since these are important in assessing the survey results they are described briefly in chapter 2. They provide more than just the general background to the issue analysed in the survey, for they exerted an important effect on some of them, and they need to be emphasized at the outset. The exercise is also of some interest in its own right. What sorts of firms own these plants, and what has been their experience of employment change and profitability? Questions such as these are rarely explored in plant-level surveys, but it is useful to try to link survey data to more general information on company characteristics.

In the next two chapters attention turns to the factory managers and their place within their firms. Chapter 3 concentrates on their careers and attitudes and on the reward systems that were used. The focus here is thus on the managers as individuals. In chapter 4 the emphasis is more on their positions at the head of their plants, the particular concern being the degree of freedom to take decisions that they enjoyed and the extent to which their activities were controlled and monitored from above. In chapter 5, a similar perspective is adopted, although the focus is now downwards to the level of the shopfloor, and in particular the ways in which labour relations were handled. Information from all three of these chapters is deployed in chapter 6 in the analysis of productivity: were the most productive firms characterized by a particular sort of managerial career, did the system of company monitoring affect productivity, and what role did labour relations institutions play? As noted above, the survey's data may not be ideal for a rigorous analysis of the determinants of productivity, but they help to throw light on several debates and to identify influences that have not hitherto been studied and that might repay further investigation. Finally, chapter 7 outlines some implications of the research, for practitioners and for researchers.

Although touching on a range of issues, the discussion concentrates on the work situation of factory managers and the systems of motivation and control that affect it. Most of the analysis is fairly straightforward: outlining the picture given by the survey, considering some of the main variations, and, where relevant, comparing the results with those of other studies. More complex statistical techniques are called for in two areas: charting the determinants of some aspects of managers' careers and attitudes, and analysing variations in productivity. It is necessary to describe in some detail the nature of the tests employed so that the analytical methods and conclusions can be scrutinized by other students. But the statistical procedures used are standard, and the reasons for the use of particular explanatory variables are explained in a non-technical way, as are the conclusions that are drawn.

The book reports most of the findings of the survey. Anyone interested in pursuing these, or in examining matters not analysed below, will find the full questionnaire reproduced in Appendix B. The data themselves are lodged at the ESRC Data Archive at the University of Essex, and they may be consulted there.

Notes

1. If the male pronoun is used to refer to a factory manager, this is because 227 of the 229 respondents were men, and there was some doubt as to whether one of the two women was in fact the senior executive on site.

2. This is not a universally accepted definition. But critics of it would generally draw the boundaries of the subject even wider than Clegg does, and it represents a minimum set of claims.

3. In the Warwick Survey (Brown, 1981: 28), 46 per cent of all respondents said that personnel and industrial relations was their main area of responsibility, which indicates that 54 per cent were non-specialists. The figure for 'specialists' rose, however, to 78 per cent in plants in the 200–499 size band and to over 90 per cent where there were 500 or more employees. A corollary is that, if the manager dealing with personnel is a specialist, the manager in charge of the whole plant will not have direct responsibility: factory managers in large plants will, with few exceptions, come from a population different from that comprising 'the managers responsible for industrial relations' (Brown, 1981: 1) studied in previous surveys.

4. Mention should also be made of studies of what managers do, in which detailed observations are made of the amount of time spent in various activities, with whom most interaction takes place, and so on (see Horne and Lupton, 1965; Marples, 1967; Mintzberg, 1970). The emphasis tends to be on a rather literal sense of behaviour, and patterns of power and authority are not revealed.

5. This of course assumes that the plant is part of a larger group and not a single, independent establishment. As shown in ch. 2, only 7 per cent of the present sample fell into the latter category.

6. The ownership of establishments was traced using trade directories and *Who Owns Whom*. Company data were extracted from Extel cards and company reports. They were attached to the data tape in such a way that the identity of individual plants and companies cannot be discovered.

7. The decline of manufacturing can also be exaggerated. In 1983 the sector accounted for 26 per cent of employees in employment. Data on potential trade union membership (employed plus unemployed) showed that in 1901 manufacturing industries accounted for 31 per cent of the total (calculated from Bain and Price, 1980).

8. Manufacturing units each employing 200 or more workers accounted in 1980 for 67.6 per cent of employment in plants with 20 or more employees: see 'Analysis of UK Manufacturing (Local) Units by Employment Size', Business Monitor PA 1003 (London: HMSO, 1982), Table 1. When estimated employment in units with fewer than 20 employees is taken into account the proportion accounted for by the 200-plus category falls to 60.8 per cent. The estimates for the 250-plus group depend on a guess about how many plants have between 200 and 249 employees.

2

The Economic and Organizational Context

In this chapter the institutional and economic environments in which the plants operated are briefly surveyed. This information provides necessary background for the following chapters. The discussion of different types of career in chapter 3, for example, rests in part on distinctions between types of firm, while the analysis of reasons for changing working practices in chapter 5 depends on an understanding of the external pressures on the plants. But the material is not just background. The forces discussed had specific effects on the issues analysed in later chapters, competitive market pressures being the most obvious example. And the present information is of some interest in its own right, for it helps to throw light on the organizational structures of large firms and on how the recent recession has been experienced at the level of the plant.

It is convenient to begin with organizational structure. As noted in chapter 1, the benefits of a multi-divisional form of structure have been widely discussed. Studies (e.g. Steer and Cable, 1978) have examined the extent to which this form has been adopted in Britain. The unit of analysis here, however, is the company, and, specifically, companies of such a size that the organization is sufficiently complex for the question of divisionalization to be germane. The present evidence allows a different perspective: not how many companies are divisionalized but what proportion of plants is owned by them. Respondents were asked whether their plants were single, independent establishments and, if not, whether there were any levels of the organization between the plant and the British headquarters of the firm.[1] Plants where such a level was mentioned can be taken to be those with some type of divisional structure, since the existence of an intermediate level implies that the firm had distinct entities such as divisions or operating companies between it and the individual plants. More detailed questioning would be needed to establish the basis and role of these levels. Even a firm with several divisions would not qualify as a fully fledged multi-divisional company unless it also treated these divisions as more than just sub-units manufacturing different products. In an M-form company each division is a self-contained unit with its own marketing functions, and the head office exercises financial discipline over its divisions. Some doubt has been expressed as to how far British firms have embraced the substance, and not just the form, of multi-divisional organization. The present survey was not designed to deal with such issues, and the evidence shows only how common some form of complex, multi-layered organization was, without being able to differentiate between types of such organizations.

The results (set out in table 2.1) show that 7 per cent of the sample consisted of single, independent establishments. A further 24 per cent were parts of multi-plant groups which did not have any levels between them and head office. But 69 per cent were parts of firms with more complex structures. Comparable data appear to be absent. The Warwick Survey (Brown, 1981: 28) showed that 72 per cent of manufacturing plants with at least 50 employees were parts of multi-plant enterprises, but did not investigate corporate structure in any more detail. The present result, from which it can be calculatd that about 45 per cent of all employees in manufacturing work for firms with intermediate levels, suggests that some form of divisional organization is widespread in British industry. Throughout this study, such firms will be referred to as corporations or corporate groups. The corporate level of management is to be distinguished from the company level, which means the top level of a firm without intermediate levels or the division or operating company in a firm with such levels. The distinction between a company and corporate groups is important at several points, for example in ascertaining, in chapter 4, whether the monitoring of plant performance is conducted by the immediate operating divisions or by the corporation.

The majority of the plants in corporate groups had only one level between them and the corporate headquarters, suggesting that they represented cases of the classic plant–division–corporation type. But in a smaller but still significant number (40 per cent of those in corporate groups, or 28 per cent of the whole sample) there were two or more levels between the plant and the headquarters. An example would be a plant that was part of a group of plants producing a similar product, with the group being one of several run by an operating company, which was in turn owned by a conglomerate corporation. The structure

TABLE 2.1
Some Characteristics of the Sampled Establishments

	(%)
Number of full-time employees (Q. 2a)	
250–499	55.4
500–999	24.4
1,000–1,999	12.9
2,000 and over	7.2
Corporate status (Qs 8–10)	
Single independent establishment	7.3
Part of group, not part of division	23.5
Part of division:	
1 level between establishment and HQ	40.1
2 or more levels between establishment and HQ	28.1
number of levels unknown	1.0
Ownership (Qs 16a, 16b)	
Single, independent establishment	7.3
Part of group:	
British owned	78.9
US/Canadian owned	8.0
European owned	5.8
Company employment in Britain (1982)	
Less than 1,000	10.2
1,000–1,999	8.9
2,000–4,999	11.9
5,000–9,999	11.5
10,000–24,999	19.6
25,000–49,999	11.5
50,000 and over	17.9
Not ascertained	8.5
Manual trade union status (Qs 20a–20h)	
No recognized trade unions	11.3
Recognition plus shop stewards (none senior)	12.4
Recognized senior stewards (not full-time)	59.0
Recognized senior stewards (some full-time)	17.3

Base: All establishments.
Note:
Numbers in brackets refer to question numbers on the questionnaire.
Data on company employment derived from published sources such as trade
directories and Extel cards.

of many firms appears to be quite complex. Allied with this organizational complexity was the very large size of firms owning the plants in the survey. The questionnaire included a question about corporate size but, because of an ambiguity in the instructions to interviewers, it was not asked in all cases where the plant was part of a non-corporate group (that is, multi-plant firms with no levels between the plant and the headquarters). Data derived from published sources are therefore reported in table 2.1. Assuming that the 8.5 per cent of cases where employment could not be ascertained were small firms that did not make data publicly available, nearly half the sample belonged to firms that each employed over 10,000 workers. This is not the same as saying that half the firms were of this size, for very large firms tend to have many separate establishments, and in some cases more than one plant of the same firm appeared in the sample. The distinction between proportions of plants and proportions of companies will be considered further below. For present purposes, the important point is the extent to which very large organizations were represented in the sample.

As shown in table 2.1, 86 per cent of the plants were owned by a British firm. In view of the small number of foreign-owned plants, it was not possible rigorously to analyse any differences between foreign- and British-owned firms in their organization or labour practices (cf. Buckley and Enderwick, 1985). In view of this, together with the fact that foreign-owned firms are not a homogeneous group and the lack of centrality of ownership to the research design, any further analysis of this point was inadvisable. But there did not appear to be any strong links between ownership and the main variables analysed in the following chapters. It is unlikely that the results would alter if ownership were included among the explanatory variables; there may be aspects of the data that interest researchers of this issue, but it will not be pursued here.

One complication with distinguishing between British- and foreign-owned firms is that the former may operate internationally and thus be as 'global' in their concerns as foreign-based companies. The need would then be to separate out different types of British-based firms. Among multi-plant firms in the present sample, 71 per cent of respondents said that their firms had manufacturing operations outside Britain (Qs 17, 18). In 44 per cent, operations were said to take place in six or more different countries. Again, there seemed to be little link between the extent of international activities and labour relations practices or company organization in Britain. This, too, is a matter that other researchers may wish to consider more carefully, but the present investigation seems not to require close attention to it. There was, for example, no relationship between foreign ownership or the extent of foreign operations and company profitability. The main significance of the evidence is in developing the picture of the firms owning plants in the

TABLE 2.2
Employment and Profitability, 1978 and 1982

	Whole Sample (N = 206)[b]		One Estab. Per Company[a] (N = 178)[b]	
	1978	*1982*	*1978*	*1982*
Average numbers employed in company (000s)	31.5	24.6	22.6	18.3
Profit as % turnover	6.5	3.7	7.1	4.0

Notes:
[a] Several companies had more than one of their establishments in the survey. To allow for this, in such cases only one of the plants has been selected in computing average figures.
[b] Where numbers are quoted for weighted samples, they are rounded to the nearest whole number. To avoid creating spuriously large Ns when weighting up, all the weights used have been divided by a constant. The total weighted N is thus 235, as against unweighted number of 229 respondents.

sample: they were large, and often had substantial interests outside Britain.

An indication of the plants' place within their firms is the fact that the great majority were profit centres, that is (and in contrast to mere cost centres) units whose financial performance was specifically assessed (Q. 15). Of the non-independent establishments, 87 per cent were profit centres with the lowest profit centre being above plant level in the remaining 13 per cent. There was no association between company size and the level of the lowest profit centre, but there was some tendency for plants not to be profit centres in their own right in foreign-owned firms. The level of the profit centre was unrelated to indices of company performance. Like ownership, it will not be considered in detail below. The fact that the great majority of plants were profit centres is, though, a useful preliminary indication of their being treated as fairly independent units: they were not mere production units but were assessed against targets set for them.

The economic environment in which these firms were operating is, in general terms, familiar: increasing foreign competition, a decline in manufacturing output, and pressures to re-structure in order to survive. Official figures put the decline in employment in manufacturing between 1978 and 1984 at 23 per cent, while output fell by 11 per cent.[2] At the time that the survey was conducted, 1982 was the most recent year for which data for all the companies represented in the sample were available, and table 2.2 therefore reports figures on employment and profitability for 1978 and 1982. For the whole sample, average company employment fell from 31,500 to 24,600. These figures relate to the position 'looking up' from the plant. That is, the 'average' plant in the survey was owned by a firm whose employment fell by this amount. Excluding the cases where more than one plant from the same firm appeared in the sample gives rather lower figures, showing that, as expected, the firms with several plants in the sample were larger than average. But the rate of decline was much the same (about 20 per cent). The consequences of the recession in terms of profitability are also clearly apparent. Several companies were making large losses in 1982, the largest being a loss of 101 per cent (indicating that the loss was slightly greater than total turnover). The differences in employment and profitability between the two years were both highly significant on the appropriate statistical tests (that is, they are highly unlikely to have arisen by chance, indicating that there was a 'real' decline over the period).

Evidence on the economic environment as it affected the plants themselves is assembled in table 2.3. The great majority of respondents said that they faced severe or very severe competition in all the markets in which they operated, and that the level of competition had been increasing over the previous three years. There were few differences between industries, except that competition was felt to be less severe in the textiles industry than it was in the other sectors chosen for special attention. Foreign competition was a significant feature of this industry but not others. Three-quarters of the whole sample felt that such competition was strong or very strong. Most of the remainder operated in markets that were primarily domestic. As would be expected, they were concentrated in the food and printing industries, for in substantial parts of these industries, newspaper production being the most obvious, there is very little foreign competition. The proportions of respondents saying that foreign competition was absent were 50 per cent in food, drink, and tobacco and 48 per cent in paper, printing, and publishing; by contrast, 97 per cent of respondents in the electrical engineering industry said that such competition was strong or very strong. The sample thus fell into two distinct groups: the majority who operated in international markets and who faced substantial competition from abroad, and the minority who operated in relatively protected markets. Even among the latter, however, the overall extent of competition was felt to be high and increasing.

Against this picture of a harsh external environment, there was some evidence that the nadir of the plants' fortunes had been passed. For some of the firms covered profits data for 1983 were available. These pointed to a slight improvement over 1982, although the level of profitability was still significantly below that recorded for 1978. As for the plants themselves, table 2.3 shows that demand was felt to have

TABLE 2.3
Aspects of the Economic Environment

	(%)
Severity of competition in all markets (Q. 146)	
Very severe	57
Severe	37
Average severity/not severe	6
Change in level of competition over previous three years (Q. 147)	
Increased	84
Stayed same	13
Decreased	3
Degree of foreign competition (Qa 148, 149)	
Very strong	45
Strong	29
Neither strong nor weak/weak/very weak	4
No significant foreign competition	22
Trend of demand for plant's products over previous two years (Q. 6)	
Rising	51
Static	24
Falling	24
Establishment's gross revenues (Q. 137)	
Well in excess of costs	30
Enough for small profit	43
Enough to break even	13
Insufficient to cover costs	15

Base: All establishments.

increased over the previous two years in 51 per cent of cases. This proportion was twice that of cases where demand was still falling. Although the overall picture was thus one of improving market conditions, this masks some diversity of experience, with some plants experiencing a recovery while others were continuing to decline.

This contrast is important in assessing the impact of the recession. It would be a mistake to assume that its effects have been uniform in their severity or timing. The intensification of competition is likely to have proceeded at different paces in different sectors, and individual firms will also vary in their ability to cushion the impact on their operating units. Relatively prosperous firms may have been able to absorb some of the effects and to rationalize on a long-term basis, while less advantaged ones will have been thrust suddenly into crisis. The present sample of plants obviously excludes establishments that were closed in the first part of the recession. The extent of diversity is thus even greater than appears within the group of plants that are still operating. But such a group exhibits considerable variation, and it is of course their situation which is relevant to assessments of future trends. Including plants that have closed would be important in assessing situations where workers were most prone to redundancy for example. But for considering the current and future pattern of labour relations it is the surviving plants that are of interest. Some of these seem to have been experiencing a recovery while others were still in difficulties. This point about diversity has to be borne in mind when overall patterns are assessed, for there can be considerable variation around the average. As shown in chapter 7, managers, in looking at the issues facing them in the future, varied in their assessments. Some stressed the consolidation of measures already introduced and looked to a reasonably secure future while others stressed the need for further redundancies and cost-cutting measures.

Diversity is also reflected in the final section of table 2.3, which reports respondents' assessments of the profitability of their own establishments. This is plainly a subjective measure, for people could differ in their views as to what constituted profit well in excess of costs. But the extent of subjectivity is limited, for whether or not a plant was making profits or losses should be reasonably clear. The majority of respondents (86 per cent) said that their plants were at least breaking even. This is consistent with the picture from the profitability of the firms owning the plants, for, as noted above, the mean profit rate was well above zero. The picture is, of course, less rosy than might appear: the company data report profit in the sense of a surplus of income over expenditure, and not whether sufficient funds were being generated to sustain a reasonable level of investment; similarly, the establishment data refer to gross revenues. If those reporting only a small profit or a worse result can be taken as representing cases in which gross profits were insufficient to support necessary capital expenditure, it appears that 70 per cent of plants were in some difficulties.

The general picture, then, was of plants which had come through a very difficult period in which profitability had been falling and competition had intensified. Some weathered the storm fairly well, and were now enjoying increasing demand for their products and improving profits while others were still in the midst of severe difficulties. Such experiences are bound to have affected respondents' views of their own position and of their relations with their subordinates. They had managed their way through a recession that was new to them in its severity. Although not in a position to be complacent, they had grounds for satisfaction at the progress that had been made. In the field of labour relations, in particular, there is likely to have been a feeling that responses to the increasingly hostile external environment had been made successfully and that management had led the work force

TABLE 2.4
Reasons for Strength of Foreign Competition

	Per Cent of Respondents Mentioning (N = 174)	Per Cent of Responses (N = 202)
Exchange rates, government policy	23	20
Market demand, overcapacity	26	22
Lower costs, better production methods abroad	49	43
Better marketing policies abroad	10	8
Other	2	2
Don't know	6	5
		100

Base: Establishments where foreign competition strong or very strong.

into a new and more constructive relationship. How far such perceptions are justified will be considered in detail in chapter 5. But the
basis of them needs to be understood at the outset.

In view of the importance of the competitive environment, it is worth
considering respondents' views in more detail before outlining some
other aspects of the institutional environment. As well as developing
the picture of the context in which the plants operated, the exercise is
of some value in its own right, for respondents were senior managers
with considerable responsibilities in running manufacturing operations.
It is of some interest to consider their views of the reasons why the
market environment had been changing.

Respondents who said that foreign competition was strong or very
strong were asked an open-ended question (Q. 150) about the reasons
for this. The answers have been categorized, as shown in table 2.4. In
this table, as in others where more than one answer is possible, replies
are counted according to how many respondents mentioned a particular
item and what proportion of total replies is represented by it. As might
be expected from a group of managers concerned with the operation
of manufacturing facilities, replies concentrated on the productive capa-
bilities of foreign firms in terms of such things as lower costs and more
sophisticated manufacturing techniques. It is already notable, however,

that specifically labour-related problems did not feature very strongly among the respondents' views of causes of the strength of foreign competition. Their views of their competitors emphasized the more general aspects of better manufacturing techniques. Internal, product-related issues, moreover, were balanced by matters external to the production process, of which two were felt to be most important: government policy on international trade, in particular the exchange rate of sterling, and the state of market demand and capacity in the industry.

Individual managers gave detailed assessments of their own positions. Two, for example, mentioned the practice of their Eastern European competitors of selling at a loss. Others emphasized systematic attempts by their competitors to raise their market shares both in general and by invading the British market. How far such views from site-based managers can be taken as accurate statements of a situation which is affected by many factors of which they may not have first-hand knowledge is, of course, hard to say. But it is plain that they were all too aware of the intensity of foreign competition and of the need for British firms to produce and sell more effectively if they were to continue to compete.

The survey also contains some data on the internal operation of the establishments. In an effort to assess how far the recession had led to short-time working and other ways of responding to inadequate levels of demand, respondents were asked to estimate the average level at which capacity had been utilized over the previous year (Q. 102). The mean figure was 78 per cent, with little variation between industries. In the absence of comparable data from other surveys it is difficult to know whether this represents an improvement over previous years. But it points to a considerable degree of idleness of capital equipment, which must have affected unit costs. When asked whether the reasons for not achieving full capacity working were mainly internal to the plant or external, only 20 per cent of respondents cited the former. It appears that external problems such as the level of market demand were the more important influence.

One way of increasing capacity utilization is to use shift working. The survey sought some information on the extent of shift work, partly to assess whether it, and therefore the utilization of equipment, had declined during the recession and partly because shift work is important in its own right. It will affect, for example, the type of worker that management aims to recruit and systems of managerial communication. In all, 82 per cent of plants reported some kind of shift system. Most popular was a double-day shift system (that is, an arrangement of two shifts during an extended day, for example 6am to 2pm plus 2pm to 10pm). This was used on its own in 22 per cent of cases and along with a permanent night shift in a further 5 per cent. Nineteen per cent of plants used some form of day and night shift working, while 25 per cent had three-shift systems that made more extensive use of capital equipment. (A system of two shifts each working eight hours a day for five days a week will run for 80 hours a week, whereas a three-shift system running from 6am on Monday to 10pm on Friday will work for 112 hours per week). Of the 25 per cent with three-shift working, the majority ran the system for five days a week, with only 7 per cent of the plants having seven-days-a-week operation, the so-called 'Continental' system.[3]

With the exception of those who already had a Continental system or who had abandoned shifts in the previous three years, respondents were asked about the feasibility of increasing the use of shifts (Q. 26). Twenty-one per cent felt that it would not be technically feasible to extend the use of shifts; 25 per cent said that it was feasible but that it had not been actively considered; and 54 per cent had considered doing so. When the last group was asked why shift working had not been increased, the lack of product demand was the main reason: 64 per cent mentioned this reason, and it was the most important reason in 56 per cent of cases. No other single reason featured prominently, the next most common 'most important' reason being the extra costs of shift work, which accounted for 14 per cent of cases.

A related issue is the extent to which shift working has been altered, a plausible expectation being that the recession will have reduced product demand and thus the need for shift working. Of those not employing shifts in the previous three years, two-fifths (or 7 per cent of the entire sample) had reduced the use of shifts while the remainder had never used shift working. In addition, some of those still using shifts had reduced their use. As against this, other plants had increased it. The result was that those ending or reducing their use of shifts were exactly balanced by those making more use of shifts, each group accounting for 22 per cent of the sample. The remainder was composed of those making no change in their use of shifts (44 per cent of the sample) and those with no shifts at all (11 per cent). There was, in short, a considerable amount of change in the use of shifts, although the result of the change was that the total extent of shift working was unaltered. The main reason for the reduction in the use of shifts was, not surprisingly, the lack of product demand, while increasing demand was widely cited by those making more use of shifts. Among the latter group, a further reason, accounting for a quarter of all the reasons for making more use of shifts, was the need to increase efficiency or the utilization of capital equipment. There was thus some consideration of the relevance of shift working to increasing competitiveness, but most of the ebb and flow in the use of shifts reflected fluctuations in market demand.

Two main conclusions emerge. First, by 1984 a significant number of large manufacturing plants were coming out of the worst of the recession, and were increasing their plant utilization as a result. But a similar number was still facing a worsening situation. Second, the unsurprising result that market demand is related to the use of shift working raises questions about the ability of firms to maximize their use of capital equipment: if they are uncertain about the future level of demand they may avoid any form of shift working or may use arrangements such as twilight shifts which give them short-term flexibility. An inability to plan production on a long-term basis may have reduced the incentive to employ more sophisticated systems.

Turning to the internal organization of the plants in the survey, it is plain that the sample was not typical of manufacturing industry. The concentration on large plants means that the formalization of procedures was greater than it was in manufacturing as a whole. As table 2.1 shows, trade unions were recognized for bargaining purposes in 89 per cent of the establishments. This compares with 76 per cent of manufacturing plants with at least 50 employees in 1977–8 (Brown, 1981: 52) and 58 per cent of establishments in the manufacturing and service sectors with more than 25 employees in 1980 (Daniel and Millward, 1983: 19). Recognition is plainly only the most basic of conditions for union organization in the workplace. One commonly used indicator of the extent of organization is the presence of one or more shop stewards who spend all their time on union duties. The proportion of plants in the present survey with such a full-time steward was 17 per cent; the comparable figures for the 1977–8 and the 1980 surveys are 12 per cent and 3 per cent. More detailed questions about such things as the closed shop, the check-off of union dues, and the existence of formal procedures for settling disputes were not salient in the present investigation. But they are likely to have been widespread. As shown in chapter 5, for example, 50 per cent of the plants reported that all the manual workers were union members, which sets a minimum bound for the extent of the closed shop; in 1977–8 30 per cent of all plants reported at least a partial closed shop (Brown, 1981: 56). Data recalculated from the survey put the proportion of all plants with 100 per cent trade union density at 36 per cent.

The role of personnel specialists within management was similarly not a central concern. But a question (Q. 88) was asked about whether the plant had a manager with specific responsibility for industrial relations. Most of them (84 per cent) had such a manager. This supports the argument in chapter 1 (p. 4) that in large plants the factory manager is very unlikely to have direct day-to-day responsibilities for personnel; hence the present sample is drawn from a population with only very small overlaps with the populations covered by previous industrial relations surveys. The information also points to the formalization of management structures: personnel specialists were reported in only 46 per cent of plants with 50 or more employees in 1977–8. Similarly, the present survey pointed to the existence of a production manager other than the factory manager in 97 per cent of cases.[4]

These differences from all manufacturing plants are, of course, to be expected. They were, indeed, one reason for focusing on large establishments, for it is here that the most sustained efforts at tackling problems of inefficiency are likely to have been concentrated. This chapter has shown that the managers in the survey had every reason to be concerned about productivity. They had just steered their plants through a deep recession in which competition had intensified and profitability had been halved. Some of the plants seemed to be recovering, as market demand improved, but others were still experiencing declining demand. Evidence on such things as the use of shift work also pointed to considerable diversity. Before examining the response in terms of changes in labour management, the position of the factory managers themselves will be considered. As shown in this chapter, many of them worked in large, multi-divisional firms. The kinds of career that they had are investigated in chapter 3, while their links with their firms are the focus of chapter 4.

Notes

1. The questions are numbered 8 to 10 in the questionnaire reproduced in Appendix B. When a question is first mentioned in the text its number is given in brackets so that the full wording may be discovered. This particular series of questions was borrowed from a questionnaire being developed in the Industrial Relations Research Unit by David Deaton and Paul Marginson in connection with their investigations of the links between plants and higher levels of firms in the management of industrial relations. Their help with these questions, and more generally with the design of the questionnaire, is gratefully acknowledged.
2. These figures express indices of output and employment in the first quarter of 1984, when the survey was conducted, in relation to the average for 1978. The indices are reported in the *Employment Gazette* (see for example January 1985, p. S.17).
3. Comparative data are hard to come by. Dawkins and Bosworth (1980) report a 1978 survey of manufacturing. Since these data relate to the number of individual manual workers employed under a given system, and not to how many establishments used it, they are not directly comparable with those presented here. But the relative importance of the various systems is similar. The authors say that 34 per cent of workers were employed on some kind of shift system. Most common were double-day arrangements (12 per cent), three-shift systems (10 per cent) and alternating days and nights (8 per cent).
4. The presence of a personnel manager was significantly related to plant size: 75 per cent of plants with fewer than 500 workers reported having such a

manager, as against 97 per cent of those with more than 500 workers. There was, however, no association with the extent of trade union organization or with the corporate status of the plant. On the latter, there was, for example, no tendency for the single independent establishments to lack specialist personnel managers.

3

Factory Managers: Careers, Roles, and Attitudes

This chapter examines the personal characteristics of the managers in the survey, in particular their careers in management and their attitudes to the managerial task. Given the aims of the survey, no data were collected on their educational or social class backgrounds or on their broad socio-political attitudes. Two considerations suggest that these absences may be less important than they appear.

First, even though many surveys of managers justify a focus on demographic data by saying that little is known about managers' backgrounds and careers, there is in fact a reasonable number of studies that chart these things. In addition to the early and frequently cited studies by Clements (1958) and D.G. Clark (1966) there were between 1970 and 1980 at least four large-scale surveys of members of the British Institute of Management (Birch and Macmillan, 1971; Melrose-Woodman, 1978; Guerrier and Philpott, 1978; Poole et al., 1981). Crockett and Elias (1984) have analysed those members of a large national population sample who could be classed as managers. Leggatt (1978) has reported on a further survey of managers in 88 companies carried out in 1970. Lee (1981) has studied the determinants of success in management. And there have been numerous studies of the social origins of directors of large companies (for example, Whitley, 1974; Stanworth and Giddens, 1974b). There would be little point in reproducing what is already known about the backgrounds of managers.

Second, general material on backgrounds and beliefs was not central to the present study. Such material has, in any event, a somewhat limited value. It does not tell us what it is like to be a manager, about the nature of the managerial role, or about the place of people called 'managers' within their firms. Case studies can throw light on these issues and help to develop an understanding of the occupation in question (two very different examples being Sofer, 1970, and Nichols and Beynon, 1977: chs 3, 7). The present study cannot emulate the detail of case studies, but it tries to use the survey method to look at issues closely related to the managers' jobs. It thus hopes to move beyond the rather unenlightening presentations to be found in much of the literature.

The first task is to use data on the factory managers' careers to compare their profile with that of 'managers' as a whole. Do factory managers stand out from the average, and if so in what ways? The place of the managers within corporate hierarchies and salary structures, including the ways in which they were paid, their experience of management development programmes, and their ownership of shares, is then investigated. These matters have not been pursued in general surveys, and little comparative information is available but they are important in assessing the job situation of managers. Attention then focuses on attitudes to the managerial task. Finally, some of the main variations identified are subjected to detailed statistical analysis. Is it the case, for example, that managers with different types of career differ in their personal characteristics or tend to work in different sorts of firm?

Managerial Careers

In providing some factual information about the age, experience, and careers of factory managers some standard of comparison is needed. The general studies mentioned above may be used to measure the characteristics of management as a whole. In view of the rather different sampling frames used by these studies, their nature needs to be briefly indicated. With the studies of BIM members there is, apart from the usual problems of response rates and so forth, the obvious point that BIM members are not typical of managers as a whole. As Melrose-Woodman (1978: 9) notes, her own sample appears to have been skewed towards large firms, reflecting the greater tendency of managers in such firms, as compared with those working in small firms, to join the BIM. Many of the older studies also looked only at managers in large companies.

Two studies help to correct this bias. Deeks (1972) looked at managers in 50 small firms in the furniture industry. Crockett and Elias (1984) have used data on the managers who were included in the National Training Survey, which was a large nationally representative sample of all adults of working age carried out during 1975 and 1976.

The authors were careful to include only people who could properly be described as managers, that is those who plan, co-ordinate, and control resources. They thus excluded first-line foremen, for example, but there are two remaining oddities about their definition. First, officers in the armed forces are included; this might be appropriate for a study of social mobility, but for a specific study of managers it seems unwise. Second, specialist managers such as chief accountants and personnel managers are excluded. The reason for this is not very clear, but for present purposes the gap is not very severe: the NTS data may not represent all managers, but they are sufficiently comprehensive in their coverage of general managers without specialist duties to act as a useful source of comparison with the factory managers in the present study.

Finally, one more specific study, namely that by Gill and Lockyer (n.d.) of 365 production managers is of some interest. The nature of this particular sample is not very clear, but it is useful here because those included within it seem to have had responsibilities similar to those of the present respondents. Thus 47 per cent of the Gill and Lockyer sample had job titles such as factory manager and production director, which correspond to the titles of the factory managers in the present sample. A further 40 per cent of Gill and Lockyer's sample had titles such as production manager or operations manager, suggesting that a fairly senior group of managers with general managerial responsibilities had been studied.

Age and Experience
The age distribution of a sample gives some indication as to its seniority; this information is also required as a 'control variable' when assessing such things as length of service with a firm and the number of moves made during a career, which are obviously age-related. The data presented in table 3.1 suggest that the factory managers tended to be older than managers in general.[1] As would be expected, it takes time to reach a relatively senior position. This is consistent with the tabulations presented by Melrose-Woodman (1978: 9) on the relationship between managers' age and their level in the managerial hierarchy, which show a tendency for older age groups to be relatively well represented in the higher echelons. The relationship was, however, far from strong: there was, for example, very little difference between the 36–45 and the 56–65 age groups according to their managerial level. This reflects a point which will run through the following discussion. Many of the supposed determinants of managerial careers exert either no effect or only a very limited effect. Although there may be a tendency for age to have some effect on careers, its effects seem to be very weak, as the Melrose-Woodman data suggest. In the present sample, moreover, there was no statistically significant difference between the mean age

TABLE 3.1
Age Distribution of Managers in Various Surveys

Age	Present Survey (1984)[a]	Guerrier and Philpott (1976)	Crockett and Elias (1975/6)	Deeks (1970)	Melrose-Woodman (1976)	Gill and Lockyer (1976)	Age
Under 30	3	8	15	15	2	20	25–35
30–39	13	35	24	20	25	36	36–45
40–49	38	34	27	20	50	35	46–55
50 and over	47	21	34	45	23	9	56 and over

Notes: Dates at head of table refer to date of survey, not publication of results.
[a] Factory managers only (N = 177).
Sources: Guerrier and Philpott (1978: 43); Crockett and Elias (1981: 7); Deeks (1972: 130); Melrose-Woodman (1978: 8); Gill and Lockyer (n.d.: 38).

TABLE 3.2
Age of Taking Up First Job in Various Surveys

Present Survey (1984)[a]		Melrose-Woodman (1976)		Gill and Lockyer (1976)	
15 or under	11	15 or under	22		
16	21	16–17	37	16 or under	47
17–20	27	18–20	19	17–20	23
21	10	21–23	16	21 and over	30
22 and over	31	24 and over	6		

Notes:
[a] Factory managers only.
Sources: Melrose-Woodman (1978: 25); Gill and Lockyer (n.d.: 24).

of the factory managers and that of the other managers.

A standard set of questions concerns managers' educational back-grounds. In Gill and Lockyer's (n.d.: 19) sample, which as suggested above has some important similarities with the present one, 45 per cent had at least two 'A' levels, and 33 per cent had a university degree. In Melrose-Woodman's (1978: 16) study the figures were 45 per cent and 28 per cent, while in the NTS sample only 6 per cent had attained any 'A' levels and 3 per cent a degree; as Crockett and Elias (1984: 36) comment, the latter figure suggests that managers as a whole have educational qualifications which are little better than those of the general population.[2] More senior managers appear to do rather better in this respect. Although the present survey did not cover qualifications, it can be inferred that the factory managers came closer to the top than the bottom of the range indicated by these studies. Evidence in support of this view comes from the distribution of the sample according to the age at which the first full-time job was taken up. As table 3.2 shows, 41 per cent of the factory managers began work at the age of 21 or older, as against 22 per cent in the Melrose-Woodman study and 30 per cent in the Gill and Lockyer study. It is likely that they had a level of educational qualifications to match. At the same time, however, a lack of qualifications is hardly a barrier to reaching a high level of management: almost a third of the factory managers had started work at the age of 16 or younger.

As would be expected, there was an association between the age of starting work and the type of job that was taken up. As table 3.3 shows, 51 per cent of those starting in manual occupations took up their first job at age 16 or younger, as against 32 per cent of the whole sample. The table also shows the distribution of first jobs. A problem in making sense of the results is the large number (29 per cent) of

TABLE 3.3
Factory Managers: Age at First Job and Level of Management of First Job

Age at First Job	Plant/dept. Manager (N = 11)	Other White-collar (N = 42)	Manual/ Apprentice (N = 67)	Mgt. Trainee (N = 52)	Other (N = 5)	All
12–15 years	6	7	18	7	0	11.0
16 years	0	29	33	4	15	21.2
17–20 years	29	16	31	24	28	25.3
21 years	0	11	5	22	0	10.7
22–4 years	32	23	11	29	57	22.2
25 years and over	32	14	1	14	0	9.6
	100	100	100	100	100	100
As % grand total	6.0	23.8	38.0	29.4	2.9	100

TABLE 3.4
Type of First Job in Some Other Surveys

	Crockett and Elias (1975/6)	Deeks (1970)	Melrose-Woodman (1976)	Clark[a] (1964)
Manual/ apprentice	57	43	15	24
Clerical/sales	26	30	25	30
Technical	3	7	26	34
Managerial	4	4	21	2
Professional	6	1	14	2
Trainee	n.a.	16	n.a.	8
Not known	6	n.a.	n.a.	0

Note:
[a] Managers in private sector only.
Sources: Crockett and Elias (1981: 15); Deeks (1972: 139); Melrose-Woodman
    (1978: 22); Clark (1966: 74).

managers who said that their first job was that of a general managerial
trainee. This must be seen as a 'genuine' result since the respondents
were given a very detailed list of occupational titles from which to
select a label appropriate to their first jobs (see Q. 36 in Appendix B).
The grading of a status such as managerial trainee is obviously difficult
without knowledge of the type of training given or what career expectations a trainee might have. What stands out from the table, however,
is the fact that over one-third of the factory managers started their
careers in manual occupations. They appear in this respect to have
fallen somewhere between all the managers included in the NTS survey
and the more elite group of BIM members. Some relevant figures are
given in table 3.4. From these data, and from what is known about the
social origins of very senior managerial groups such as the boards of
directors of large corporations, it can be concluded that management
as a whole is not a particularly 'closed' occupation. The NTS data in
particular show that managers are far from being an elite in terms of
educational background or qualifications. As one moves higher up
the scale, however, social closure increases so that directors of large
companies are drawn very heavily from elite social backgrounds. Factory managers seem to fit within this pattern.
    Aspects of their careers in management suggest that they may be
distinctive in terms of their mobility between firms and jobs. Almost
a quarter (24 per cent) of the factory managers had spent all their
careers in their present firms, and a further 21 per cent had worked

for only one other firm. The figure of 24 per cent is higher than that in a number of other surveys. Birch and Macmillan's (1971: 3) survey of BIM members gave a figure of 17 per cent; Guerrier and Philpott (1978: 7) had a figure of 13 per cent; and Poole *et al.* (1981: 52) quote 14 per cent. Only the early study by Clark (1966: 82) gives a higher figure, of 34 per cent, but given the unrepresentative nature of this sample it is hard to know how to treat the result. At least in comparison with recent surveys, the factory managers seem to have been rather immobile. This point is reinforced by their length-of-service distribution, reported in table 3.5: they had been with their present employers for rather longer than respondents to two large BIM surveys. Their length-of-service profile is similar to that of all Deeks's (1972) sample, but this reflects the inclusion in that sample of a substantial number of owner-managers, who obviously tend to remain in their own firms. The non-owner-managers had shorter lengths of service than managers in the present survey. In short, the factory managers had stayed longer with their present firms than had managers in other

TABLE 3.5
Time in Present Organization and Job Recorded in Various Surveys

	Present Survey (1984)[a]	Melrose-Woodman (1976)	Poole et al. (1980)	Deeks (1970)	
				All	'Managers' Only[b]
Time in organization (years)					
0–2	5	11	12	23	37
2–5	10	18	27		
5–10	16	22	19	44	45
10–20	29	22	24		
20 and over	40	27	19	33	18
Time in present job (years)					
0–2	41	25	22	39	57
2–5	28	37	48		
5–10	22	24	17	46	38
10–20	6	12	9		
20 and over	3	2	3	15	5

Notes:
[a] Factory managers only.
[b] In Deeks's survey, there were 94 owner-managers, 87 other managers without an ownership stake in their firms, and 48 supervisors. Data in this column relate to the second group only.
Sources: Melrose-Woodman (1978: 29); Poole *et al.* (1981: 54); Deeks (1972: 144).

surveys. Their age profile may have something to do with this, but is unlikely to be the whole explanation, since it was not dramatically different from that in the other surveys.

The broad similarity between factory managers and other managers is also borne out in comparisons within the present survey. There was no significant difference between the mean length of service of the 177 factory managers and the 58 other managers, a point which also applies to the total length of the career (that is, the time between taking up one's first job and the present). There was, however, a difference at the 5 per cent level of significance between the number of other firms worked for, with the factory managers having the higher mean figure.[3]

This is not to suggest that the managers were immobile in terms of total managerial experience. They were asked whether they had ever had any 'significant changes' in functional responsibility such as a move from production to finance both during their careers outside their present firms and while they had been with their current employers (Qs 40 and 45). Of those who had worked for other firms, 59 per cent reported having changed functions during this time, and 56 per cent said that they had done so during their careers with their present firms, giving a figure of 85 per cent who had changed functions at some time during their careers. Comparable data on this point seem to be scarce, but Melrose-Woodman (1978: 28) reports that 17 per cent of her sample had had no changes in managerial function, with 20 per cent having one change and 63 per cent two or more changes. In interpreting these results a good deal obviously turns on the meaning attached by the respondents to 'significant', and on how changes in function were defined in the Melrose-Woodman study. It seems, though, that the factory managers were roughly on a par with managers as a whole.

It appears from these comparisons that factory managers do not constitute part of a managerial elite. The age at which they started work and the type of jobs in which they began do not mark them out from the general run of management. Neither do they appear to be particularly experienced in different managerial functions.

The last point may be considered further by examining the industrial sector in which they started work and comparing it with the sector in which they were currently working. In order to have sufficient numbers, the analysis has to be limited to the five industries chosen for special consideration. In all, 69 per cent of the 112 managers concerned had begun work in an industry which could be considered to be similar to that of their present industrial sector; that is, someone working in chemicals had begun there, but in addition the mechanical and electrical engineering sectors were considered to be similar, so that one of the electrical engineering managers who had started work in a mechanical engineering firm would count as being in a similar position. Career continuity was highest in the textiles industry (81 per cent had started in the industry) and lowest in chemicals (40 per cent). It is, of course, possible that there were some movements out of an industry and back into it during the course of a career, but the evidence suggests that the overall breadth of experience was quite narrow.

In short, the factory managers were relatively immobile between firms. It may be that the surveys of BIM members have included those managers who see themselves as managerial professionals and who move between firms readily. The factory managers seem to have represented a different approach based on a rise within one firm. The difference between the two career paths of internal promotion and movement between firms may now be considered by looking at sources of variation within the sample.

Influences on Career Paths
It is possible that those who work in divisionalized corporations have moved between firms less than those working in smaller organizations because large corporations provide internal career structures. In fact, however, there was no clear relationship between the corporate status of a plant and the number of other firms in which its senior manager had worked. Nor was there a tendency for those in divisionalized firms to have had more jobs within the firm than other managers (see Q. 44, relating to how many separate jobs a manager had held between joining the firm and taking up his current position).

More positive results emerge in connection with the two career paths, that of moving up inside an organization and that of having several moves between organizations. Thus there was a tendency ($r = -0.21$, significant at better than the 1 per cent level) for those with a large number of moves between firms to have had a small number of jobs within their present firms. This is consistent with another piece of evidence on the shape of managers' careers. Respondents in multi-plant firms were asked whether their careers had been within the one plant or in other parts of the organization and, if the latter, whether this had involved any time at headquarters in a planning or strategic capacity (Qs 46, 47, and 48). Overall, one-third (33 per cent) had worked only in the one plant, 31 per cent had worked elsewhere but not at head office, and 37 per cent had planning or strategic experience at headquarters. The proportion in the last category is, in view of the generally unexceptional position of factory managers, surprisingly high. Given also the clear reference in the question to overall planning duties, it seems unlikely that the replies were based on a misunderstanding of its intent. It is possible to speculate that, while factory managers are little different from other managers in where they come from and in their first steps on the managerial ladder, those who begin to move upwards are marked out by their firms and are groomed for further progress with experience within the strategic aspects of their operations.

What is clear is that experience in these aspects was associated, although not strongly, with having worked in a small number of other firms; that is, it can be seen as part of a career progression inside companies.

Further evidence on these two types of career comes from the relationships between having changed functions during one's career, the number of firms previously worked in, and the number of jobs held in one's current firm. The number of firms worked for was associated with changes in function outside the present firm and with no changes in function in the present firm. The number of jobs exhibited the reverse pattern, having a strong association with changes in function during the career in the current firm and an association with no change of function in previous firms. There was no overall association between any change of function (that is, either in the current firm or previously) and the number of firms worked for, the number of jobs in the current firm, or length of service in the current firm. But different types of functional change do seem to be associated with different types of career. A final piece of evidence is the connection between the size of the firm and the number of previous firms for which a manager had worked. After controlling for the effects of age and length of service, there was a slight tendency ($r = 0.10$, $p = 0.067$) for those in large firms to have had a small number of previous firms. This is consistent with the view that there are different sorts of career, for large firms can provide a manager with internal career development whereas small ones are more restricted in this respect.

It must be emphasized that these relationships are far from strong. The idea of different career paths is an analytical abstraction that finds some confirmation in the data, but there are many overlaps and mixed situations such that it would be impossible to divide the managers into movers between firms and careerists within firms. It is doubtful whether the respondents would recognize themselves in such stereotypes. This is of some importance, not only in considering the present results but also interpreting the general BIM reports. These provide various cross-classifications of the data and infer a relationship between, for example, age and the type of first job. Yet the strength of the relationship is not always clear. In seeking patterns in the data there is a danger, particularly when tables are inspected without any indication of the statistical significance of the results being given, of implying that the patterns are clear-cut. In fact, it would appear that managerial careers do not fall into clear patterns. In the present survey this can be shown by comparing factory managers with the other managers. A variety of independent variables such as age, type of first job, length of career in management, number of other firms worked for, and experience of other managerial functions was unable to make any differentiation between the two groups.[4] This is in contrast to Lee's (1981: 103) finding that the level of the first job is the best predictor of success later. Several reasons may be suggested for this. In Lee's study a wider range of managerial careers was considered; specifically, 118 executive directors in 41 manufacturing organizations were studied, and compared with 48 other managers who had not progressed as far. When the top reaches of managerial hierarchies are considered, it is likely that social origins and career histories will influence success more than when middle levels of management are the focus. Even then, however, the correlations between the measure of managerial success devised by Lee and the independent variables were not large: a good deal continues to depend on personal drive and other factors that cannot be incorporated in a formal model relating success to background characteristics. In the present survey, success in the sense of attaining the position of factory manager cannot be explained by conventional demographic variables.

Conclusions
The factory managers do not appear to have differed much from managers in general in terms of their educational qualifications, age, or mobility between firms: comparisons with the other managers in the present survey and with other surveys indicate few substantial differences. This finding is surprising to the extent that distinct career paths are expected. In fact, as studies of social mobility of the population as a whole show, there is considerable fluidity in the social structure (Goldthorpe, 1980). If an individual's broad class position is far from being determined by his or her family background and educational experience, this is even more true of access to a particular occupational position such as that held by the factory managers in the present survey. There are many career paths in management, and these are not determined by individuals' background characteristics. Analysis of variations within the group of factory managers has pointed to some of the different paths that can exist. A slow rise through the ranks has been contrasted to relatively rapid promotion based on qualifications and expertise. A surprising finding was the number of factory managers who claimed to have had experience of a strategic or planning role at headquarters. This finding warrants more detailed investigation, to see whether such managers stand out from others. Possible explanations include, however, exposure to formal salary structures (on the argument that firms with such structures have a more strategic view of their managers than do others, and that this is associated with giving factory managers headquarters responsibility) and the managers' own attitudes. Examination of the determinants of types of career is best left until these matters have been explored.

Rewards and Development

Having considered how factory managers have reached their present positions, we may examine their present roles. Three aspects of their rewards and development will be highlighted. First, how are they paid: do their jobs fall within clear grading structures or is pay determination relatively informal? Second, how common is it for this stratum of management to own shares in their firms, and what significance does the pattern have? Third, in what kinds of training and development have they been involved? These issues are of considerable importance for understanding the work situation of managers but there is unfortunately little information on them in other surveys, and discussion will have to concentrate on the factory managers in their own right. It is hoped that, if the analysis is of any value, it will stimulate studies on these lines.

Salary Arrangements

Factory managers working for single-establishment companies can be taken to be the managing directors of their firms, and asking about salary structures would be inappropriate. The remainder were asked, 'Are you paid according to a formal salary structure, i.e. within a specific band or grade?' (Q. 67a). It might be expected that the recent growth and bureaucratization of firms in general, together with the reform of payment systems in particular, would have encouraged the development of formal salary structures for senior managers. There are no data on trends, but the survey shows that 40 per cent of factory managers working for multi-plant firms said that they were not paid according to formal structures. Not surprisingly, there was a strong relationship with the size of the company. Of those working in firms with fewer than 2,000 employees, 71 per cent were not paid according to a formal structure; the figure fell to 24 per cent for those in firms with 25,000 or more employees. But it is notable that even in the very large firms almost a quarter of the factory managers were not located within formal grading structures.

Those paid within such structures were asked what levels of management were covered by them. Just over half (56 per cent) said that they covered only plant managers and other senior managerial personnel at estasblishment and headquarters levels; 43 per cent said that middle and junior management were also included. In all, therefore, three-quarters of factory managers were either not included in formal grading systems or were covered by schemes which related only to very senior managerial positions.

As would be expected, objective indices were the most important in determining into what grade of a structure a particular post went. Thus

77 per cent of those paid within such structures mentioned the level of responsibility as a criterion; 35 per cent mentioned the size of the plant, and 23 per cent the use of job evaluation techniques. There was also, however, some evidence that less clear-cut measures were used: 23 per cent mentioned, on their own initiative, personal merit. Those not spontaneously mentioning personal merit were asked whether the company's evaluation of a manager's merit influenced the band to which he or she was allocated (Q. 68c). Combining the results with the number mentioning merit themselves gives a figure of 56 per cent of those in salary structures saying that personal merit was a criterion. There was little variation according to company size. It thus appears that, even among those factory managers paid according to salary structures, formal and bureaucratic procedures for allocating jobs to grades were far from universal.

The picture of informal arrangements is supported by the evidence on the ways in which increases in managers' pay were determined (Qs 70a, 71b). Very few factory managers (6 per cent) had their pay increases tied to the sums negotiated by trade unions representing other grades of staff. Just over a quarter (27 per cent) reported annual awards that were tied to profitability or some other measure of company performance. But the majority either had annual awards, with the amount of the increase being at the company's discretion, or depended on the firm for the timing as well as the amount of the increase (43 per cent and 22 per cent respectively). Remuneration thus seems to be an area in which the factory managers' direct links with their firms were far more important than were collective agreements. As table 3.6 shows, there were some variations according to company size, with the importance of complete company discretion declining as company size increased. The decline was, however, matched by a rise in the prevalence of annual awards whose amount depended on company discretion. Overall, therefore, there was no marked rise in more rigid systems of pay determination as company size rose, the only notable tendency being a concentration of arrangements tying factory managers' pay to increases negotiated with other groups among the very largest companies.

In addition to the basic salary, managers' total compensation can vary according to a large number of fringe benefits and bonuses. It was not feasible to ask detailed questions about fringe benefits, but it was decided to try to ascertain how far pay varied according to performance-related bonuses. The relevant question (Q. 70b) asked whether pay varied according to bonuses or profit-sharing schemes. Just over half (52 per cent) of factory managers reported that their pay varied in this way, with there being no variation with either plant size or company size. Those whose pay varied were asked how much, on average, variable elements added to their total salaries. The addition was fairly

TABLE 3.6
Means of Determining Pay Increases for Factory Managers, by Company Size

	Company Size (No. Employees)				
	Under 2,000 (N = 28)	*2,000– 4,999 (N = 20)*	*5,000– 24,999 (N = 46)*	*25,000 and over (N = 54)*	*All*
Company discretion	34	30	20	15	22
Annual award, amount at company discretion	29	36	43	53	43
Annual award tied to company performance	28	34	34	19	26
Annual award tied to negotiations with TUs	0	0	4	12	6
Other	9	1	0	0	3

Base: Factory managers in multi-plant firms (*N* = 164).
Note: Total figures include cases where the size of the company was not ascertained.

low, the mean being 13 per cent, with 58 per cent of the managers reporting an addition of 10 per cent or less.[5] It appears that direct performance incentives were relatively unimportant. This is supported by the evidence on the type of bonus schemes in operation. Respondents in multi-plant firms were asked whether bonuses were related to plant performance or overall company performance, or both. More mentioned the latter than the former (62 per cent and 38 per cent, respectively, of all mentions), suggesting that bonuses were more dependent on the performance of the firm than they were on the individual manager's success in attaining targets specific to his own plant.

The evidence on pay suggests, then, that companies did not treat their factory managers in a very bureaucratized manner and that direct incentives were not very prominent methods of motivating such managers. Less formal and clear-cut procedures appeared to be quite common.

All but one of the factory managers were covered by a company pension scheme. For present purposes the important question about such schemes is not so much what level of benefits they provide but how far the rights accumulated in them are transferable to other jobs, for this says something about how tied the managers were to their present firms. The results, set out in table 3.7 indicate that for the majority of managers transferability was restricted: only 30 per cent said that rights were totally transferable, while 41 per cent said that the rights were either not transferable or transferable only within the firm. As shown above, most of the managers had spent considerable periods of time with their firms. Their accumulated benefits must therefore have been substantial. Whether or not the managers saw these benefits as a constraint on moving to other firms, and if so whether they were worried about it, it is impossible to say. But there may have been some tendency in this direction.

Share Ownership
A further way of assessing managers' relationships with their firms is to consider the pattern of share ownership: how many managers held shares in their firms and how large was the typical holding? Thirty-nine per cent of all factory managers held some shares in their firms (Q. 74). As would be expected, ownership was most common in firms where the factory manager was close to the top of the managerial hierarchy; as noted above, a factory manager in an independent establishment will be the managing director of the whole firm. In such establishments, 69 per cent of respondents owned shares, as against 43 per cent in non-divisionalized groups and 35 per cent in divisionalized corporations. The size of the firm had no effect on the extent of ownership but affected the way in which shares were acquired. Overall, 62 per cent of those owning shares said that they had bought them

TABLE 3.7
Transferability of Pension Rights of Factory Managers

	(%)
Transferable:	
Within company only	20
To some other companies	14
Totally	30
But degree of transferability not known	7
Not transferable	21
Not known	6

Base: Factory managers in company pension schemes (*N* = 174).

through company schemes offering special terms to employees, but the figure was 85 per cent for those in firms with 25,000 or more employees, compared with 24 per cent where company employment was 2,000 or less.[6]

How large was the typical share holding? Respondents were asked to think of their normal basic salary as 100 per cent and to estimate the relative capital value of their shares. The mean estimate of capital value was 132 per cent of the annual salary, but this figure was the result of one or two very high estimates, the largest being 2,000 per cent, or 20 times the average salary. Fifty-five per cent of the share-owners put the value of their holdings at 10 per cent or less of their annual salaries. When this figure is taken together with the number of factory managers owning no shares in their firms, it emerges that 83 per cent either owned no shares or had only a small holding.

In view of current arguments that giving employees a stake in the firm is a way to increase commitment, some correlates of share owner-ship were analysed. There was a clear tendency for share-owners to have had longer periods of employment with their present firms than non-owners, and they had also worked for fewer firms before joining their present organizations. It is not, however, clear whether share ownership increases commitment, as measured by such things as length of service, or whether having stayed in a firm for some time simply makes it more likely that a manager will qualify for share option schemes or will think it worth his while to buy some shares. The latter possibility seems the more likely, for it is unlikely that owning some shares creates any powerful ties to the firm. There was also no tendency for the share-owners to differ from the non-owners on two of the attitudinal dimensions analysed in detail below, namely the preference for personal flexibility and the attitude towards the company. Most significantly, as shown in detail in chapter 6, the expectation that share ownership will be associated with a high level of productivity was not borne out; on the contrary, firms where the factory manager owned shares performed worse than did others.

This is not to suggest that share ownership is unimportant, although it is unlikely that having managers who own shares will, in and of itself, increase commitment to the firm. To be effective, schemes to extend share ownership need to be made part of much broader policies of involvement. As suggested in the conclusion to this chapter, links between factory managers and their firms can be strengthened. In the context of a developed policy on this, share option schemes may have a part to play, but in the absence of an overall policy they may have little impact.

Appraisal and Development
The final issue examined in this section is the prevalence of formal
systems to evaluate the managers' performance and of schemes of
management development. All those paid within formal salary structures were asked whether they were subject to any regular system of
management appraisal; 82 per cent (representing 46 per cent of all
factory managers) said that they were subject to systems of appraisal.
Just over three-quarters (78 per cent) of those subject to appraisal said
that the results of the evaluation affected the overall level of their
remuneration. This means that about one-third of all factory managers
were subject to fairly highly formalized monitoring: they were paid
according to established salary structures, they were subject to performance appraisals, and the results affected their pay.

There was no strong tendency for the use of appraisal systems to
increase with the size of firms: they were almost as common among
the smallest firms as among the largest. This is not, of course, to say
that small firms use formal pay systems as often as do large ones. As
shown above, the existence of salary structures was strongly related to
the size of firm. But once such structures have been introduced the use
of appraisal systems appears to go along with them regardless of the
size of the firm. The type of firm made more of a difference: appraisal
systems were reported by 54 per cent of those in non-divisionalized
firms and by 89 per cent of those in divisionalized corporations (a
highly significant difference on the relevant tests). In establishments
using appraisal systems for their factory managers, the systems were
used more widely within the management hierarchy. Every manager
subject to appraisal said that similar schemes operated for other managers in his plant. And when asked what was the lowest level of staff
for whom the schemes operated, 75 per cent said that they extended
down to the level of supervision or below. When appraisal systems are
used, they are used widely and, not surprisingly, it is the complex
divisionalized firms that have most use for them.

A related issue is the use of management development programmes.
These may be defined as schemes which go beyond training in the
narrow sense of providing specific skills to embrace attempts to develop
the talents of managers, to make managers aware of the overall goals
of the enterprise and, possibly, to identify 'high-flyers' who can be
moved between jobs in order to give them the experience necessary
for taking on larger responsibilities in the future. Since the term management development can cover such a wide area, it was decided to
give only a broad indication of its scope by asking (at Q. 119), 'does
the corporation employ management development programmes to
widen the experience of managers at your level?' Respondents do not
appear to have had any difficulty with seeing what the question was

about: there were only two 'don't know' replies. Of those working for multi-plant firms, 67 per cent reported the presence of development programmes, and of these 80 per cent had personal experience of them. When asked what the programmes involved, most managers, not surprisingly, mentioned training courses inside or outside their firms; but just under a third also cited new experience in other functions or parts of the firm. This last category reflects one of the more important aspects of development, namely deliberately moving managers around the company in order to increase their experience. A substantial minority of firms appear to be doing this with their factory managers, which could be a pointer to future developments wherein firms treat their managerial resources in an increasingly strategic way.

As would be expected, the use of development programmes increased with the size of firms and was also most common in divisionalized organizations. The use of programmes involving experience in new managerial functions was also related to firm size, but there was no link with the complexity of organizational structure. In neither case, however, was there any association with such indices of company success as profitability or the rate of growth of turnover (the latter being measured over the period 1978–82). It might also be expected that experience of a development programme might lead to a favourable attitude to the company, but in fact there was no link between such experience and the measures of attitudes discussed below.

These results suggest that the most successful firms were not those most involved in the advanced forms of management development. It may be that, faced with the impact of the recession, relatively unprofitable firms, as much as profitable ones, have tried to restructure their internal organization in order to release managers' capacities of initiative. In any event, management development programmes do not appear to be restricted to particular types of firm.

Attitudes to the Managerial Role

The final way of assessing factory managers' involvement in their firms was to turn to their attitudes to their jobs. Four specific issues connected with the managerial role were investigated. First, the measure of personal flexibility introduced by Ellis and Child (1973) in their study of managers in 78 organizations was employed. It assesses how much variety managers desire in their work. It has two main values here: in examining how factory managers score in comparison with other managers, in particular whether they turn out to be more flexible than the supervisors in two factories who replied to the same questions (Child and Partridge, 1982); and in seeing whether certain types of firm are associated with flexibility or inflexibility. The second issue was

TABLE 3.8
Job Flexibility of Factory Managers

	Degree of Flexibility				
	High	*Med. High*	*Med.*	*Med. Low*	*Low*
Job which is changing	47.5	29.3	14.6	4.9	3.7
New circumstances	51.5	28.9	14.0	4.2	1.4
Regular pattern of working day[a]	22.1	40.9	23.5	8.1	5.4
Doing things that I am used to[a]	19.8	41.6	23.6	6.4	8.7
Taking on new problems	64.6	28.0	4.0	2.0	1.4

Note:
[a] The statements for these two items were phrased in favour of an 'inflexible' response, e.g. 'I like to have a regular pattern in my working day'. Scores have been reversed to ease comparison with the three items.

the views of managers in multi-plant firms concerning the extent to which company management knew about events at local level and respected the position of establishment managers. The questions aimed to assess the extent to which those in operating units were alienated from higher management. Third, questions were asked about the organization of management and the extent to which different levels of management were felt to have a role to play in the organization. Finally, some broader questions were asked about the ways in which managers felt that people like themselves were evaluated by various groups in society.

Ellis and Child (1973) used a set of ten questions from which, on the basis of factor analysis, they chose five which correlated quite closely together and seemed to give a consistent measure of personal flexibility. These five were used here, with a five-point scale (Q. 84). Two of the statements are phrased to give regularity and not flexibility a positive rating (for example, 'I like to have a regular pattern in my working day'); scores on these were reversed. An index of flexibility was created by adding together scores on all five questions, low scores indicating a high level of flexibility. The scores on each item for factory managers are given in table 3.8; in line with the earlier evidence on the absence of differences between factory managers and the other managers in the survey, there were no significant differences between the two groups.

Replies were fairly heavily weighted towards the 'flexibility' end of the continuum. This was particularly so with taking on new problems, while there was more preference for regularity in the items referring to a pattern to the working day and doing 'something that I am used to rather than something different'. This may have reflected the wording of these questions which stresses predictability. Overall, however, a preference for flexibility emerged strongly. This is confirmed by comparison with Child and Partridge's (1982) data on supervisors in two Birmingham factories. From the raw data very generously provided by Bruce Partridge, it can be calculated that on the first question, for example, 28 per cent of the supervisors chose the flexible option as against 48 per cent of factory managers. A chi-square test on this and two other questions pointed to a highly significant difference between the two groups: an unsurprising but useful result.

The six questions on the company's responsiveness to local needs and problems were designed to form part of an assessment of the place of factory managers within their organizations (Q. 124). Do they feel that they are isolated from the decision-making centres of the organization, or do they see themselves as having knowledge of and influence over the decisions that affect them? The results (table 3.9) point in general to a reasonably high level of satisfaction with the activities of company management. Satisfaction was highest with respect to the amount of consultation over allocation of funds for investment and with taking local advice in implementing pay awards. There was rather more dissatisfaction about being kept in the dark about the development of strategic plans, but most dissatisfaction focused on the interchange of personnel between the operational and the strategic levels of company operations, with the number of dissatisfied managers balancing the number who were satisfied.

Since similar questions have not been asked in other surveys the results are difficult to interpret: are the replies more or less favourable to the company than might have been expected? There is obviously a strong possibility that answers were biased towards the 'favourable' end of the spectrum, for managers may be unwilling to enter strong criticism of their employing organizations in questionnaire surveys of this sort. It may therefore be that the impression of satisfaction with the company is exaggerated. There is no way of assessing the extent of bias, but, unless it was very strong, there appears to have been no substantial discontent among the factory managers with the ways in which their firms treated them.

The third set of attitudes to be investigated was the managers' opinion of the contribution of different functional specialisms and levels of management (Q. 96). The results for the four areas chosen are set out

TABLE 3.9
Factory Managers' Attitudes Towards Company-Level Management

	Very Favourable	Fairly Favourable	Med.	Fairly Unfavourable	Very Unfavourable
Pay attention to advice re pay award	41.9	26.9	16.2	7.2	7.8
Accounting system and needs of individual plants[a]	22.7	29.8	24.5	18.3	4.8
Out of touch[a]	23.9	40.6	29.3	3.5	2.7
Consultation on allocation of investment funds	48.2	34.8	11.4	3.8	1.9
Strategic planning at HQ[a]	21.3	27.0	35.3	11.1	5.3
Interchange of personnel	12.7	22.0	29.3	24.8	11.2

Base:
Factory managers in multi-plant firms (N = 164).
Note:
[a]The statements on these three items were phrased in favour of a critical view of the company: see Q. 124. The scores have been reversed.

in table 3.10. As would be expected factory managers did not feel that the generalist had been superseded by the specialist. On a scale running from 1 to 7, with 7 representing the view that the generalist still had an important role to play, the mean score was 5.4, and most of the managers gave the extreme score of 7. On the next two issues, on whether specialists tend to take an overly narrow view of the business as seen in terms of their own specialisms and on the amount of discretion that should be granted to junior managers, the managers opted for a more middling view; replies were concentrated around the middle of the range. Finally, the managers strongly dissented from the view that supervisors had few responsibilities left; more than half of them chose the opposite extreme of seeing supervisors as important members of line management. Although unsurprising, this pattern of replies indicates that factory managers were strongly of the view that generalists, both in management as a whole and at the level of first-line supervision, were important while not dismissing the contribution of specialists. Prospective members of a managerial elite might be expected to be more critical of the contributions of junior managers and supervisors. The evidence is consistent with a picture of these managers as middle managers. As shown above, they did not stand out from management in general in terms of backgrounds or careers, and their attitudes reflected a balanced judgement in which the contributions of different functions and levels of management were recognized.

Finally, some questions were asked about how the managers felt they

TABLE 3.10
Factory Managers: Views on Managerial Specialisms

	Mean score	Mode	Per Cent Choosing Modal Option
General manager superseded by specialist	5.4	7	31
Specialists take a narrow view of business	4.1	5	24
Junior managers need discretion	3.8	4	26
Supervisors are important	1.9	1	55

Note:
Respondents were asked to rate pairs of statements, on a scale from 1 (totally agree with one statement) to 7 (totally agree with other). Full wording is at Q. 96. Above statements are those at the low end (score 1) of the scale.

had been doing in terms of pay, both in relation to the cost of living and in relation to other groups within their firms (Qs 81 and 83); and they were also asked about how they felt they were evaluated by other groups (Qs 85 and 86). On pay, there was substantial satisfaction: 84 per cent of factory managers felt that their pay in recent years had kept pace with the cost of living, as against 16 per cent who did not. In relative terms, those perceiving an improvement in managers' pay outnumbered those who felt that there had been a worsening: in relation to non-manual workers, for example, 31 per cent of factory managers felt that their relative pay position had improved, as against 10 per cent perceiving a worsening, with 59 per cent saying that there was no change.[7] Similarly, most managers felt that other key groups placed a high value on their contribution: 88 per cent of factory managers employed by multi-plant groups felt that their company as a whole rated their contribution highly or very highly. The figure fell to 63 per cent on the perceived evaluation by manual workers, and to only 15 per cent for how the managers felt that people in society as a whole saw their own contribution. The last figure is consistent with a widespread feeling in manufacturing industry that working in it is valued far less highly than working in accounting, finance, or the liberal professions. The factory managers seem to have shared this feeling. At the same time, however, they were broadly satisfied with their own role, not only in terms of pay but also in how their companies responded to them.

The measures of personal flexibility and company attitudes were designed to tap some underlying dimension of attitudes. Previous uses of the former have demonstrated that the items are sufficiently inter-correlated to produce a reliable scale (see, for example, Child and Partridge, 1982: 221). This was also true in the present case. The practical result is that scores on the five measures can be added together to form one index of flexibility. The results for attitude to the company are less clear-cut, but a reasonable degree of inter-correlation was observed, so that one scale may be used. For the third set of attitudes, that assessing managers' views of the role of functional specialists and different levels of managers, no underlying dimension was expected, and the items do not form a reliable scale.[8] Multi-variate analysis of the determinants of flexibility and company attitude is thus feasible. The results are discussed in the following section.

Some Determinants of Career Patterns and Job Attitudes

The foregoing sections have described the main results of the survey and have considered some of the more obvious of the possible influences on them, for example the link between company size and the existence of formal salary structures. It is also worth investigating whether any more complex patterns of association are observable. Three issues stand out as meriting special attention. First, as noted in the first section, a surprisingly large number of factory managers claimed to have had experience of working at company headquarters in a strategic or planning role. Do these managers stand out from the rest? Second, were there any systematic influences on the degree of personal flexibility exhibited by factory managers? Third, did those with critical attitudes towards their firms differ from those who were more satisfied?

Two main sets of influences on each of these three measures may be studied. The first is fairly straightforward and relates to the managers' own characteristics. Were the older or longer-serving managers more likely, for example, to express satisfaction with their firms? Second, and more directly linked to the concerns of this study as a whole, are measures of the type of firm. Does the presence of such a factor as a formal salary structure affect the level of satisfaction? If certain types of firms tend to have certain types of manager, the assessment of links between firms and managers will be extended, for it will be shown that careers and attitudes are determined by structural as well as personal influences. In other words, some types of firm attract specific types of manager to work for them. The policy implication would be that, rather than using uniform criteria of ability when recruiting managers, firms should seek the type of manager who is likely to fit their own particular needs.

Career Paths and the Headquarters Role
The question about the characteristics of those with headquarters experience is part of a twofold investigation of career paths. It was suggested above that there may be two extreme types of managerial career, one exemplified by the 'high flyers' with experience at headquarters and the other by the 'slow risers' who have moved gradually up the managerial hierarchy and are unlikely to progress further. What features distinguish each group from other managers?

The appropriate technique here is discriminant analysis. In brief the programme is given two or more groups and a set of independent variables. It aims to use these variables so as to maximize the distance between the groups. A perfect analysis would be able to use scores on the independent measure to predict into which group an individual fell. Further technical details of the method are given in Appendix A.

In the present case it is in principle possible to try to distinguish between three groups: those with careers limited to one plant; those working in more than one plant but not at headquarters; and those having a headquarters role. Since, however, these groups can be seen as forming a continuum of experience it is unlikely that two distinct dimensions can be identified. Using two discriminating functions may not help much. On a more substantive note, there may be distinct features of the first and last groups which warrant particular attention. Two separate analyses will therefore be carried out: distinguishing between those with careers in only the one plant and the rest of factory managers; and distinguishing those with headquarters experience from all others.

Several sets of independent variables can be identified. The first relates to the personal characteristics of the managers. Length of service is obviously important, for a new recruit will have had little opportunity of moving around the firm; length of service will then be positively related to having a career in only the one plant. (For brevity, this dependent variable will be called ONEPLANT, while HQ represents cases where headquarters experience was reported. Throughout, a measure quoted in capital letters indicates a variable used in one or more of the multivariate statistical analyses reported in this and other chapters.) A manager's age, the number of firms that he has previously worked for, the number of posts held in his present firm, and the number of separate parts of the organization that he has worked in (AGE, NFIRMS, POSTS and PARTS) might also be expected to affect his career pattern. Do those with experience in a large number of other firms, for example, gain in so far as their present firms recognize this experience by giving them headquarters responsibilities? These, and the other variables used in the final model, are listed in table 3.11 which summarizes the discussion in the text as an *aide-mémoire*. Variables are listed in the order of entry into the model (see table 3.12).

The age at which a manager started full-time employment (AGESTART) may also be significant: those starting work late in life are likely to have the highest educational qualifications, and it is possible that they enjoy benefits in terms of their careers. Two other variables index the level at which the first job was taken up. As suggested above, it is not advisable to try to produce a single continuous variable measuring this level since it is unclear where starting as a managerial trainee, for example, should fit into a hierarchy: is it 'higher' or 'lower' than starting as, say, a supervisor? In order to avoid this problem, one variable, TRAINEE indicates that a manager's first job was as a general management trainee. A second, HISTART, shows that the first job was in one of the unambiguously 'high' job grades; specifically, it takes the value 1 if the first job was clearly managerial with other than merely routine levels of responsibility. Finally, managers' attitudinal characteristics may be important. A reasonable expectation is that managers who like change and new challenges will be those who tend to have had headquarters experience. There would then be an association between the measure of personal flexibility, FLEX, and career paths. Given the scoring of the measures, this means a positive coefficient for FLEX in

TABLE 3.11

Independent Variables Used in Prediction of Managers' Careers

Variable	Meaning	Expected Association with	
		Career in One Plant (ONEPLANT)	Having Had HQ Planning Role (HQ)
AGE	Manager's age	+/−[a]	+
LS	Length of service with firm (years)	+/−[a]	+
SALSTR	Presence of formal salary structure in firm	−	+
SHARES	Manager owns shares in firm	−	+
FLEX	Manager's score on job flexibility measures (a low score means high preference for flexibility)	+	−
IND1, IND2 etc.	Dummy variables controlling for industrial sector	0[b]	0[b]
AGESTART	Age at taking up first job	−	+
PARTS	Number of parts of firm previously worked in	−	+
POSTS	Number of posts previously held	−	+
NFRMS	Number of firms previously worked for	−	+
COSIZE	Size of company	−	+
HISTART	First job at a managerial level	−	+
TRAINEE	First job as general managerial trainee	?[c]	?[c]

Notes:

Predictions are not necessarily the author's own; they represent plausible arguments that warrant investigation.

[a] Arguments for positive effects (e.g. those with careers in one plant are 'slow risers') and for negative effects (e.g. a short period of service makes it likely that only a restricted career path can have been followed) are both possible.

[b] No predictions made: variable used to control for any industry specific effects (e.g. chemicals firms are more 'progressive' than others).

[c] No predictions made: effect is uncertain.

the model predicting ONEPLANT and a negative coefficient in the prediction of HQ.

A second set of variables reflects the characteristics of industries and firms. It is possible that firms in different industrial sectors differ in their needs for managerial talents and in their traditions of operating their businesses. A relatively traditional area such as textiles, for example, might see factory management as a fairly self-contained activity, with managers not needing to move around the firm, while, in more rapidly changing fields such as chemicals, firms might take a more strategic view of their managerial personnel. Whatever the precise mechanisms involved, there may be some systematic industry effects which need to be allowed for. The size of the firm (COSIZE) is also of obvious relevance, since the chances of movement are likely to be higher the larger the firm, although it is also possible that as firm size increases so does the distance between operating units and headquarters, the result being that the chances of gaining headquarters experience would fall with increasing firm size.

A final set of variables indicates something of the connections between firms and their managers. SALSTR indicates that the company had a formal structure for determining the grade into which a factory manager's job went. SHARES indicates that a manager held shares in his company. Why might the holding of shares be expected to affect the type of career that a manager had? The answer to this question indicates a fundamental point about the assumptions on which the exercise is carried out. It is not being hypothesized that holding shares in a firm makes the individual manager more or less likely to have a particular career pattern. Instead, share-holding should be seen as a reflection of a particular type of firm, namely one in which managers are encouraged to involve themselves in its fortunes. Ownership of shares might then be expected to be reflected in experience at headquarters. Or, to put the point slightly differently, the type of manager who is likely to have such experience and to be a high-flyer may also be likely to own shares and to take a personal interest in the company's development. A similar and more obvious argument applies to SALSTR: the use of formal salary structures may be one part of a more general policy of developing systematically managerial resources. Thus firms with such structures may also have a policy of developing the skills of their managers by giving them experience at headquarters level.

It must be emphasized that these various hypotheses are no more than suggestions of some very broad tendencies. The connection between share ownership and career patterns, for example, is very unlikely to be any more than a weak association. Neither should great expectations be held for the overall model of career development, for whether or not a manager has had a particular kind of experience is likely to be affected by a range of influences tied up with his personal history, the chance of a particular post's becoming available at a particular time, and so on. Some such influences can be very roughly captured in variables such as POSTS and NFIRMS but there is bound to be a large part of the variation of the dependent variables that cannot be explained by them. It should also be stressed that some of the hypotheses to be investigated are plausible possibilities that can be deduced from commonly held expectations, and not necessarily arguments that would be endorsed by the writer.

With these points in mind, the results can be considered; they are set out in table 3.12. One preliminary point must be made. It is possible to enter the independent variables concurrently, with them all competing for inclusion in the model. It is also possible, however, to experiment with the effects of sub-sets of variables, forcing their consideration by the statistical programme before other sub-sets are included. Such an approach is indicated in the table by listing the variables in blocks: all those in Block *A* were entered before those in Block *B* were included, and so on. One approach would be to take personal characteristics as one block and company measures as another; this would be appropriate if the effects of personal characteristics were of particular interest to the investigation. In the present case the interest was more exploratory and the constituents of the blocks developed from a process of experimentation. At a preliminary stage several variables were considered. For example, the effects of industrial location were considered by entering five variables, each taking the value 1 for one of the five industries selected for special attention and zero otherwise. In fact, only the dummy for industry number two (IND2: the chemicals industry) had any effect. The model represented by Block *A* is the result of some initial experimentation; Block *B* shows a second set of variables added to see if any further effects could be identified; and Block *C* considers the effects of the type of first job held. For most purposes, the final model is the most interesting, with the results for each block being pertinent only in so far as they influence the order of inclusion of the variables: those in Block *B* could not be included ahead of those in Block *A*, and consideration of the order of inclusion needs to take this into account.

Overall, in view of the caveats mentioned above, both models perform quite well with Wilks's lambda being significantly below its maximum level of unity and with moderately high canonical correlation coefficients. The coefficient of 0.7 indicates that 49 per cent of the variance in the dependent variable, ONEPLANT, was accounted for, although, as will be seen, this was a somewhat artificially high figure; but the coefficient of 0.54 for HQ, where artificial influences were absent, was quite high. Some of the expectations outlined above were not met. Thus the measure of length of service, LS, was included to take account of the common-sense argument that the chance of moving between posts will depend on having been with a firm for some time. But, as the zero under the inclusion level shows, it did not appear in the model predicting HQ. It entered the model for ONEPLANT, but not only was its coefficient small but its sign was also not that expected: the positive sign indicates a tendency for those with longer periods of service to have careers limited to the one plant. As suggested above, there may be different paths of career development, with one path being that of the relatively slow developer who rises gradually in a firm and whose career has a limited range. The results on the LS and AGE variables support this view, with age and length of service being positively associated with remaining in one plant. On other aspects of personal characteristics, both POSTS and NFIRMS have positive associations with ONEPLANT, indicating a good degree of moving about between and within firms before attaining the current position. Although far from decisive, this evidence is again consistent with a career path of many rather short-range moves. The results for FLEX, the measure of personal flexibility are also pertinent: since a low score represents a high level of flexibility, the negative coefficient means that those restricted to the one plant were relatively inflexible in their attitudes to their jobs. And the negative coefficient for HISTART shows that those starting their careers in the higher reaches of management were least likely to be restricted to the one plant: a further result suggesting that those with careers limited to one plant tend not to be the high-flyers.

The results for the model predicting HQ are broadly consistent with this interpretation. Length of service played no role in the model: simply staying with the firm a long time did not help. Having a preference for change was very important and having started at a high level of management or as a managerial trainee was also important. What the results for the last two variables means is best seen by reference to the category that they exclude, namely manual and routine white-collar jobs. Starting in such jobs reduces the likelihood of working at headquarters level: a suitable first job is important to the manager's subsequent career. The picture is not, however, unambiguous. The positive result for AGE shows that being older is associated both with staying in the one plant and with having headquarters experience. It is possible to rationalize this by arguing that very junior managers are unlikely to attain a strategic planning role, so that age is likely to be associated with such experience, while also arguing that age can also be associated with a slow rise through the ranks. But there is a further problem with the AGESTART coefficient which, on the view that high-flyers are highly qualified, should be positive whereas in fact it is negative. There is no obvious explanation of this result. One tenuous *ex post* argument goes that, once the positive effects of HISTART and

Table 3.12
Models for Explanation of Factory Managers' Experience Within Their Firms

	Model as to Whether:					
	Career Limited to One Plant[a] (ONEPLANT)			Career Includes HQ Planning[b] (HQ)		
	Order of Inclusion	Sig. (p)	Coeff.	Order of Inclusion	Sig. (p)	Coeff.
Independent variables						
Block A:						
AGE	3	0.000	+0.15	3	0.000	+0.44
LS	2	0.000	+0.05	0		
SALSTR	1	0.000	-0.27	1	0.005	+0.63
SHARES	0			5	0.000	+0.16
FLEX	4	0.000	+0.17	2	0.000	-0.93
IND2	0			4	0.000	-0.29

BLOCK B:						
AGESTART	0	0.000		7	0.000	−0.32
PARTS	5	0.000	−0.92	0	0.000	+0.38
POSTS	7	0.000	+0.29	6		
NFIRMS	6	0.000	+0.39	0		
COSIZE	0			0		
Block C:						
HISTART	8	0.000	−0.29	8	0.088	+0.37
TRAINEE	0			9	0.000	+0.22
Summary statistics						
Wilks's lambda	0.51	0.000		0.70	0.000	
Canonical correlation	0.70			0.54		

Notes:

[a] High score indicates career limited to one plant.

[b] High score indicates career includes time in planning role.

Inclusion level zero indicates that variable was included in the model but did not attain the criteria for inclusion in the predicting equation. For other explanation, see text.

TRAINEE have been taken into account, any further tendency to start one's career late has a depressing effect on the chances of having a planning role: starting as a routine white-collar worker at the age of, say, 22 is unlikely to lead to being marked out as a high flyer.

Turning now to company characteristics, perhaps the most notable result is the lack of significance of company size in either model. As suggested above, the size effect could operate in either direction. If this is so, the positive and the negative effects seem to have cancelled each other out. Such a result should not be taken lightly. It may seem to be 'obvious' that large firms have bureaucratic structures which make it difficult for operating managers to play a planning role. If this expectation were confirmed, a statistical analysis might be criticized for finding out what was already known. In fact, such analysis permits at least some apparently commonsensical expectations to be refuted.

The results for SALSTR and SHARES, two variables included very much on an experimental basis, are clearer. In both models SALSTR was the first variable to be included; the signs of the coefficients show that firms with formal structures were least likely to restrict their factory managers to single plants and most likely to give them headquarters experience. The results for SHARES, although less impressive, point in a similar direction, with share ownership being associated with headquarters experience. Although it would be dangerous to place too much weight on such evidence, it at least suggests that there are different types of firms and that some firms treat their factory managers in a long-term strategic way.

Finally, the result for PARTS warrants comment. Its inclusion in the model predicting ONEPLANT is the reason why the canonical correlation coefficient for the model was termed artificially high: the variable measures the number of other parts of the enterprise that a manager had worked in, and if his career was in the one plant he could not have worked in any other parts. The variable's substantive importance is in the HQ equation, for, as against some expectations, how many different parts of the organization a manager had worked in had no effect on his chance of having had headquarters experience.

To summarize, the results are, in view of the obviously difficult nature of the exercise, quite encouraging. There is some evidence that managers staying in the one plant tend to be the relatively slow developers and to have a preference for stability and predictability in their jobs. By contrast, those with headquarters experience were much more likely to stress a desire for change, and for them being in the firm for a long time was unimportant. They also tended to work in firms in which formal salary structures were used and in which share ownership was encouraged. There are, then, some pointers, admittedly not very strong or clear ones, suggesting that there are different types of career

paths and that these depend not just on managers' individual characteristics but also on the nature of the firms for which they work.

Personal Flexibility
Several possible sets of influences on the level of managers' personal
flexibility can be identified. First, there are their own characteristics.
It is likely, for example, that increasing age and experience in a firm
are associated with a decline in willingness to accept change. The index
of flexibility would thus be expected to be inversely related to such
measures as age, length of service in the present firm, and total length
of career since starting work. On the other hand, someone who has
had numerous changes of position and changes in functional responsibility might be expected to be more flexible in his approach than
someone with a more limited range of experience. The number of firms
previously worked for, the number of posts previously held in the
present firm, and experience of significant changes in functional
responsibility during the career would all then be positively related to
flexibility. Investigating such relationships has some value, but the most
that it can really do is confirm some more or less obvious expectations
about managers' personal attributes. Of much more substantive interest
is the question of whether firms with different structural characteristics
tend to contain managers who are particularly flexible. Are the more
successful firms associated with flexibility and, if so, can a causal link
between these things be inferred? The nature of the firm and the nature
of the market environment need to be distinguished. On the former,
it is possible to see whether size, profitability, the firm's rate of growth,
and the plant's own economic performance are related to flexibility.
On the latter, it is possible that managers working in some sorts of
market and with some sorts of technology require more flexibility than
others. Highly competitive product markets and technologies that are
liable to disruptions may attract managers with a liking for change and
uncertainty, whereas more stable conditions may appeal to those with
a preference for regularity and order.

Since the main interest was in the structural characteristics of firms,
product markets, and technologies, the first step was to test the effects
of measures of these things. Twelve independent variables were identified. Two, the size of the individual plant and the size of the whole
company, measured the size of the organization in which the manager
worked. A priori expectation of the effects of size are, as in many
other aspects of organizational behaviour, far from simple. It could be
argued that size will bring increasing responsibilities and an ability to
deal with changing circumstances, so that it will be directly associated
with flexibility. Alternatively, size might be seen, as it has been by
several writers, as an index or correlate of bureaucracy, the result being
that large organizations will be seen as stultifying initiative and as

encouraging conformity to rules; those seeking change and new challenges would then avoid such organizations. The size measures are thus entered with no prior expectation as to the direction of their association with flexibility.

Three other measures reflect company and plant performance. These are the rate of profit (profits as a proportion of turnover) in 1982; the proportionate rate of growth of turnover between 1978 and 1982; and a measure of the plant's financial performance. The last stems from a question to respondents about the profitability of their own establishments (Q. 137). The measure is a dummy variable taking the value 1 if the plant was said to be making very large or satisfactory profits (the first two categories of the question) and zero otherwise. A reasonable hypothesis to test here is that high levels of performance are associated with managers who are flexible. Three further variables measured aspects of the company's organization. Two dummy variables indicated whether a plant was part of a divisionalized corporation and whether it was a single, independent establishment. As with the measures of size, expected associations with flexibility are uncertain. A third dummy represented establishments that were owned by foreign companies. It is often argued that foreign companies have a more dynamic approach to management than do British ones. Thus Ellis and Child (1973: 248) found an association between flexibility and employment in American-owned firms.

Finally, four variables indexed product market and technological conditions. Two dummies representing the extent of competition were employed, one indicating those cases in which competition in all the establishment's markets was felt to be severe or very severe, and the other those cases where the level of competition was felt to be increasing. Both are expected to be positively related to the manager's flexibility. Two, admittedly rather limited, measures of technical conditions were used. The first indicated that there was shift working for a significant group of manual workers in the establishment. The expectation is that shifts will involve problems of co-ordination and will require more flexibility than will operations without shift work. The second represented cases where a breakdown in one part of the production process brought the whole sequence of operations to a halt (see Qs 3, 4, and 5). Again, it is expected that managers working in environments where stoppages can occur will require more toleration of change and uncertainty than those in more predictable environments.

In addition to these twelve variables, dummy variables for industrial location were used. It is possible that, in addition to any effects due to technical and product market characteristics as measured by the variables just discussed, there are some other aspects of these characteristics that affect managers' flexibility. Perhaps, for example, the food, drink, and tobacco sector is more ordered and predictable in terms of the variability of demand and the nature of the production process than is, say, the printing industry. Five dummies were created for each of the five industrial sectors given special attention in the study. They are used simply to control for extraneous influences not measured by other variables included in the analysis.

A multiple regression model was estimated. Of these 17 variables, including the five industry dummies, only three, the two dummies for competition and the dummy representing single independent establishments, attained significant levels of association with the measure of flexibility. The association of the first two was in the expected direction, that is, competitive conditions were associated with a high level of flexibility. The same was the case with the measure of being a single, independent establishment. There is thus some support for the view that being in a small organization is associated with a preference for change. But the lack of significance of the other measures of size suggest that it would be unwise to conclude that there is a clear relationship between size and a growth of bureaucracy and inflexibility.

It now has to be seen whether these already far from impressive results stand up when aspects of managers' personal characteristics are brought into the picture. Table 3.13 summarizes the variables used. In the first column of table 3.14 the results of the model which best fits the data are reported. The dependent variable, FLEX, is the measure created by adding together the results of the five questions about personal flexibility.[9]

Six measures of personal characteristics are given in the table, of which three had significant degrees of association with flexibility. The variable AGESTART gives the age at which a respondent started full-time work. The significant negative coefficient indicates that flexibility increased with the age of starting work; the implication is that the more educationally qualified managers who started work later than their counterparts were more likely to be flexible, a result which accords with common sense. A second significant measure, labelled EXP, indicates a change in functional responsibility prior to joining the present firm; again as expected, such experience is associated with a high degree of flexibility. Yet it does not seem to be changes in functional responsibility as such which are important: a variable indicating any change in responsibility, either before joining the present firm or during the career with the firm, failed to attain any significant association with flexibility. Experience outside the present firm seems to be crucial. One aspect of the career within the present firm did affect flexibility. This was the number of separate posts held between joining the firm and taking up the present post; as expected, a large number of job moves was associated with a high degree of flexibility. Other aspects of personal experience did not affect flexibility. Most notably, age did not attain a significant level of association, although its effect was in

TABLE 3.13
Variables Used in Predicting Personal Flexibility and Attitudes to Firm

Variable	Meaning	Expected Association with	
		FLEX[a]	COATT[b]
AGE	Manager's age	+	−
LS	Length of service	+	−
EXP	Experience in other functions prior to joining present firm	−	+/−
AGESTART	Age at taking up first job	−	−
POSTS	Number of posts previously held	−	−
NFIRMS	Number of firms previously worked for	−	+/−
INDEP	Firm is single, independent establishment	−	n.a.
COMP1	Competition in markets is severe or very severe	−	?
COMP2	Competition is increasing	−	?
LOCOST	Production costs below average for industry	?	−
FLEX	Personal flexibility score	n.a.	+

Notes:
Variables are those reported in table 3.14; other variables included in preliminary analysis are excluded. See table 3.11 for conventions used.
[a] Low score = high flexibility.
[b] Low score = favourable attitude to firm.
n.a. = not applicable.

the expected direction, that is with increasing age being associated with declining flexibility. The same point applies to length of service with the present firm. Finally, the number of firms previously worked for, NFIRMS, failed to exhibit any relationship with flexibility.

This is a very mixed set of results. Some biographical variables performed well while others, which on a priori grounds might also be expected to affect flexibility, did not. But there is at least some indication that such variables had an effect on flexibility. In addition, one of the structural variables considered above, namely that measuring a high level of product market competition (COMP1), continued to perform impressively. The other structural variables lost significance.

The model explains 22 per cent of the variance of the measure of flexibility. By the standards of analyses carried out in the area of, say, industrial economics this is not a high figure. But in the light of the

TABLE 3.14

Determinants of Factory Managers' Personal Flexibility and Attitudes to Their Companies

	Dependent Variable		
	FLEX[a] (N = 175)	COATT[b] (N = 157)	COATT[a]

Independent variables: beta coefficients
  (t statistics in brackets)

	FLEX[a]	COATT[b]	COATT[a]
AGE	0.15 (1.57)	−0.37*** (3.78)	−0.43*** (4.43)
LS	0.11 (0.88)	0.32** (2.55)	0.29** (2.45)
EXP	−0.20** (2.31)	−0.15 (1.64)	−0.08 (0.84)
AGESTART	−0.25*** (3.43)	−0.14* (1.83)	−0.05 (0.66)
POSTS	−0.22** (2.23)	−0.29*** (2.72)	−0.22** (2.07)
NFIRMS	0.00 (0.03)	−	−
INDEP	0.08 (1.19)	−	−
COMP1	−0.24*** (3.42)	−	−
COMP2	−0.10 (1.48)	−	−
LOCOST	−0.05 (0.63)	0.13 (1.62)	0.13* (1.77)
FLEX	−	−	0.29*** (3.64)
Summary statistics			
$\bar{R}^2$	0.22	0.14	0.20
F	5.93***	5.21***	6.71***

Notes:
[a] Low scores represent a high degree of flexibility.
[b] Low scores reflect a favourable attitude to the company. Only managers in multi-plant firms were asked these questions.
  * = significant at 10% level.
 ** = significant at 5% level.
*** = significant at 1% level.

nature of the dependent variable it is not to be dismissed. Crockett and Elias (1984) were able to explain 47 per cent of the variance of the earnings of male managers in the National Training Survey, but earnings are a fairly unambiguous measure and are likely to be reasonably closely related to a range of independent influences. The desire for change in one's working environment, by contrast, is much more of a personal attribute reflecting one's views of oneself. It is less likely to vary systematically with independent influences since it is to a substantial degree an expression of personal preference and not an unambiguous characteristic of a manager's position. In view of this, explaining as much as 22 per cent of the variance of the measure can be taken to be a reasonable achievement. In particular, the finding that the most flexible managers are found in the most competitive product markets is robust, and suggests that firms operating in such markets may want to consider whether they have managers with the appropriate attitudes to changing conditions. Now it may be suggested that the correlation is not all that powerful, because we do not have an independent measure of competitive circumstances: what is being correlated is one set of attitudes (personal flexibility) with another (the manager's belief that he is in a highly competitive environment). But it is reasonable to suppose that assessments of the extent of competition were tolerably objective. As noted in chapter 2, for example, the assessments fitted with the industrial distribution of respondents, with managers in the sectors that an independent observer might consider to be the most competitive being most likely to rate competition as strong.

As noted above, the FLEX measure has been used in two previous pieces of research. It is difficult to make direct comparisons since the issues of interest are rather different. Child and Partridge (1982), for example, related supervisors' flexibility scores to the amount of authority that the supervisors felt that they had over a number of areas of decision-making; they also related them to the supervisors' managers' assessments of the influence that the supervisors had. The mode of analysis is also different, for Child and Partridge, and also Ellis and Child (1973), felt that for their purposes a series of zero-order correlations was sufficient to indicate the main connections with personal flexibility. Although such an approach may be suitable for the description of relationships between pairs of variables, there is the weakness of not being able to assess the joint effects of several variables; in particular, the impact of one variable may be far greater than that of another, so that a significant zero-order correlation becomes insignificant in a multi-variate analysis. Since such an analysis of the determinants of flexibility has not, to the writer's knowledge, been carried out elsewhere, the present results therefore stand alone. But some comparisons with Ellis and Child's results are possible.

Ellis and Child (1973: 250) found that, in their sample, flexibility was inversely related to age, positively related to the level of educational qualifications, and inversely connected with length of service and with the length of time spent in the current post. The present findings broadly confirm these results; as noted above, for example, rising age and length of service were associated with declining flexibility, while the age of starting work, which can be taken as a rough proxy for qualifications, was associated with rising flexibility. In addition, however, they also suggest that the effects of age and length of service are not significant when other variables are taken into account. Thus it should not be concluded that the older manager is inflexible, nor that those who have spent a long time in their present organizations become set in their ways. This finding may have some implications for those charged with the career development of managers, for it suggests that older and longer-serving managers are not necessarily lacking in the flexibility to take on new challenges.

Ellis and Child also found that the size of the organization and ownership by an American firm stimulated flexibility. In the present sample there was no evidence to support either finding. This difference may reflect differences in sample design, for Ellis and Child chose 78 organizations across a wide range of sizes and may thus have had a better spread of organizational sizes than the present survey. Even so, total organizational size in the survey varied considerably: from 300 employees to 160,000 employees. Even if the effects of plant size on attitudes and behaviour cannot be adequately assessed in the present survey, because of the limitation to fairly large plants, organizational size varied over a wide range. In view of the continuing uncertainty about the nature and direction of the 'size effect' on many aspects of organizational behaviour, it is not surprising that conflicting results should emerge here; in many, far more thoroughly researched areas, there remain disputes about whether a size effect exists and about how a theoretical account of an observed effect should be developed. In the present case, the safest conclusion is that there is no simple tendency for managers' personal flexibility to reflect the size of the organizations for which they work, although more systematic analysis may reveal a more complex pattern of relationships. A similar point probably applies to the country of ownership of the organization.

In short, and as is to be expected, managers' personal characteristics had a more powerful effect on their preferences for change than did the organization structure of their employing organizations or the economic performance of these firms. There was, for example, no evidence that flexible managers were concentrated in the most profitable firms. There was some suggestion, however, that flexibility was associated with the presence of highly competitive product market conditions.

Explaining Attitudes to the Company
What explains how satisfied factory managers working for multi-plant companies are with the way in which the company responds to them? As with personal flexibility, a number of hypotheses can be suggested. Large firms, particularly multi-divisional ones, might be expected to be remote from the concerns of each operating unit and to promote discontent in its managers. Successful ones might encourage feelings of satisfaction. As for managers' personal characteristics, it is possible that those with experience of working in other companies will be more critical of their present firms than those without such external sources of comparison; alternatively, movement to the present firm might represent finding a company which fitted one's personal preferences, while those who have not moved firms might experience a sense of being stuck. The likely effects of previous work experience are thus unclear. The expectation for length of service is clearer: those who have stayed in an organization a long time are likely to be satisfied with it. Similarly, older managers can be expected to be more satisfied with their firms. One reason for this is that, among factory managers, the older managers are the least likely to have aspirations for further career development while the younger ones hope to move on and take a more critical view of the ways in which the company responds to them. It might also be expected that length of time in the present post would be associated with satisfaction.

The relevance of some of the other variables discussed in connection with personal flexibility is less clear. Thus there is no particular reason to expect the technology or the product market environment to affect the managers' views of their firms. This in fact turns out to be the case. None of the product market and technical conditions variables (including the industry dummies) had any relationship with the measure of attitude to the company.

As with the flexibility measure, several possible influences on attitudes to the company, measured by the variable COATT, in fact turned out to be absent. The size of the firm, the rate of profit, and the rate of growth were not associated with managers' attitudes to the firm. Several aspects of managers' career also failed to have any explanatory role. Most notably, whether or not a manager had had experience of a headquarters planning post did not affect his views of the company's responsiveness to him. Neither was the length of time in the present post related to attitudes to the company.

Some more positive results are reported in the second column of table 3.14. As suggested above, age was significantly associated with attitudes to the firm, with increasing age being associated with satisfaction. Perhaps surprisingly, however, the effects of length of service went in the opposite direction, with increasing service with one firm being associated with a decline in satisfaction. Part of the explanation for this result may lie in the results for the POSTS variable, measuring the number of posts held between joining the firm and taking up the present post: having held several posts was associated with a favourable attitude to the company. After the effects of this variable and that of age have been allowed for, it appears that increasing length of service was associated with a growth in unfavourable views of the firm. That is, allowing for the tendency of older managers to be less critical and for experience of several posts to increase satisfaction, any remaining effect of having worked a long time for a firm was to stimulate unfavourable attitudes. One possible reason is that a long stay in a firm, with few changes of responsibility, leads to feelings of frustration and discontent. Finally, there was some tendency for those starting work late in life to have favourable views of their firms. The result is consistent with that for the flexibility variable, where a late start encouraged flexibility. It seems that those with relatively low levels of educational qualifications were the least likely to be flexible and the least likely to have favourable views of their firms.

In the final column of table 3.14 the flexibility measure is added as an explanation of the managers' attitudes to their firms. In statistical terms, the measure works well: the two measures were strongly associated, with flexibility and favourable views of the firm going together, and the overall explanatory power of the equation improved. But what is the theoretical rationale for treating personal flexibility as causally prior to attitudes to the firm? To the extent that a preference for change is a fixed characteristic of an individual, it can be taken to be independent of attitudes to any particular company. As shown above, moreover, the flexibility measure was not strongly related to the organizational characteristics of firms. It is thus reasonable to ask whether managers with a flexible approach tend to develop favourable views of their firms. The answer is that they do. This is quite an important finding, for it suggests that those managers who dislike change and prefer a stable working environment tend to adopt a critical position towards their firms. It may be that they resent demands for change and feel themselves somewhat isolated from the mainstream of thinking in the company and thus grow to be critical of the way in which the company responds to them. Together with the evidence on the variables measuring length of service and the number of separate posts held, it appears that there was a group of managers who had experienced little movement within their firms, had however worked for them for some time, had little desire for changed circumstances, and felt distanced from their companies. A syndrome of frustration and a feeling that decisions are taken by high flyers who have little understanding of the position of those stuck in their present jobs was the result.

It must be emphasized, however, that managers with such feelings formed a very small minority of the present sample. As shown above, the overall position was for a strong preference for flexibility and a favourable set of attitudes to the company. Most factory managers did not feel distanced from decision-making in their firms. In view of this, the characteristics of those managers who expressed any strong criticism of their firms were investigated further. Specifically, anyone choosing one of the two most unfavourable options on the five-point scale on any of the six items measuring attitudes to the firm was identified as taking a 'critical' stance. The rationale for this procedure was that those expressing unfavourable opinions on any item may be expected to differ from those who were satisfied in all the relevant respects. Fifty-seven per cent of factory managers were critical on at least one of the six items.

One obvious possibility is that managers who are tightly constrained from above are dissatisfied with their lot. This may be considered by examining two issues that are assessed in their own right in chapter 4: the locus of decision-making and the extent of monitoring of plant performance. The former was investigated by asking managers to state where the decision rested on a number of matters. For the latter, they were asked how closely their firms monitored performance on five issues. On decision-making, there was no association between the extent to which decisions were taken outside the plant and the express- ing of critical attitudes. On monitoring, the results were surprising. On three of the five issues listed at Q. 125 there was no association between the closeness of checking and critical attitudes to the firm. On two, the monitoring of production schedules and of quality standards, the results ran against expectations: criticism was highest where monitoring was least strict. On the monitoring of quality, for example, 40 per cent of those where monitoring was very close were critical, as against 78 per cent where the monitoring was not at all close. A plausible *ex post* rationalization of this result is that, on matters of day-to-day operations such as keeping a check on production and quality, factory managers want their companies to take a close interest and are dissatisfied when they do not do so, feeling perhaps that senior company managers cannot be bothered with the day-to-day issues that take up so much of the managers' own time.

Some other possible predictors of critical attitudes did not perform well when taken individually although, as will be seen below, some were useful in multi-variate analyses. The size of the firm, whether or not it was divisionalized, and whether or not it was foreign owned did not affect the occurrence of critical attitudes. Of managers' personal characteristics, age made a difference, with the 'critical' managers being younger than others, but length of service, the number of other firms worked for, and the age of taking up the first full-time job did not.

Neither did company profitability or the rate of growth of turnover affect the expression of critical attitudes.

In order to explore some of these connections further, a discriminant analysis was carried out. This aimed to distinguish those expressing critical attitudes in the sense defined above from those who did not. A first step was to specify a model similar to that used in the prediction of the continuous measure of attitudes to the company, COATT. The results are reported as Model 1 in table 3.15. In line with the bivariate results just reported, company growth and profitability were not associated with a critical attitude, and neither was length of service an important discriminating variable. The remaining nine variables all played a role, as indicated by the significance of their contributions to the reduction of Wilks's lambda and by the similar sizes of their coefficients. The measures of personal background and attitude performed as expected, with increasing age, for example, reducing the likelihood of having a critical attitude and with a preference for flexibility having a similar effect. The size of the firm also played a role, with size reducing critical attitudes, contrary to the expectation that size leads to bureaucracy and a distance between top management and the operating units. The result for LOCOST shows that managers feeling that their costs were lower than average were critical of their firms, while that for COMP2 suggests that increasing competition made managers less likely to be critical. The low order of inclusion in the model suggests, however, that the effects of competitive circumstances were far from clear-cut. Finally, CLOSE is a dummy variable indicating that a very close check was kept on quality standards. It is designed to capture the tendency, mentioned above, for those with close checking to report satisfaction; as expected, the variable was associated with an absence of critical attitudes.

In the second model of table 3.15 some of the variables that helped to explain patterns of managers' careers (see table 3.12) are introduced. The number of firms previously worked for (NFIRMS) was inversely related to having critical attitudes, as was having started work as a management trainee. The other measure of career background, HISTART, played no role, however. From the earlier evidence it might also be expected that firms with salary structures and with share-ownership among their managers might promote feelings of satisfaction. In fact, neither SALSTR nor SHARES entered the model.

The third model drops the unsuccessful variables and introduces some new ones. It performs better than the first two, as shown by the lower value of Wilks's lambda and the increased canonical correlation coefficient. The variables PARTS (number of other parts of the firm worked in), HQ (having had headquarters planning post) and ONEPLANT (career in one plant only) are introduced to assess how careers within

Table 3.15
Models Predicting Critical Attitude to Company

	Model 1[a]			Model 2				Model 3			
				Dependent Variable: CRIT (Dummy, High Score = Having a Critical Attitude)							
	Order	Sig. (p)	Coeff.	Block	Order	Sig. (p)	Coeff.	Block	Order	Sig. (p)	Coeff.
Independent variables											
AGE	2	0.008	−0.35	B	4	0.004	−0.57	A	6	0.000	−0.52
LS	0			B	0						
EXP	1	0.015	−0.57								
POSTS	4	0.004	−0.47	B	6	0.005	−0.37	A	4	0.001	0.17
NFIRMS				B	5	0.005	−0.50	A	5	0.002	−0.04
AGESTART	9	0.001	−0.28					B	8	0.000	−0.21
HISTART				C	0						
TRAINEE				C	7	0.002	−0.43	A	7	0.000	−0.35
PARTS								B	0		
HQ								D	12	0.000	−0.33
ONEPLANT								D	0		

Variable	n	Model 1 Coeff	Grp	Order	p	Model 2 Coeff	Grp	Order	p	Model 3 Coeff	Grp	Order	p
FLEX	6	+0.36	A	3	0.002	+0.48	A	3	0.054	0.45	A	3	0.000
COSIZE	5	−0.44	A	2	0.002	−0.48	A	2	0.043	−0.23	A	2	0.002
GROWTH	0		A	0			A	0			B	0	
PROFITS	0		A	0			A	0			B	9	
LOCOST	7	+0.43			0.002					−0.25			0.000
HIPROF	0											10	
COMPI												1	
COMP2	8	−0.39			0.001								
DIVCO						−0.55			0.027	−0.25			0.000
CLOSE	3	−0.42			0.006		A	1	0.002	−0.64	A		0.001
SALSTR			A				A	0					
SHARES			A		0.001		A	0			C	11	
VARPAY										−0.23			0.000

Summary statistics

	Model 1	Model 2	Model 3
Wilks's lambda	0.81 (0.001)	0.84 (0.002)	0.71 (0.000)
Canonical correlation	0.44	0.40	0.54

Note: a In Model 1, all independent variables were entered in one block.

Key:
Variables are as previously defined, plus:
HIPROF = Profits high or very high (inverse relation with CRIT expected).
DIVCO = Divisionalized firm (positive sign expected).
CLOSE = Close monitoring of plant performance (positive sign expected).
VARPAY = Pay varies according to bonus elements (inverse relation expected).

firms affected attitudes. Only HQ entered the model; as might be expected it reduced the likelihood of having a critical attitude. Having worked in only one plant had no effect one way or the other. These two results suggest that experience of a strategic role at headquarters helps to make managers feel satisfied with their firms, whereas being limited to one plant makes no difference. This is consistent with the view that high-flyers value movement within the firm whereas slow risers are content to work their way up within a plant and are not worried about a lack of experience elsewhere in an organization.

Of the measures of plants' economic performance, LOCOST failed to enter the model, which may reflect the inclusion of the variable called HIPROF. This takes the value 1 when the highest category of plant profitability (revenues well in excess of costs) of the five available was chosen at Q. 137; it is zero otherwise. As table 3.15 shows, managers running such profitable plants were, not surprisingly, less critical of their firms than were others. The variable DIVCO indicates that the firm had a divisionalized structure. Its inclusion in the model shows that, in addition to the effects of company size, the structure of the firm made a difference. The effect of the variable, like that of company size, goes against the view that bureaucratization leads to discontent: those in divisionalized firms were the least likely to adopt a critical stance. Finally, VARPAY indicates that a manager's pay varied according to bonus or profit-sharing arrangements. It was included to assess the view, associated with Williamson (1970: 151–2) for example, that giving operational managers bonuses that are directly related to the performance of their own units will stimulate performance by providing them with an incentive to hit targets. Williamson also feels that share ownership may be relevant only to senior company directors, whose behaviour in managing the firm can influence the value of the shares; for more junior managers, owning shares may make no difference because the performance of the shares is remote from their own work situations. For Williamson to argue that systems of reward affect managers' performance, he must be able to identify some factor intervening between the reward structure and behaviour, and it is reasonable to suggest that this factor is the manager's own willing pursuit of his duties, which ought to be correlated with his satisfaction with his firm. VARPAY would then be associated with a lack of critical attitudes, while SHARES made no difference.

As table 3.15 shows, this expectation was borne out. Not only was VARPAY inversely associated with CRIT, but the performance of the model including it (Model 3) was also better, as shown by the summary statistics, than was that of the other models. The difficulty for Williamson's argument, however, is that, as noted above, both personal flexibility and satisfaction with the company were unrelated to the profitability or the growth of the firm. The mechanism linking reward structures to overall performance seems to be absent. Thus it is true that having some kind of bonus pay encourages factory managers to be satisfied with their firms, which is quite an important finding. The larger claims that might be made about the benefits of such an association seem, however, to be not proven.

Conclusions

The results reported above help to assess some expectations about the determinants of managers' careers and job attitudes that might be derived from common sense or specific theoretical arguments. On careers, the discriminant analysis supports the argument advanced earlier that high-flyers and slow risers represent two contrasting types of career progression. For the former, having started work at a fairly senior level and having a preference for change were important, but staying with a firm a long time had no effect. Of the company characteristics investigated, the size of the firm, as against some expectations, was unimportant but there was a tendency for managers in firms using formal salary structures and for those owning shares in their firms to have experience of work at headquarters in a planning role. This supports the view that some firms may treat their factory managers in a strategic way: experience of this role was not randomly distributed but was concentrated in firms that would be seen as 'progressive'.

As would be expected, managers' individual characteristics were particularly important in the explanation of personal flexibility. But the finding that the most flexible managers were found where market competition was strongest was quite robust and suggests that flexibility may be particularly important here. There was no evidence that managers with a liking for change were concentrated in the most profitable or the fastest growing firms, which goes against some expectations that those with this characteristic are 'dynamic' and likely to contribute to the success of firms employing them. Flexibility was, however, strongly related with attitudes to the firm: the most flexible were also the most satisfied with the ways in which they were treated by their companies. The obverse of this, namely that a preference for stability tends to go with critical attitudes, is also important in suggesting that the 'slow risers' with little movement within their firms and with little chance of further promotion tend to be those among whom discontent is concentrated.

Perhaps the most surprising finding was that close monitoring of the plant by the firm was associated with satisfaction and not dissatisfaction. This suggests that factory managers prefer an interest being taken in their activities to being left to their own devices. This aspect of company behaviour was more important than were such features of company organization as size and the formalization of salary structures. There was also no tendency for measures of company performance to be related to attitudes to the firm or to personal flexibility. This suggests that ideas that there are direct connections between managers' attitudes, their behaviour, and the performance of the firms for which they work are inaccurate. This question is pursued further in chapter 6.

Overall, the results show that careers and attitudes varied in explicable ways. Some of the possible explanatory variables, of which company size is the most obvious, did not in fact enter the account, while other variables performed in ways that might not have been expected. In view of the vast range of factors which influence a variable such as a manager's preference for change, the results are quite encouraging.

Conclusions

The most obvious, and in many ways the most important, conclusion to emerge from the above analysis is that factory managers were, in general, satisfied with their positions within their firms. This applies even to those showing most dissatisfaction, for even here the overall amount of discontent was limited, and 'dissatisfaction' was relative to the very wide degree of satisfaction with treatment from their firms that marked the sample as a whole. One possible influence on the extent of satisfaction was the large number of managers who had experience outside their plants in some kind of planning role; and multi-variate analysis confirmed that such managers were less likely than the remainder to hold attitudes critical of their firms. There was, moreover, no tendency for alienation from the firm to increase with the size of the company. Most measures of size had little effect on careers or attitudes, and where other possible indicators of bureaucratization, such as whether or not a firm had a divisionalized structure, were related to managers' attitudes the tendency was for bureaucratization to be associated with increased satisfaction with the firm.

There was no tendency for the success of the firm, as measured by its growth or profit rate, to be related to managers' satisfaction with their roles. In so far as this finding may help to correct the assumption that managerial satisfaction, managers' performance, and company success go happily together, it may also encourage a close analysis of the factors which aid or hinder such a connection. Plainly, there can be circumstances in which all three things are related and mutually reinforcing, but this appears not to be a general rule. A lack of direct connections is not really surprising, in view of all the factors that influence both managers' perceptions and company performance. But unsurprising results can none the less be important, particularly when schemes to increase managers' sense of involvement in their firms are being canvassed for the economic benefits that they allegedly contain. This is not necessarily to argue against such schemes but only to suggest that they are unlikely to have automatic effects and that, to work effectively, they may need to be made part of an overall policy for rewarding factory managers, developing their managerial potential, and integrating them into their firms. One other finding of the survey, namely the distinction between high flyers and slow risers, is relevant here. It is only the former who are likely to benefit from this type of programme, and it may prove possible to find means to distinguish the two groups and to develop career development packages that suit members of each. It would be a mistake to treat all factory managers as identical just because they currently hold similar jobs.

There may, moreover, be some indirect patterns of association that hint at connections between attitudes, company structure, and success. This may be seen in relation to the links between managerial attitudes and labour issues. In general, there is no particular reason to expect a close connection between a factory manager's attitude to his job and the labour relations arrangements of his plant, and such connections indeed proved to be largely absent. But there was one link, of a policy rather than an institutional kind. Managers were asked about the importance of labour matters in general business decision-making. Those who rated these matters as being important tended to be those with headquarters experience. The implication is that managers with a 'strategic' type of career give more weight to personnel management than do those with more limited careers. As noted in chapter 1, writers such as Peters and Waterman (1982) see 'people orientation' as an important characteristic of successful firms. Although in the present survey types of managerial career and policies of labour management were not directly related to company success, the presence of connections between careers and attitudes to labour management, and between careers and attitudes to the managerial role, suggests that some less general and direct effects may have been at work. That is, across the whole sample company success was not related to career types or personnel policy, but there may have been particular cases in which a strategic type of management career, a 'people orientation', and satisfaction with the managerial role among factory managers went together to create a syndrome of success. In any event, the tendency for those with strategic careers to have attitudes to the managerial task in general and to labour management in particular that differed from the remainder of the sample reveals some important connections between careers and attitudes.

These contrasts within the sample notwithstanding, the career structure of the factory managers as a whole did not seem to stand out markedly from that of the 'average manager'. Qualifications and experience for example seemed to be similar to those observed in general samples of managers. It might have been expected that factory managers' location within the production function would have marked them out from managers in the more fashionable specialisms of sales or finance: they might, for example, have had few career moves and little experience of functions outside production. This seems not to have been the case. The one major difference from other samples was the relatively long spell of service with one firm and the small number of jobs in other firms observed in the present sample. Career development within one firm, and not spiralling between several firms, was the norm. But the factory managers seem to have had considerable experience within their present firms: they were not mere functionaries without experience beyond their own plants.

This evidence may be compared with the results of Gill and Lockyer's (n.d.: 28–31) survey of production managers. As noted above, the authors defined this group as managers who fell between the levels of production directors and supervisors and who took responsibility for production and the costs thereof. Asked about relationships with other functions, 67 per cent reported satisfactory relationships with senior management, as against 10 per cent saying that they were unsatisfactory. The marketing function gained the highest score of dissatisfaction (17 per cent found the relationship unsatisfactory, as against 41 per cent finding it acceptable). The main sources of dissatisfaction were frustration due to labour problems (47 per cent mentioned this), the neglect of production considerations by sales departments (33 per cent) and the status of production in the organization (26 per cent). Finally, 66 per cent felt that their salaries were equitable in comparison with those paid for equivalent jobs. A broad satisfaction with pay and with senior company management also emerges from the present survey. Gill and Lockyer's results show, too, that resentment at the position of production in the company was far from universal. It must also be stressed, however, that their survey looked only briefly at the tensions and frustrations attached to the managerial task and that the present survey did not ask directly about dissatisfactions. It should not be concluded that factory managers find life easy. In the context of the recession their jobs over the last few years have plainly been difficult and exacting. What can be said, however, is that in dealing with the inevitable problems that arise in managing complex production facilities factory managers do not in general experience the activities of their companies as an additional constraint; on the contrary, they are reasonably satisfied with the relationship.

Complacency would, however, be unwise. Two sets of changes suggest that the role of the factory manager will become increasingly important. First, there is the general pressure to increase productivity and quality standards and to adapt products to changing market demands. Second, as discussed in chapter 5, companies have been altering their policies of labour relations to stress involvement and commitment. The latter not only increases the duties of the factory manager, as the person charged with applying the policy at establishment level; it also affects his or her own position, for if firms are giving more attention to the management of human resources at all levels then they also need to consider senior managers, who may feel somewhat neglected.

Two areas in particular warrant attention. One is the interchange of personnel between operating and strategic levels of the company, together with the whole area of management development. The main area in which factory managers were dissatisfied with their firms was that of the movement of managers between establishment level and company headquarters. It has also been shown that those who had experience of strategic roles were most likely to express satisfaction with their firms. On management development, one-third of those with personal experience of development programmes (which represents just over one in six of all factory managers in multi-plant firms) reported that the programmes included moving managers between functions to increase their experience. If firms see managerial resources in strategic terms, that is if they wish to develop the skills of their managers and if they want to plan the careers of their high flyers, there may be a case for giving detailed attention to policies on managerial development, in particular the systematic movement of key managers between levels and functions within the firm.

The second area is that of payment and reward systems. The survey revealed a surprising amount of informality in pay arrangements, in the sense that many factory managers were not paid according to formal salary structures and had their pay increases determined largely at the discretion of the company. And just over half the factory managers said that their pay varied according to bonuses and other performance-related measures. It would be wrong to suggest that there is one best set of pay arrangements that will suit all firms. What is appropriate in one firm may cause great problems in another. But, in view of the general importance of pay and the ways in which payment systems affecting other groups of staff are changing (for example, through the extension of 'staff status'), pay systems for factory managers may warrant consideration: what is the system for, how far does it fit into other attempts to increase managers' motivation, is there a case for retaining bonus elements in pay and if so what form should they take, and so on?

This chapter has concentrated on the managers as individuals, although in the discussion of their careers and attitudes considerable reference has been made to the type of firms for which they worked. In the following chapter, the connections between the managers and their firms become the main focus of attention.

Notes

1. The Gill and Lockyer results appear to be considerably out of line with those from the other studies; there is no obvious reason for this. Note also the different age categories used in different surveys.
2. The precise figures for the NTS survey are reported in more detail in a discussion paper (Crockett and Elias, 1981: 11–14) than they are in the published paper.
3. There was also a statistically significant difference between different functional groups in their length of service: the 19 deputy factory managers had a mean length of service of 22.8 years, and the 17 production managers averaged 21.7 years, against the factory managers' average of 16.8 years. The 14 personnel managers averaged only 10.6 years.
4. The dependent variable here is a dichotomy (whether or not the manager was a factory manager). There is considerable dispute about the use of regression techniques in such cases. The analysis was therefore carried out using discriminant analysis as well as regression. The results were similarly negative. Discriminant analysis is described briefly in Appendix A.
5. Comparative data exist in the survey of 6,477 'higher-ranked staff' in 616 firms carried out by the management consultants Inbucon: see *Financial Times*, 10 October 1985. Of all executives in the survey, 44 per cent received bonuses; the figure was 43 for general managers and 50 per cent for managing directors. Bonuses increased basic pay by an average of 13 per cent, a figure identical to that in the present survey. There had been no change in the proportion of earnings accounted for by bonus elements since 1980, suggesting that this form of incentive has not been increasing in importance.
6. The Inbucon survey shows that 35 per cent of managers had a share option scheme, and 13 per cent a share-buying scheme. These figures cannot be compared directly with the present survey's data, which refer to actual holdings. But since 62 per cent of the 39 per cent of the sample who owned shares had acquired them through a company scheme at least 24 per cent of factory managers must have had a share-buying scheme. This puts them somewhat above the average, reflecting presumably the size of their firms. The Inbucon results also point to a sharp rise in share option schemes (up from 10 per cent of all managers in 1980) and share-buying schemes (5 per cent in 1980). For further details of these results, see *Industrial Relations Review and Report*, Pay and Benefits Bulletin no. 146, October 1985, p. 122.
7. These perceptions are in line with reality. The Inbucon survey found that the pay of all executives rose by 68 per cent between 1980 and 1985, as against a rise in average earnings for all employees of 50 per cent and an increase in prices of 41 per cent.
8. For the flexibility measure, the mean of the inter-correlations between the five items was 0.29 (Ellis and Child report a figure of 0.30). The reliability coefficient Cronbach's alpha was 0.67. For the measure of attitudes to the company these two figures were 0.6 and 0.49, while for the view of specialisms they were 0.09 and −0.06. Adding scores to form a single scale seems reasonable for the first but not the third. As for the second, the indices are acceptable while raising some question about the additivity of the scale. As

explained below, therefore, in addition to the company attitude variable, COATT, a second dichotomous measure of attitudes was also created; this focuses on managers taking a critical view on any of the items (see below, p. 78).

9. FLEX is, as shown in table 3.8, highly skewed towards the 'flexible' end of the range. A logarithmic transformation was therefore used. This explains, incidentally, why a high level of flexibility is given a low score. Taking logarithms produces a more nearly normal distribution when a variable is negatively skewed, a familiar example being the size distribution of firms. Strictly speaking, the transformed version of FLEX should be used. But the results were identical to those using the untransformed version, and the latter are therefore reported in the text.

4

The Plant and the Company: A 'Loose–Tight' Relationship

Introduction: Autonomy and Control

As noted in chapter 1, there is a massive literature on the strengths and weaknesses of bureaucratic forms of organization and the delegation of responsibilities within hierarchies. This study does not aim to examine issues of organizational design in general. Instead it focuses on the specific questions of how much responsibility manufacturing firms delegate to plant level, of the extent to which decision-making is further delegated within the plant, and of how performance is monitored and controlled. In view of the particular concern with the management of industrial relations, issues with labour implications are given special attention; but some matters of a broader nature are also investigated so that the overall position may be assessed.

The picture to emerge may be described in terms of one of the characteristics of successful firms identified by Peters and Waterman (1982: 318), 'simultaneous loose–tight properties'. These involve 'the co-existence of firm central direction and maximum individual autonomy ... Organizations that live by the loose–tight principle are on the one hand rigidly controlled yet at the same time allow (indeed, insist on) autonomy, entrepreneurship, and innovation from the rank and file.' It appears that factory managers were given considerable discretion in running their plants, but that they were also subject to close monitoring of the outcome of their efforts. This is not directly to confirm the Peters and Waterman argument, for it rests on the presence of clear values about the organization that are developed at the centre and are continually reinforced, the result being a strong corporate culture. A policy of giving discretion to operating units is only part of this. The obverse also holds: a firm can grant discretion without its having a strong culture. The fact that discretion is widespread does not mean that most firms have loose–tight properties; indeed, it cannot do so, since the crux of Peters and Waterman's argument is that these properties characterize the minority of 'excellently managed' firms. What it does show is that the relationship between plants and firms is loose and tight in a different but complementary sense: establishments were granted considerable freedom but the results of using it were monitored. As will be seen in chapter 6, moreover, a moderate degree of control is associated with a high level of productivity, a result which represents an extension of Peters and Waterman's arguments.

Plant managers may, however, have an exaggerated view of their own autonomy. Should it not be investigated by studying managers higher in the organization? This point has been pursued in some recent contributions about labour management. It underlies much of the analysis offered by Purcell (1983), who argues that many of the key decisions are taken above plant level. It has been extended by Kinnie (1985), who argues that local autonomy may well be a myth. He suggests that survey evidence, notably that provided by Marsh (1982), indicates that managers at head office level consider plant managers to be tightly constrained in their activities. And he draws on his own investigations of four organizations to point to several controls over local discretion: financial targets are clearly specified, and a plant's failure to meet them will lead to close investigation; plant performance in other respects is closely monitored; pay bargaining is co-ordinated, although the illusion of plant autonomy is permitted and a little local custom and practice is tolerated (indeed, autonomy can also be used to tighten central control because plant agreements can be linked to local productivity, thus making plants sink or swim on their own performance); and senior managers are encouraged to adopt the company and not the individual factory as their main focus of identification. Since the evidence presented below points to a belief among factory managers that they have a high level of autonomy, these points need to be considered carefully.

The evidence for central co-ordination is not, however, quite as strong as may appear. Thus Kinnie and Purcell quote Marsh's (1982: 161) view that 'there can be few multi-establishment companies which have by this time failed to provide for co-ordination on pay and conditions claims of some kind'. This is a very guarded statement, and Marsh's survey did not investigate in detail how much central direction or co-ordination there was. His overall conclusion (for example, pp. 218, 232), moreover, is that companies tend to have only very broad labour relations policies at company level; the traditional preference for settling issues at shopfloor level and for avoiding detailed substantive rules at company level was as strong as ever. This suggests that the extent of specific control of plants' activities may be limited. It is also consistent with other evidence. Thus Peters and Waterman's argument is that a strong corporate culture is a rarity. And Hill and Pickering (1986: 37) show that the chairmen of large British companies generally see not only industrial relations but also marketing, production, and buying decisions as the responsibility of operating subsidiaries.

Assessment of the survey evidence also depends on one's initial assumptions. If the starting point is a model of total plant autonomy, the evidence on co-ordination is quite impressive. But it is equally plain that individual plants do not slavishly follow a policy laid down from above. Indeed, Marsh suggests that clear and detailed policies are rare. The question concerns the extent and form of control over plants, and how far clear substantive rules are promulgated from above. Different types of firm are likely to differ in this respect, and it may be that Kinnie's four companies represent an extreme case, although he presents insufficient information on their organizational structures for a proper judgement to be made. In any event, a larger survey may be able to throw some light on the typicality of his findings, while also addressing some rather more specific issues than Marsh's survey was able to do.

It also appears from these studies that plant autonomy is not entirely illusory: local managers are given the power to make decisions, even if their range of choice is limited and the consequences of the decisions are closely monitored. 'Constraint' may be a better term than 'illusion'. There are thus two models of organizational control of plants. One is based on direct control through the issuing of rules. The other involves indirect control, with only broad guidelines or limits being set and with control being accomplished by measuring performance against targets instead of specifying how those targets should be sought. Kinnie's evidence seems to point to the latter, in so far as targets and broad co-ordination, as distinct from direct rules of behaviour, are stressed. The present evidence points in a similar direction. In short, autonomy is constrained, but the constraints are attained more by setting standards to be met than by directive. And the nature of this autonomy is important to grasp. The current fashion seems to be to give local managers the freedom to develop their own ideas. The freedom is also a responsibility in so far as it is necessary for managers to demonstrate that they have ideas and that they can see them through. Freedom is not just offered but is required, in the sense that not developing new ideas will be penalized; and the criterion of success is not self-fulfilment but profit.

But how can such points be assessed by looking only at the level of the establishment? A preliminary point is that one aim of the survey was to consider how far the factory managers took decisions themselves and how far they delegated them to other managers: the intra-plant and not the intra-company structure. For this purpose they were the key respondents, for they could provide a better assessment than could, say, personnel managers of their own involvement in a wide range of matters. They also provide a useful basis for looking upwards, for they are likely to have a wider knowledge of the ways in which their companies monitor them than are specialist managers. There is, of course, the danger that they will exaggerate their own autonomy, either through a natural tendency to inflate one's own importance or through ignorance of the extent to which their activities are monitored and controlled. It is difficult to assess how far this took place. But ignorance is unlikely to have been substantial, given that these managers were responsible for substantial manufacturing operations, and given also the evidence presented in chapter 3 that many of them had experience elsewhere in the organization: they were influential managers who surely knew what was going on, even if the finer details of company policy were unknown to them. Another piece of evidence from chapter 3 is also relevant: the factory managers were generally satisfied with the degree to which their firms took account of their own views when policy was being formulated. This is consistent with the factory managers' being in a position to operate freely: they did not feel over-burdened by directives from above or that they were kept in the dark about long-term strategic developments. A tendency to exaggerate their own importance is of course a possibility. But they were asked some fairly specific questions about where decisions were taken on certain issues and about the closeness with which the company monitored aspects of the plant's performance. These ought to minimize any bias in the answers, even though they cannot guarantee against it.

The following evidence may, then, be treated as a reasonably 'objective' picture of the pattern of managerial decision-making. Local autonomy may not be as illusory as an image of a large firm as an integrated organization with clear goals and policies may imply. Such autonomy is, however, powerfully constrained. These points are pursued in turn, first by considering the pattern of decision-making, and second by examining the monitoring and control techniques employed by companies.

Managerial Decision-Making

As already indicated, two questions informed the analysis of decision-making: how far the factory managers were themselves involved with the detailed operation of their plants, and the extent to which decisions had to be cleared with the higher levels of the organization. The former question relates to all the factory managers, while the latter is germane only to those in multi-plant groups. For comparability, and in view of the small number of independent establishments, discussion of both will be limited to the factory managers of multi-plant firms. The two questions imply two distinct dimensions for replies. The problem of gaining accurate replies rapidly was solved by giving respondents a card on which the two dimensions were identified. The card is reproduced in Appendix B. As will be seen, respondents were asked to say whether a decision could be taken within the plant, whether a higher level was consulted, or whether the final say rested elsewhere in the organization; and there were six categories representing different kinds of personal involvement. The 12 decision areas considered, mainly but not exclusively of a labour relations type, are listed at Q. 95. The replies have been collapsed into six categories, as shown in table 4.1.

It is, of course, recognized that this method cannot capture the subtleties of managerial decision-making. But a similar exercise by Hill and Pickering (1986: 36) seems to have worked well: company chairmen were asked whether a particular organizational level always or normally had responsibility for a given issue, whether responsibility was shared, or whether it was rarely or never responsible. The present questions, moreover, focused on some fairly specific matters and indicated the type of involvement of interest. That is, they did not ask respondents to assess where power 'really' lay but to state whether higher levels of management were normally involved in the making of decisions. This is to provide a reasonably objective focus which should indicate the overall pattern if not all the complexities. Certainly, respondents seem to have had few problems with the method.

Patterns of Decision-Making

The least controversial results relate to the extent to which factory managers were involved in decision-making within their factories. Several of the decision-making areas listed, for example the re-deployment of workers within the establishment, related specifically to matters internal to the plant, the aim being to assess how far the factory managers were themselves involved in these day-to-day matters. The evidence points to a considerable level of involvement. On re-deployment, for example, 72 per cent of factory managers said that they were involved in the decision. As would be expected, the extent of involvement was greater on issues of a broad or strategic significance than on those of a more routine nature. Thus only 3 per cent said that they delegated decisions on redundancy without themselves being involved at all, whereas the figure was 40 per cent for the setting of overtime requirements. Even here, however, personal involvement remained quite high, with a third of respondents saying that they made the decision. Involvement in disciplinary matters was also quite high. The formulation and application of disciplinary procedures is sometimes seen as one of the central areas of personnel management expertise, but the final authority to dismiss need not lie with the personnel specialist. Thus 63 per cent of factory managers said that they took the final decision to dismiss for disciplinary reasons. Comparable data are rare, since the many surveys that have covered disciplinary procedures have concentrated on the formalization of procedures and not on the levels of management involved. But a survey in 1978 covering several sectors apart from manufacturing reported that the final authority to dismiss lay with factory managers in 39 per cent of organizations and with personnel managers in 32 per cent (Institute of Personnel Management, 1979: 41). And it seems to be quite common for procedures to specify a number of stages, with the factory manager being the final stage. In short, the factory managers were involved in all areas of the running of their plants in which general matters of principle were likely to arise. They were even more likely to take the decision in the apparently individual and specialized area of dismissal than they were on such general matters as dealing with plant breakdowns.

The main variable likely to affect the extent of delegation within the establishment is the size of the plant. The present sample cannot test this properly since small plants, where delegation is likely to be most constrained, are excluded. But there did not seem to be any marked increase in the degree of delegation of several decisions as plant size increased. This is to be expected. A matter such as the redundancy of a large number of workers is as likely to require the attention of the factory manager in a large plant as it is in a small plant. On more day-to-day matters there was some tendency for the amount of delegation to increase. The pattern was, however, not simple. On the issues of keeping to production schedules and applying discipline short of the sack, for example, the proportion of managers reporting any delegation was identical in plants with fewer than 500 employees and in plants with 500 or more workers. That is, factory managers delegated the issues in the same proportions. What differed was the form of delegation: in the larger plants the factory manager was more likely to delegate the decision without himself being involved. For example, in the smaller plants 69 per cent delegated the decision on discipline short of the sack, as against 71 per cent in the larger plants. But the 69 per cent in the smaller plants divided into 40 per cent who retained some personal involvement and 29 per cent who did not, whereas in the larger plants the figures were almost reversed (28 per cent and 43 per cent respectively). The implication seems to be that plant size does not encourage delegation as such but that, if a manager is inclined to delegate at all, he is more likely to take the process further in a large plant than in a small one.

More difficult to assess is the evidence on plant autonomy. The factory managers reported high levels of independence. In some areas,

96

TABLE 4.1
Levels of Managerial Decision-Making in Multi-Plant Companies (%)

	Decision Taken Outside Plant	Higher Level Consulted At All	Respondent Decides: With Consultation Above Plant	Respondent Decides: Without Consultation	Decision Delegated and: Respondent Involved	Decision Delegated and: Respondent Not Involved	Other/ Don't Know
Keeping to production schedules	2	6	2	44	34	15	0
Monitoring quality	1	3	0	42	33	22	0
Dealing with plant breakdowns	0	2	1	38	36	23	0
Selection/ promotion of supervisors	1	8	6	35	33	24	0
Pay negotiations for manual workers	18	15	12	50	7	7	3
Recruitment (numbers employed)	4	20	17	55	13	9	0

Redundancy of substantial number of manual workers	9	32	28	50	2	3	5
Re-deployment of workers within establishment	1	3	2	38	34	24	0
Setting overtime requirements	2	3	2	34	21	40	0
Use of short-time working/layoffs	3	21	15	56	10	7	5
Dismissing for disciplinary reasons	3	10	8	55	18	15	(..)
Applying discipline short of the sack	1	2	1	28	32	38	0

Base: Factory managers of multi-plant companies (N= 166).
Note: Figures do not necessarily sum to 100 across rows because the third column is included within the second column.

TABLE 4.2
Discretion of Subsidiary Plants in 1977–1978 (%)

	Complete or Almost Complete Freedom	Discretion Within Broad Rules or Advice	Limited Discretion Within Detailed Rules	Virtually No Freedom	Other Reply
Manual workers' pay	34	32	18	16	(..)
Redundancies	37	31	18	11	3
Dismissals	71	21	6	2	(..)
Industrial relations generally	48	43	8	(..)	1

Source: Calculated from the Warwick Survey (see Brown, 1981). Data relate to plants that were not single independent establishments and that had 250 or more employees (*N* = 185).

such as the re-deployment of workers within the establishment, this is to be expected. Higher levels were involved more often in broader areas of manpower policy such as recruitment and redundancy, and also of course in determining rates of pay. Yet even here the extent of plant autonomy was surprisingly high. The proportion of plants reporting any higher-level involvement was greatest for redundancy decisions, but even there it reached only 41 per cent. Perhaps even more surprising is the evidence on pay negotiations, with only a third of plants reporting any higher-level involvement and with the final authority being said to lie above the plant in only 18 per cent of cases.

These results may be compared with those from the Warwick Survey of manufacturing plants employing at least 50 workers which was conducted in the winter of 1977–8 (Brown, 1981). Respondents were, as noted above (p. 4), managers responsible for industrial relations. They were asked about the amount of discretion enjoyed by local management over a range of issues. The data have been re-analysed, and to make them comparable with the present evidence plants with fewer than 250 workers have been excluded. The issues similar to those covered in the present survey are listed in table 4.2. The results are consistent with those given above. The 66 per cent of respondents who said that local management had complete or considerable discretion in setting manual workers' pay, for example, parallel the 64 per cent in the present survey who said that pay negotiations for manual workers took place without consultation above the level of the plant. The Warwick data also confirm the relatively high level of autonomy in the handling of dismissals. Their main point, however, is to counteract one possible explanation of the present results. This is that factory managers exaggerate the extent of local autonomy because they are unaware of the degree to which personnel managers at head office monitor and co-ordinate the pay settlements of individual plants. If this were the case, the personnel managers in the Warwick Survey would surely have reported less local autonomy than they in fact did. The perception of autonomy is not peculiar to factory managers.

The Warwick data also help to point to the conditions promoting plant autonomy.[1] Those plants in which pay bargaining was conducted at 'corporate' level, that is, at the level of the head office of the whole organization or at some other level within the company above the plant itself, reported low levels of autonomy. For all the plants in the survey, discretion on manual workers' pay was complete or almost complete in 33 per cent of cases, while in those subject to corporate agreements the figure fell to 19 per cent (Brown, 1981: 36). There was also a tendency for the presence of an industrial relations specialist at a higher level in the organization to be associated with a limited level of plant discretion. The conclusion drawn was that the local personnel manager 'acts more as a commissar for company policy than as a decision-maker in his own right' (p. 37) when the firm has corporate bargaining and a personnel department at a higher level. This point warrants emphasis. The sorts of company with which Purcell and Kinnie are concerned are precisely these corporate bargainers. The survey suggested not that plants are autonomous but that this form of bargaining powerfully constrains local discretion.

The present data confirm this view. In the top panel of table 4.3 the level of outside involvement in pay matters is cross-tabulated with the level of pay bargaining. In cases where bargaining took place at the establishment plus other levels in the firm, which can be taken as roughly approximating to the corporate bargainers, outside involvement was much higher than it was in any of the other modes of bargaining. The lower panel relates local discretion to the size of the plant in the organization. The most appropriate measure of size here is not the absolute size of the plant or the size of the company (the effects of the latter are considered below). It is the relative size of the plant, as measured by the proportion of total company employment accounted for by the plant itself. Thus more than three-quarters of the plants were owned by the large firms, such that they themselves comprised less than 10 per cent of total company employment. There was a clear tendency for plant autonomy to rise with the importance of the plant

The Plant and the Company

TABLE 4.3
Plant Autonomy on Pay Issues, By Bargaining Level and Company Size (%)

	Decisions on Manual Pay Taken			
	Within Plant	With Consultation above Plant	Outside Plant	All
Level of pay bargaining				
Estab. only	75	20	5	61
Estab. plus others in co.	43	20	38	26
Estab. plus other companies	100	0	0	3
Outside co. only	73	6	21	10
				100
Estab. employment as % total company employment				
Less than 2	44	28	28	32
2 and less than 10	62	22	16	35
10 and less than 50	92	8	(..)	21
50 or more	97	4	0	12
				100

Base: Establishments in multi-plant companies (N = 218).

within the firm as a whole. Again, the impression from the works of Purcell and Kinnie is that these writers are concerned with large, multi-divisional corporations in which each plant represents a small part of the firm's operations. The data suggest that plant autonomy is particularly likely to be constrained in such firms, while also underlining the obverse of this point, namely that these firms do not account for the whole of manufacturing employment and that in other types of organization local autonomy may be quite substantial.

Marsh's survey evidence is also pertinent. As noted above, Marsh suggests that some kind of co-ordination on pay is probably the norm. Thirty-three per cent of his respondents at head office level reported that their pay system applied to all their divisions and establishments; and 62 per cent of the remainder said that they attempted to co-ordinate the separate pay settlements made at lower levels (1982: 177). Thus 75 per cent of the whole sample had some co-ordination or central direction. Marsh also reports (p. 224) the independence that head office respondents ascribed to their subsidiaries. Only 6 per cent said that they were wholly independent while 27 per cent felt that they were mostly or entirely subordinate. The largest group (52 per cent) said that they were partly independent, with most of these respondents saying that they gave periodic advice and direction to subsidiaries or that certain actions needed their own approval. Plant autonomy is thus constrained, but this does not mean that it is non-existent. It is notable that 25 per cent of Marsh's respondents apparently claimed to exercise no co-ordination of pay, particularly in view of the fact that personnel managers at head office are likely, given the salience of pay and the need to demonstrate that they influence activities in their subsidiaries, to stress their own importance. That is, just as local respondents may exaggerate their own autonomy, so head office managers may overstate their ability to shape decisions at local level. The kind of advice and direction given to subordinates is also relevant. Marsh asked about the giving of guidance to subsidiaries on various matters. The results (p. 228) show that fewer than two-thirds of head office respondents claimed to give guidance on any matter. And 'guidance' is a very general term. It would be surprising if large firms did not give some assistance to local managers, but it remains an open question how far they give detailed instructions to them.

This is not to suggest that plants can do as they like within only very general guidelines. As will be seen below, the present respondents reported considerable monitoring of their activities; and companies are plainly likely to make known their general preferences even if they do not lay down precise rules. The evidence of table 4.1, particularly that on pay bargaining, cannot be taken at face value. But some firms apparently undertake only a very broad supervision of their plants. And those that engage in a more rigorous form of co-ordination do not thereby constrain plant autonomy out of existence. Plants may well be given a degree of leeway in the precise pay settlements that they make. Alternatively, or additionally, they may be given a global figure for increases in the wage bill, with the distribution of the moneys involved, and the balance between wage increases and cuts in manning levels, being left up to them. As Kinnie (1985) suggests, such arrangements can bring two kinds of benefit to firms: they make plants responsible for their own destinies, thus stimulating an interest in efficiency; and they help to reduce the challenge from trade unions, for bargaining at establishment level will encourage an establishment focus from the union negotiators and reduce the danger of comparability claims and, even worse from the firm's point of view, attempts to bargain at company level about such things as investment plans which have traditionally lain outside the bargaining agenda.

There are, then, grounds for arguing that the level of plant autonomy reported by the factory managers was not spurious. The day-to-day management of the plant was largely in their own hands. On issues of broader significance they may have consulted higher levels in the firm, and it is very likely that they received broad policy guidance. But the final decision rested with them. On issues going beyond the individual plant, of which pay is the most obvious, the managers again reported that they took the final decision. But reference above was more common, particularly where pay bargaining was co-ordinated and where plants were only small parts of their organizations. And it is also likely that, even where the decision was made at plant level, broad ranges of acceptable figures were suggested from above. Companies may also reap some important benefits from granting their establishments some autonomy. Plant autonomy means not total freedom but the requirement as well as the ability to take the responsibility for decisions. This is more likely to suit companies than is an attempt to impose specific rules on a large number of disparate units, for such an attempt may lead to resentment among managers and an erosion of the formal rules.

Some Correlates of Levels of Decision-Making

What explains the pattern of variation observed in table 4.1, that is, why do some respondents report more autonomy than others? Given the preponderance of replies stressing local autonomy, there is rather little variation to be explained. In particular, reference above the plant was too rare for substantial multi-variable analyses to be performed. But the effects of some fairly obvious influences may be briefly considered.

Company size is one such influence. On most of the issues listed in table 4.1 there was no tendency for the size of the firm to affect either the extent of reference above the plant or the degree of delegation within it. On pay negotiations, however, there was, in line with the evidence presented above on the relative size of plants, a tendency for decisions to be taken above the plant, and for delegation to be rare, in large companies. There was a similar pattern in the case of redundancies. Overall, however, neither plant size nor company size appears to have had a powerful effect on levels of decision-making.[2]

One way of summarizing the data is to create an index counting the number of issues on which the decision was taken without reference above the plant; a high score thus indicates a high degree of autonomy. Some significant correlations with this crude measure emerged. As would be expected from the above discussion, autonomy tended to be low where firms were large and where plants were small. There was also a tendency for it to be low where trade union density was high, which is possibly explicable in terms of the power position of unions: where their organization is strong, they pose a challenge to management, and company management may have to make a more careful and thorough assessment of the implications of, say, a pay settlement or the dismissal of a worker than it would where the union was too weak to challenge a decision made at local level. Union organization may constrain local management not directly in terms of preventing them from making changes but indirectly, by encouraging company managers to take an interest in the decisions that are made.

Finally, discretion was low in those firms that had a high level of turnover per employee. This last variable will be considered in detail in chapter 6, for it is one of the key indicators used by economists in assessing company efficiency: when the appropriate controls, most importantly for the amount of capital employed, have been made, a high level of turnover per worker can be taken as an indication of a high level of productivity. The present result is thus a pointer to further investigation. Firms that give their subsidiaries little autonomy appear to have the highest levels of productivity. One implication is that there is a causal connection between the two things, with tight control preventing plants from adopting cosy and unimaginative attitudes. This requires careful consideration in the light of other relevant evidence. It is also possible that high productivity can 'cause' a low level of discretion, in that efficient firms keep their houses in order and ensure that their subsidiaries fit within the overall direction of company policy; a ramshackle and inefficient firm may fail to integrate its plants into any coherent strategy. For the present, it is safe to conclude only that there was a tendency for autonomy and low productivity to go together, with the reasons requiring further study.

One possible influence on decision-making levels is the importance of industrial relations considerations in the issues in question. Is there a tendency for managers ascribing a high level of importance to labour matters either to involve managers above the plant or to take a close personal interest in the relevant decisions? This question may be assessed by looking at two of the issues listed in table 4.1 on which a question was also asked about the importance of labour considerations in making decisions on them. These issues are overtime and redundancy. (The question on labour considerations is Q. 100; the results are discussed below on p. 129.) Overtime decisions were generally taken within the plant. Was there a tendency for factory managers to be involved more when they saw labour matters as exerting an influence on managerial decision-making? The answer was that there was not. A similar result emerged for a matter where higher level involvement was greater, namely redundancy decisions: there was no tendency for this involvement to be greater, or for the manager's own involvement to rise, when labour considerations were rated as important. The implication is that labour matters, although important in their own right, were not of sufficient weight to affect the level of firms' decision-making. This helps to put their role in perspective: managers felt that they were significant but this did not override other aspects of their decision-making arrangements.

Overall, there were few very clear or strong influences on levels of decision-making. This is not very surprising. The process of reaching decisions is complex, and its nature can be captured only imperfectly through survey methods. The methods have some value in giving an overall picture, but the 'dependent variable' cannot be measured very precisely; efforts to explain it are thus necessarily very unlikely to find any powerful determinants. In addition, the extent of the delegation of responsibility will reflect an individual manager's preferences, and these may be as important as structural variables.

Limits on Expenditure
A further way of assessing plant autonomy is to consider how much freedom establishments were given to retain their own revenues and to engage in capital expenditure without approval from higher authority (Qs 130–3). Almost a third of plants in multi-establishment companies were able to use their own revenues to finance their own capital expenditure. Over half (57 per cent), although unable to do this, were given their own allocation of capital by the company. Only 11 per cent were not given their own capital funds. The great majority (80 per cent) were set a limit on capital expenditure that did not require higher approval. Of those with a limit the average figure was £37,500, the highest being an exceptional £3 million; there were five other cases where the limit was between £250,000 and £1 million. In view of the size of the plants and the costs of new pieces of equipment, these figures do not seem very high. When the six plants with very high limits are excluded, the average limit was £14,800. Set against the costs of employing a few extra workers, this is a far from high figure. There was some tendency for the size of the limit to increase with the size of plant and little variation between industries, except for a higher than average figure in paper, printing, and publishing; this last result is curious in that one might have expected a capital-intensive industry such as chemicals to be associated with high spending limits.

Some interesting associations with limits on spending emerged. Neither the right to retain revenue, nor the granting of a capital allocation, nor the existence of a limit on capital expenditure was related to the size of the firm. There was a similar lack of association between these expenditure constraints and such measures of company performance as the rate of profit and the rate of growth of sales between 1978 and 1982. There was, however, a relationship with turnover per head, which was high where plants could not retain their own revenues and where there was a limit on capital expenditure. This again points to the possibility of a connection between productivity and company controls, with tight controls apparently leading to better performance. But, in addition to the problem of the direction of causality mentioned above, the lack of association with measures of performance other than turnover per head suggests that company performance may have a number of elements which are not closely related and that any contribution of controls of plant expenditure differs between them.

Conclusions

The evidence on limits on expenditure begins to point to a number of constraints within which factory managers made their decisions. They felt that they had, none the less, quite a substantial degree of discretion, and there is no reason to suppose that they were exaggerating their own importance: they did not have higher-level managers constantly watching over every decision, and even on matters such as pay determination they had a degree of autonomy. This autonomy varied according to the extent to which pay bargaining was centralized within the company. Neither the present survey nor previous workplace surveys suggest that plants have complete freedom. The evidence indicates some of the influences on the degree of autonomy, and underlines the fact that not all firms are well-organized multi-divisional organizations with thorough systems for the co-ordination of pay settlements. The surveys also at least raise the question of how far firms have developed anything more than *ad hoc* methods of ensuring that company policy, to the extent that there is one, is followed at plant level. Company constraints on plants seem to rely more on measures of the outcomes of what plants do than on detailed instructions on how to do it. Seen in this light, the reported level of discretion enjoyed by factory managers is not surprising. The constraints on the use of this discretion must now be investigated.

Company Monitoring of Performance

Extent of Monitoring

Respondents in multi-plant firms were asked (at Qs 125–9) how closely the company level of management monitored their performance in five areas, and whether there was a regular system of measuring performance against formal criteria or targets. 'Company' in this context means the head office for establishments with no divisionalized structure (that is, those in firms where there was no level of the organization between the plant and the head office), and the divisional level where there was such a structure. Those in the latter group were asked how far corporate management, that is, management at the top level of the whole firm, took an interest in the issues in question. The results for these three sets of questions are set out in tables 4.4 to 4.6.

There was plainly a substantial amount of checking of plant performance. As might be expected, this was highest in the area of profit targets, with 96 per cent of respondents reporting a close or very close

TABLE 4.4
Company Checking on Plant Performance (%)

	Profit Targets	Quality Standards	Production Schedules	Movements of Pay Outside Negotiated Settlements	Industrial Disputes
Very close	83	33	32	44	42
Close	13	27	17	25	32
Not very close	(..)	22	28	14	18
Not close at all	2	18	22	16	5
Don't know/ not answered	1	1	1	1	4
	100	100	100	100	100

Base: All respondents in multi-plant companies.

TABLE 4.5
Presence of Formal Systems for Monitoring Plant Performance

	Respondents Reporting Presence of System as Percentage of:	
	Those Reporting Close or Very Close Check on Each Area	All Respondents in Multi-Plant Firms
Profit targets	98	94
Quality standards	96	58
Production schedules	94	46
Pay movements	73	50
Industrial disputes	64	47

Note:
The relevant question (Q. 126) was asked only of those reporting a close or very close check on performance in each area. It is possible that in some cases where such close checking was not reported there was still a formal monitoring system.

TABLE 4.6
Degree of Corporate Interest in Plant Performance (%)

	Profit Targets	Quality Standards	Production Schedules	Pay Movements Outside Negotiated Settlements	Industrial Disputes
Great deal	63	19	14	22	27
Some	7	19	16	13	21
Little	0	4	6	10	5
None	26	58	63	53	45
Don't know/ not answered	3	0	0	2	2

Base: Establishments in corporate groups (*N* = 162).

check at the company level, 94 per cent of them saying that there was a formal monitoring system, and 63 per cent of those in corporate groups reporting a great deal of interest by corporate-level management. An earlier question (Q. 15) had established that 81 per cent of plants in multi-plant firms were treated as profit centres, that is, as units for which revenues as well as costs were calculated. The monitoring of other aspects of plants' activities was less common but still quite important. The relatively day-to-day matters of quality standards and production schedules were monitored less often than were the labour-related issues of pay movements and industrial disputes. It seems that the more routine and predictable areas are left more to the local managers than are those which can have important implications for the firm as a whole: an industrial dispute can affect other plants, either because the demands from which it emerges are generalized or because of the indirect consequences of breakdown in the flow of products between plants. As table 4.5 shows, however, in those plants where quality and production issues were closely monitored a formal system was almost universal whereas such systems were less common for the two labour-related matters. On the former pair of issues firms seem either to have little direct interest in plants' activities or to have developed fairly formal procedures for assessing performance. On the labour issues a more *ad hoc* approach was more common. But even here about half the plants reported not only company interest but also the presence of formal monitoring against specific criteria or targets.

On corporate-level involvement the picture is straightforward. There was generally a high level of interest in plants' performance against profit targets but very little interest in any of the other areas: in between a half and two-thirds of cases little or no interest was reported. The evidence on pay movements throws a further light on the previous consideration of plant autonomy in setting pay rates. In 63 per cent of plants little or no interest in movements outside negotiated settlements was reported. Even allowing for some possible understatement of the degree of corporate interest, it still appears that corporate managements tended to show little interest in wage drift at local level. This must raise some question about the detail with which pay matters are co-ordinated by these managements.

Correlates of Monitoring

As would be expected, there was a close relationship between the extent of company and of corporate interest in pay movements. There was also some tendency for close company interest to be associated with the taking of decisions on pay settlements above the level of the plant, and a stronger tendency for corporate interest to be linked with decision-making at this level. There is, of course, no necessary reason why such relationships should exist, for firms could determine pay settlements at company level while showing little interest in wage drift at local level, or could alternatively permit plant managers to set wage rates while keeping a close eye on actual pay movements. The relationship was, indeed, far from strong, which again suggests that firms' arrangements for dealing with pay matters may be rather undeveloped. That is, a firm with powerful central direction of pay decisions would ensure that negotiations were under central control while also keeping a close check on movements at local level away from negotiated rates. This pattern was far from dominant in the sample. On other issues there was no relationship between the level of decision-making and the extent of company interest in the issue.

It might be expected that the size of the firm could influence the degree of checking of plant performance, one possible hypothesis being that large firms will be relatively distant from their individual plants and that they will therefore tend not to check closely on plant performance. There was in fact no connection between company size and either company-level or corporate-level monitoring. Neither was the relative size of the plant as described above (see table 4.3) a significant influence, except in the area of quality standards. Here the expected tendency, namely an increase in company interest as the size of the plant relative to that of the company rose, was evident. Why a size effect should be present for only this one area is far from clear. If it were present for other areas a reasonable explanation might be essayed. As it is, the safest conclusion is that there was no tendency for the absolute size of firms or the relative size of the individual plant to affect the extent of monitoring of plant performance.

There was an interesting pattern of association with the importance attributed to industrial relations matters in managerial decision-making. Although, as shown above, such importance was not linked to the level of decision-making, there was a link with company monitoring. On four of the five areas considered there was a statistically significant tendency for the importance attributed to industrial relations to be higher the closer was the degree of company monitoring. On the fifth area, namely profit targets, a high importance was attributed to industrial relations where monitoring was either very close or not close at all, with a lower level of importance being associated with the two middle categories of monitoring. Since, however, 'very close' checking was the overwhelming response on this issue, not too much should be made of this particular pattern of variation. The overall picture is one of close monitoring tending to go along with the ascription of an important role to labour matters.

But what does 'importance' mean? Does it mean that managers perceived problems with union restrictions, such that they could not act without fear of strikes? If so, these correlations would suggest that companies monitor their plants closely when they fear labour unrest. Alternatively, importance can refer to the value that is placed on workers' contribution to the enterprise and to a 'people orientation' in managerial decision-making. As shown in chapter 5, the latter interpretation fits the evidence much more closely than the former. Managers reported labour-related constraints on their operations only rarely, and the great majority said that they had made changes in working arrangements without opposition. There was also no association between the closeness of company monitoring and such possible indicators of union resistance as the extent of shopfloor union organization and experience of strikes (see Qs 20 and 23). Even the extent of monitoring of industrial disputes was unrelated to whether or not the plant had had a strike in the previous two years.

The 'obvious' explanation for the link between monitoring and the importance ascribed to labour matters thus does not work. A rather more complex influence may have been present. The most likely direction of causation runs from monitoring to importance. It is unlikely that giving importance to labour matters causes firms to monitor plants' activities closely. But it can be argued that managers who are subject to close checking of their performance feel that they have to get all aspects of their internal management, including relations with the work force, in order if they are to meet the targets that they are set.

Looking at the matter in terms of direct cause and effect may not, however, be the most illuminating approach. Underlying the model of organization developed by Peters and Waterman is the view that organizational characteristics are related to each other: excellently run firms have cultures that embrace a set of values that reinforce each other. A similar approach runs through other discussions. The most sensible way of considering how firms generate a sense of commitment among their workers is not to treat each aspect of their employment policies as separate but to explore the ways in which they fit together to produce an interlocking structure of control (Burawoy, 1979; P.K. Edwards, 1986a). In the present case, monitoring and ascribing importance to labour considerations may have been parts of the 'culture' of the firm as a whole, in which a high level of freedom in the making of decisions also played a part. Thus firms may give plants freedom while also monitoring their performance, and this approach may go along with promoting a 'people orientation'. The link between monitoring and seeing labour matters as important may be not a direct relation of cause and effect but an indirect reflection of the way in which monitoring and placing weight on people management both stem from a corporate culture of the type discussed by Peters and Waterman.

It is hard to produce concrete evidence in support of this interpretation, since by their nature survey data are better at examining relationships between two or more variables than at explaining how in a particular case a corporate culture is created. But other possible accounts do not seem to work, and the interpretation thus stands as the best available. And there is one other relationship in the data which supports it. As shown in chapter 6 there was a clear link between monitoring and productivity: a particular style of company management associated with a 'loose–tight' link between plants and the head office does seem to carry the claimed benefit of improving productivity. This strengthens the idea of a corporate culture.

The evidence is certainly not clearcut. Thus there was no link between productivity and the importance attributed to labour matters. But this absence may not be surprising. In addition to points relating to the accuracy and adequacy of the measures used, there may be reasons not to expect a direct connection. The argument about a culture is that there are distinct types of firm with clusters of characteristics. The presence of one characteristic, treated in isolation, may be less important than the cluster as a whole. The survey evidence can do two things: assess whether a posited relationship between two parts of a culture holds across all plants; and examine the connections that are found to exist in the light of plausible accounts of the causal mechanisms at work. In the present case, it is possible to show that company monitoring and a people management orientation went together across all the plants in the survey. This can be explained in terms of the place of both within a broader approach to the operation of individual firms.

Conclusions

In chapter 3 the links between firms and operating units were investigated by examining the individual career structures of factory managers. In this chapter the focus has been on the plant as an organizational entity. The main conclusion is simple. Plants were given a good deal of autonomy in managing their own internal arrangements, but the results of the exercise of this autonomy were carefully monitored by companies. Exactly how the discretion was used cannot be assessed through survey methods, but in the important area of pay settlements various suggestions were made as to how companies could set broad guidelines for the principles to be followed or establish global figures for the size of the wage bill. A survey at plant level cannot pin down these influences or compare plant-level perceptions with views higher up the organization. Work currently under way is attempting to deal with this problem.[3] But the present survey has been able to address several pertinent issues. Most obviously, it has pointed to the substantial role played by the factory managers in all areas of the operation of the plant: a style of direct, 'hands on' involvement seemed to be preferred to one of delegation.

It has also been suggested that the autonomy claimed by factory managers was far from illusory. Not only was the actual running of the plant, a duty whose responsibilities should not be minimized, left to them with little outside interference. They were also able to take decisions which potentially had important ramifications for the rest of their firms. It is very unlikely that they would have taken such decisions without reference to what was going on elsewhere or to company guidelines, but it is also true that they were not merely following out orders from above. Just as company managers can co-ordinate and monitor pay settlements, so plant managers can lobby those responsible for corporate policy to try to make this policy more suitable to their own needs. Systems of bargaining and influence can be used by different groups for different purposes. Despite this, the monitoring of plants' performance was substantial, and the results of the monitoring are likely to have affected corporate management's perceptions of a plant and hence its ability to attract investment funds and even its chances of remaining open. This fact must have had a powerful effect on how the factory managers conducted themselves. But it would be a mistake to suppose that corporate managements are simply accounting machines, directing investment funds to plants in direct proportion to their financial performance. Some firms may not possess the necessary sophistication of accounting techniques or, more importantly, the decision-making apparatuses to carry out what the financial results suggest. (This is apart from any uncertainty about the objectivity of the accounting techniques themselves.) And those that do have the necessary attributes may well have to take other considerations into account. A plant which is central to a firm's operations, be it for historical reasons or because it is an important supplier to other plants, is in a stronger position than one on the periphery of the firm's operations. The factory manager of the former type of plant may well have been able to bargain about corporate policy. Financial results have to be interpreted through intra-managerial political processes.

The factory managers were thus neither totally autonomous nor the pawns of higher management. They carried out some complex duties which could not be specified in detail without a stultifyingly rigid set of rules being laid down. Their position also gave them some bargaining power within their firms. In a sense, even the idea of constraint, which was counterposed in the introduction to the chapter to the idea that plant autonomy is illusory, may not do justice to their position. It implies that there were clear and fixed limits within which the factory managers operated, whereas in fact company rules and monitoring procedures are likely to contain areas of uncertainty and ambiguity. The plants were parts of their firms' political structures, and they had political resources as well as being limited by constraints that were in part, political in form. They were relatively autonomous in that they had areas of local discretion while also having to meet corporate goals.

The evidence of this chapter thus fits with that presented in chapter 3 where it was shown that the factory managers were a confident and satisfied group, with many of them having had considerable experience of different areas of their firms' operations. These facts strengthen the argument that they were knowledgeable and influential people and that they are likely to have had a clear idea of how the structures of power and influence analysed in this chapter worked. There is also a substantive point, namely that factory managers appear to be influential people in the management hierarchy as shown by their careers and by the powers that they exercise. They have also been shown to have considerable involvement in issues of a labour relations type. How they viewed the management of labour relations is examined in the following chapter.

Notes

1. One possible argument, namely that plant size affects perceived discretion, is refuted by the data. The results for all plants in the Warwick Survey (Brown, 1981: 36) are very similar to those given in table 4.2. If anything, they suggest that discretion was felt to be greater in the smaller plants. On industrial relations matters generally, for example, 58 per cent of the whole sample claimed complete or almost complete discretion, as against 48 per cent of those in plants with at least 250 employees.

2. One other association worth noting is that with the reported performance of the plant relative to other plants in the company (Q. 145). As relative performance increased, so local discretion in decision-making rose. Since both sets of replies are obviously the subjective views of respondents, not too much should be read into the result. But it suggests that plants which are seen as successful may be given more autonomy than those seen as having problems, a point which case study work might usefully explore further.

3. This is the 'Higher Level Survey' which is following up the 1984 Workplace Industrial Relations Survey by examining industrial relations arrangements above the level of the individual establishment. Specifically, unlike Marsh's (1982) survey, it takes a sample of establishments and matches each plant to a higher level in the organization, namely the head office of the whole organization and, where it exists, an intermediate level such as a division or operating company. Differing perceptions of decision-making, and also the character of links between plants and higher levels, can be investigated. The survey's fieldwork was carried out during 1985. The results are being written up by a team based at the IRRU, Warwick University.

5

The Management of Industrial Relations

The previous chapter has shown that the factory managers were quite heavily involved in decisions with a labour element. In this chapter, attention turns to the management of industrial relations in its own right. For the most part, the unit of analysis is the factory: for example, what changes in working practices have been introduced recently? The whole sample will therefore be used. But it is also of interest to compare factory managers' attitudes to the management of labour with those of personnel specialists. Some analyses will thus be restricted to the factory managers in the sample.

As noted in chapter 1, labour relations should not be equated with the institutions of collective bargaining. The management of labour involves all the ways in which firms recruit, motivate, and control their employees. The survey followed through the implications of this argument by asking respondents to assess the importance of industrial relations in their overall decision-making and to summarize their broad policy or philosophy on labour matters. Since they did not seem to have any difficulty with these questions, there is some evidence to suggest that they, too, saw labour management in a broad sense. It is also necessary, however, to consider institutional matters. The key question here is what changes have been made in firms' methods of handling labour relations: has there been an offensive against shop steward organizations, have there been widespread attacks on the 'restrictive practices' that are often seen as the companions of these organizations, and has the role of personnel management declined as problems of labour relations have evaporated? The chapter begins by examining these questions before moving on to outline the broader approach to labour management that underpinned managerial action on them.

The central argument is that, although changes in working practices have been widely introduced, the main reason for them was the external threat of competition and not problems of labour control. Attacks on steward organizations have been rare, and the institutional framework of industrial relations is little altered from what it was in the late 1970s. What has changed is the approach to labour that is adopted. The present evidence, together with that from other sources, suggests that managers are increasingly concerned with the 'involvement' of the work force in the business. The emphasis is less on negotiation and more on persuading workers as individuals that their interests are best met by co-operating with management. Involvement, together with another vogue word, 'participation', does not mean that firms believe in giving workers an increased say in decision-making. Quite the reverse. They are willing to provide information on the firm's activities, and they seek a spirit of co-operation on the shopfloor, but workers' power of decision is limited to their own immediate tasks. Although still in existence, organizations such as shop stewards' committees may be less able to challenge managerial decisions than they were in the past. The approach of seeking commitment on an individual basis will be called a policy of enlightened managerialism.

There has been a good deal of debate about current trends of labour management, much of it focused on the notion of 'macho management' (Purcell, 1982). The following discussion does not use this debate to organize the presentation of the findings because the concept of macho management does not grasp the complexities of recent developments: it assumes an all-or-nothing approach by management wherein attacking steward organization goes along with a reassertion of the right to manage. Managerial authority can be established in other ways, and enlightened managerialism is arguably tougher, because it is more sophisticated, than an all-out attack on existing practices. The following discussion will outline the policies associated with enlightened managerialism. The final section of the chapter returns to debates in the literature to consider the approach, in particular, how far it characterizes all British industry or only one specific part of it.

Industrial Relations Institutions and Working Practices

Institutional Arrangements

It was quite widely thought, when the survey was carried out, that there was a systematic managerial onslaught on trade union organization in the factory, reflected in reductions in the number and influence of shop

TABLE 5.1
Changes in Bargaining Arrangements with Union Representatives

| | Respondents Mentioning as % of: | |
	Those Making Changes	All Respondents
Encouraging awareness of need for change	75	16
Reducing number of shop stewards	13	3
Reducing number/influence of senior stewards	14	3
Reducing facilities for stewards	0	0
Ending closed shop	0	0
Decentralization of bargaining	17	4
Other	6	1

Base: Respondents with recognized unions (N = 209), and those making changes in bargaining arrangements (N = 42).

stewards and attempts to dismantle institutions such as the closed shop. These pressures, together with the wider economic environment, might have been expected to have reduced the combativity of workers, as reflected in their proneness to take strike action.

As noted in chapter 2, trade unions were recognized for bargaining purposes in 89 per cent of plants. Respondents in these plants were asked, 'Have you made any changes in the way in which you bargain with your trade union representatives in the past two years?' (Q. 112).[1] Seventy-nine per cent of them said that they had made no change. The minority who had made changes were asked what these involved. As table 5.1 shows, the most common response was the general encouragement of the need to accept change. In only 13 per cent of cases where changes had been made in methods of bargaining (representing only 3 per cent of the whole sample) was a reduction in the number of shop stewards mentioned. A more subtle approach, of removing the facilities available to stewards while continuing to recognize them, was also absent, as was any direct attack on the closed shop.

To assess patterns of change some basis of comparison is needed. For present purposes the most useful is the Warwick Survey (Brown, 1981) mentioned in chapter 4 (p. 98). For comparison with the present results the data have been re-analysed to exclude those with fewer than 250 workers. A question of comparability plainly arises, for the Warwick Survey interviewed the manager at each plant responsible for personnel and industrial relations; in large plants this was almost always a personnel specialist and not a general manager. On matters of perception, for example the importance of the personnel function, differences between respondents are likely to swamp any changes between 1977 and 1984. But on straight matters of fact, such as whether a plant had a full-time shop steward, there should be little difference between types of respondent.[2]

The key contrasts to the Warwick Survey are set out in table 5.2, with data for the whole of the Warwick Survey sample included for comparative purposes. On the indicators of trade union presence, there was very little difference, the presence of recognized senior stewards, for example, being reported in 76 per cent of plants in 1984 as against

TABLE 5.2
Comparison with Previous Survey

	1984	1977–8	
	Plants with 250 or more Employees	All Plants
Per cent plants reporting Recognized manual union	89	93	76
Recognized senior manual stewards	76	79	54
Full-time manual stewards	17	25	9
100% manual union density	50	49	36
Any industrial action	63	66	46
Any strike	36	48	33
Any other action	51	48	29
Establishment most important level of pay bargaining	60[a]	50	42
IR function 'much more important'	19	56	36
Presence of joint consultation committee	78	63	42

Note:
[a] Percentage saying bargaining took place at establishment only. A further 29 per cent said that bargaining took place at other levels in the company or corporation. Respondents were not asked the most important level where more than one was involved. The figure of 60 per cent is thus a lower bound.
Source: 1977–8 figures recalculated from the Warwick Survey data; Brown (1981) reports details of the survey. Figures are on comparable basis to present survey, i.e. they relate to plants with 250 or more full-time employees and are weighted.

118 The Management of Industrial Relations

79 per cent in 1977–8. There was some decline in the presence of full-time stewards, from 25 per cent to 17 per cent. These results are consistent with those reported by Batstone (1984: 210–16). Batstone compared the figures in his sample of personnel managers with those arising from an appropriate re-weighting of the Warwick Survey.[3] He found no change in the extent of union recognition or in the presence of senior or full-time stewards, and there may have been a slight rise in the prevalence of the closed shop. The last datum is again consistent with the present findings. Although no direct questions were asked about the closed shop, that is arrangements whereby workers have to be union members to keep their jobs, the institution must have been widespread: union density among manual workers of 100 per cent was reported in 50 per cent of the plants, as against 49 per cent in the Warwick Survey.

The comparison may be taken further by considering separately each of the five industries chosen for special examination. As table 5.3 shows, union recognition remained widespread. It had even increased in chemicals, although this was more than off-set with declines in food, drink, and tobacco and in electrical engineering. Given the small numbers involved, there is a large margin of error, and the results are not in general statistically significant.[4] But there seem to have been some differences between industries, with reductions in the extent of recognition of senior stewards being most prevalent in electrical engineering and textiles, while food, drink, and tobacco, chemicals, and textiles showed the greatest propensity to reduce the number of full-time stewards.

Paper, printing, and publishing is a special case, with a slight fall in the frequency of recognition being balanced by a rise in the prevalence of senior and of full-time stewards. As the table shows, and as will be seen in more detail below, the industry stands out in other respects. It has of course been the site of some of the most significant conflicts over the introduction of new technology. It is the only one of the five industries where an increase in strike action is recorded in the present survey. Managements here seem to have been particularly active in altering their working practices and in facing strikes if necessary.

But this has not gone along with an attack on union organization as such. Indeed, those recognizing unions seem to have been willing to increase the status of shop steward organizations. A possible explanation is that they have felt a need to retain or extend some form of shopfloor organization so as to be able to negotiate the introduction of change, while being firm on the need for change to be introduced. The general impression from press reports of the industry is that, while managements have been making sweeping changes in work organization which have been directed at undermining the traditional power of the unions, there has been no widespread attempt or even desire to operate

TABLE 5.3
Comparison with Earlier Results, within Industries

	FDT		Chemicals		El. Eng.		Textiles		PPP	
	1984	1977–8	1984	1977–8	1984	1977–8	1984	1977–8	1984	1977–8
Per cent reporting										
Recognized manual trade union	85	95	91	86	81	89	94	95	97	100
Recognized senior manual stewards	73	79	74	76	66	82	52	66	76	70
Full-time manual stewards	10	15	23	30	23	25	6	12	18	14
Any industrial action	63	73	63	55	45	68	40	42	85	71
Any strike	37	60	31	41	15	43	16	36	57	43
Estab. most imp. level of pay bargaining	34	32	65	50	73	77	30	29	45	15
Industrial relations function much more important	17	69	20	48	18	69	20	37	21	62

Notes and Sources: See table 5.2.

on a non-union basis. It is the role and not the presence of unions that has been under attack.

The presence of unions may not have changed much since 1977, but other features of labour relations have altered. Most obviously, and in line with the official statistics, the prevalence of strike action has fallen, with just over a third of plants reporting a strike in 1984 as against nearly a half in 1977–8 (Q. 23). These figures are very similar to those reported by Batstone (1984: 293). There appears to have been a less steep fall in the use of industrial action other than strikes, with 63 per cent of plants reporting some form of action in 1984 as against 66 per cent in 1977–8: Batstone notes a rather sharper decline in his data, from 71 per cent to 57 per cent, but suggests that the use of action other than strikes has held up more than the use of strikes, which may point to the use of more subtle forms of industrial pressure. This view is upheld even more strongly in the present data, which show a slight rise in the use of sanctions other than strikes.

There has been considerable speculation over the years about the connections between strikes and other sanctions. One common argument about the 1960s, when strike activity was rising in Britain and many other countries, was that strikes represented only a small part of the total number of sanctions and that non-strike activity was probably rising more rapidly. A plausible corollary is that, in a recession, managements are unwilling to tolerate the overtime bans and go-slows that they may have to live with during an up-swing. If workers were to use industrial action at all, they might be forced into a strike. It would follow that fluctuations in strike activity would be less sharp than fluctuations in the use of all forms of industrial action. This model does not fit the recent recession, where the use of strikes seems to have fallen more sharply than that of other forms of action.[5] It would be unwise to treat this as a general rule, for the wish to use industrial action and the ability to sustain it will depend on a wide range of economic and institutional factors. At another time the pattern may be different. But it seems that in the present case the decline in strike activity has exaggerated the weakness of workers in sustaining industrial action.

The level of pay bargaining is a further important indicator of institutional arrangements. The data suggest an increase in the importance of the establishment level of bargaining. This is in contrast to Batstone's (1984: 203) finding of a decline in the importance of the establishment, which was matched by a slight rise in the importance of company bargaining above plant level and a sharper rise in the number of plants reporting that there was no bargaining at all. Several reasons can be suggested for this contrast: a difference due to plant size, with the large plants in the present survey having more establishment bargaining while smaller plants were shifting away from this form of bargaining;

differences in the wording of questions; and different perceptions between factory managers and personnel managers. Batstone found only a weak relationship between plant size and bargaining level, which suggests that the first factor may not be the reason. The other two influences are harder to evaluate. The factory managers were not asked to assess the importance of different bargaining levels, but only to say at what level bargaining took place (see Q. 21). The present figures may thus actually understate the importance of the establishment level. Against this, however, is the possibility that factory managers do not know at what levels apart from the plant itself pay bargaining takes place. It is certainly safe to conclude that there has been no sharp shift away from establishment bargaining in large plants. It is also possible that autonomy in such plants has been rising. Batstone's sample contained only 133 plants, and this may not have been large enough to assess any size effect. The view that large plants, if not all establishments, have had increasing discretion is consistent with the evidence presented in chapter 4 that discretion is considerable in several areas of managerial decision-making, and also with press reports that suggest that the current fashion is to devolve decision-making to and increase the accountability of local managers.

A final institutional feature of importance is the presence of joint consultation committees. Such committees were reported to 78 per cent of plants, as against 63 per cent in 1977–8. A rise in their prevalence is consistent with other evidence. In the Warwick Survey 38 per cent of the plants with at least 250 workers had introduced their committees over the previous five years. The 1980 Workplace Industrial Relations Survey found that, in industry as a whole, committees had been introduced, over the previous three years, in 9 per cent of plants and abandoned in only 1 per cent (Daniel and Millward, 1983: 132). In the present survey, 16 per cent of plants had introduced committees over the previous three years. Their introduction was most marked in the paper, printing, and publishing industry, where 30 per cent were less than three years old. From being below average on the presence of committees (42 per cent were three years or more old, as against the average of 62 per cent) the industry has come near to the overall average, a further indication of the move away from traditional modes of bargaining in the sector. The significance of the committees was, however, limited here. Respondents with committees and with recognized unions were asked to rate the relative importance of the two means of dealing with the work force. Overall, 28 per cent rated joint consultation as the more important, but in paper, printing, and publishing the figure was only 13 per cent; the proportions rating negotiations as more important were, respectively, 14 and 25 per cent. Finally, 31 per cent of all those who had had committees for at least three years felt that their importance had increased, while only 9 per cent noted a decrease; there was little variation here between industries.

This evidence suggests that, far from disappearing, consultation has had something of a revival. The significance of this should not, however, be exaggerated. As Joyce and Woods (1984) note, in their survey (carried out in 1982) of members of the London Chamber of Commerce and Industry, joint consultation appeared to be growing in popularity. They point out, however, that this may have reflected external circumstances, with firms setting up consultation committees to tell workers the problems caused by the recession and to persuade them to accept changes in working practices. There need have been no desire to involve workers more fully in the operation of the enterprise. MacInnes (1985) has argued that there is little evidence of a long-term increase in the prevalence of committees, and he uses this, together with case study material on the influence of committees, to suggest that their role may have been exaggerated. Be that as it may, there is evidence of a recent upsurge in the use of committees, even if the long-term significance of this is questionable. MacInnes may also be correct to ask how far the committees are really used for joint worker–management discussion, as distinct from being mere means of communication. As shown below, managers in the present study were keen on 'involvement' but they meant by this not co-determination but persuading workers to see and accept the managerial point of view. Joint consultation committees could be a useful vehicle, even though the amount of genuine joint activity may have been slight.

The contrasts to earlier results suggest, then, that the institutional framework of workplace industrial relations has been little changed, although some of the practices within that framework, notably a decline in the presence of industrial action and a rise in the use of joint consultation, have been altering. This latter point may be pursued by looking at changes in working practices.

Working Practices and Limits to Efficiency

Respondents were asked whether, over the previous two years, they had made any changes in working arrangements or introduced any schemes to increase the efficiency of labour utilization (Q. 106). At least one change has been introduced in 84 per cent of plants, with three or more distinct types of change being mentioned in 43 per cent of cases. In Batstone's (1984: 242) survey, 'major' changes in working practices were reported to have been introduced, in the previous five years, in 86 per cent of plants. As table 5.4 shows, the main types of change in the present survey were the introduction of new technology and increasing the efficiency of existing equipment (mentioned by 76 and 66 per cent respectively of those making changes). Changes of a specifically labour relations kind, such as changing demarcation lines and attacking unions' restrictive practices, were mentioned less fre-

TABLE 5.4
Changes in Working Practices

	% of All Respond-ents	Type of change[a]	% of Times Men-tioned	% of Respond-ents Mentioning
Number of changes mentioned				
None	16	New technology	26	76
1	21	Increased efficiency with	23	66
2	20	existing equipment		
3 or 4	30	Flexible working	19	54
More than 4	13	Cutting overtime	11	32
		Change demarcation lines	8	24
		Remove other TU restrictions	6	18
		Change pay systems	4	10
		Change plant layout	2	4
		Other	1	4
			100	

Note:
[a] Base is number of respondents introducing at least one change (N = 197).

quently.[6] There was little variation between industries, except that the introduction of change was particularly marked in paper, printing, and publishing. Thirty per cent of respondents here identified more than four different sorts of change, as against an average of 13 per cent and a figure of only 1 per cent in textiles. They were also more likely than other respondents to include changes in demarcation lines and other trade union restrictions. This adds weight to the previous argument that the industry has been marked by particularly rapid change over the last five years or so and that this has involved a high level of overt conflict together with challenges to existing shopfloor controls of effort.

This raises the question of the extent to which changed working practices were introduced to deal with constraints on efficiency that were internal to the plant, and in particular constraints of a labour relations kind. When asked whether there were any internal constraints on attaining full-capacity working (Q. 103), only 20 per cent of man-

124 *The Management of Industrial Relations*

agers said that there were such constraints. There was little variation between industries, except that constraints were particularly rare in electrical engineering. The types of constraint identified are classified in table 5.5. Technical production problems were the most significant, being mentioned by 64 per cent of those reporting constraints. These were either the only constraint mentioned, or were the most important of two or more constraints, in 40 per cent of cases. Trade union restrictions and overmanning were less significant, being the most important constraints in 15 per cent of cases, which represents 3 per cent of the whole sample. Thus 97 per cent of managers did not see unions' restrictions as the major constraint on achieving full-capacity working.

These results may underestimate the extent of labour-related constraints. It may well be that, had managers been asked about them three or four years previously, they would have been reported in greater numbers, but they had been eroded by 1984. The question also asked about limits on working at full capacity and not about the efficiency of

TABLE 5.5
Constraints on Attaining Capacity Working

	Respondents Mentioning		Most Important	
	As % Those with Internal Constraints	As % All Respondents	As % Those with Internal Constraints	As % All Respondents
Technical production problems	64	13	40	8
Quality of management	34	7	6	1
Maintenance problems	13	3	0	0
Trade union restrictions, overmanning	33	7	15	3
Lack of worker effort, absenteeism	29	6	10	2
Shift system	12	3	10	2
Lack of labour, worker inflexibility	21	4	17	4
Other	2	(..)	2	(..)
			100	20

Base: Those mentioning internal constraints (*N* = 47).

labour utilization. It is possible to work at capacity while having manning levels and labour costs that management considers to be excessive. It is, however, doubtful whether respondents put such a strict interpretation on the question. Anyone for whom problems of manning levels and inefficiency loomed large would have been likely to say that there were obstacles to working to full capacity, for it is unlikely that, in a plant where these things are significant, operations simply run smoothly, albeit with a level of labour utilization that management finds unsatisfactory. It is much more likely that they will be associated with frequent disputes which hold up production, and with a perception among managers that labour problems are a significant issue. This would certainly have been the case in various factories with powerful shop steward organizations that have been the subject of case studies (Batstone *et al.*, 1977; Edwards and Scullion, 1982b). The evidence in the survey is consistent with such a view. There was a strong association between having a strike and the presence of trade union restrictions that were said to interfere with working at full capacity (14 per cent of plants with strikes also had these constraints, as against 3 per cent of plants without strikes). This is not of course to say that there is a close correlation between strong steward organizations and constraints on efficiency. Such organizations are necessary but not sufficient for significant challenges to managerial authority to develop. And they are not even necessary for firms to experience problems of efficiency arising from other sources.

Managers had a further opportunity to cite labour difficulties. They were asked (at Q. 138) about their costs of production, and those who said that these were above average were asked whether the sources of problems in this respect were internal to the plant and, if so, whether labour productivity was a significant influence. This was rare, with only 7 per cent of all plants citing labour productivity as a problem.

In assessing the characteristics of plants with labour-related constraints, it is important to see whether the various constraints go together, that is, whether there is a distinct syndrome of labour problems. This would appear not to be the case. Three constraints were examined: that just mentioned arising from excessive costs of production, plus union restrictions (together with overmanning) and a general lack of worker effort (from the question about constraints on attaining capacity working). Of the (unweighted) total of 229 plants, 32 had at least one of the constraints, but 25 had only one, 5 had two, and only 2 had all three. This suggests that there was not a distinct group of plants with severe labour relations problems, a point supported by various comparisons between the 32 plants and the remainder. There was no difference in the managers' perceptions of the degree of plant utilization over the previous year; and the introduction of new working practices or of new methods of bargaining with union representatives was as common in the 197 plants with none of the constraints as it was in these 32.

This suggests that changed working practices were not the result of factors internal to the plant, for not only were these practices not associated with union-related problems but they were also far more common than were any sorts of internal constraint, whether labour related or otherwise. Batstone (1984: 242) similarly reports that in his plants where changed working practices were absent unions were not seen as a significant obstacle to change, which suggests that union restrictions were not important in the prevention of change. In the present survey, of those introducing changes, 73 per cent reported that there had been no resistance from the work force while a further 18 per cent said that there had been bargaining followed by the acceptance of change. In 1 per cent, industrial action had forced management to back down, and in another 1 per cent opposition prevented change without the need for such action (strikes or other action that failed to prevent changes accounting for the remaining 7 per cent).

If change was introduced without serious shopfloor resistance, and if internal constraints were relatively rare, why were changed working practices so widespread? The survey data as a whole suggest that it was not internal problems but external ones which stimulated managements to make changes. As shown in chapter 2, competition was widely felt to be severe and to be increasing in strength. In such a market environment firms are likely to have felt that they had to increase their labour efficiency even if there were no specific labour problems to overcome.[7] This view is supported by a comparison between the plants that had introduced new working practices and those that had not. There was no significant association with the density of union membership or the status of union organization (that is, whether there was no recognition, recognition without senior stewards, the recognition of senior stewards, or the presence of full-time stewards). Neither did industrial location make a difference.

The introduction of new working practices was associated, albeit not very strongly, with four characteristics: being subject to a high level of competition; facing increasingly strong competition; reporting the average level of production per worker to be higher than that in the rest of the relevant industry; and seeing industrial relations considerations as important in business decision-making. The effect of the first two is obvious. The third may perhaps be seen as more a consequence than a cause of change, but in fact causality may not be clear-cut, with the more efficient plants tending to be those that have the resources and the managerial confidence to introduce change, which tends to make them more efficient; there may be a mutual reinforcement between change and the level of productivity. The fourth factor was introduced to assess whether managers in plants making changes in working practices took account of labour matters in taking their decisions. The fact that they do has to be interpreted in the light of two other pieces of evidence: that labour relations constraints were rare and that, as shown below, 'importance' appears to have meant not that managers saw labour issues as creating limits on their freedom of action but that they saw workers as a significant part of the business. The correlation with the introduction of new working practices suggests that it was the plants which had the most positive view of labour matters, in the sense of seeing these as important in the pursuit of wide business goals, which were the most likely to make such introductions. To put the point another way, the absence of new working practices was associated with a lack of a developed view on labour matters: the minority of plants that did not make changes tended to have low levels of productivity and not to see labour as important in business ends. These things may have gone together to form an overall climate of stagnation and lack of consideration as to how efficiency could be raised.

This argument is consistent with some other patterns of association. As noted above, the 32 plants reporting some form of labour-related obstacles to increased efficiency were no more likely than the remainder to have introduced changes in working practices. The presence of such obstacles was, however, related to changing bargaining relationships with the unions: 40 per cent of those citing union restrictions as limits to achieving full-capacity working had altered their methods of bargaining, as against 20 per cent of those not citing restrictions. There was also a tendency for those with restrictions to report low levels of labour productivity (Q. 144).

These results point to the existence of three types of plant; or, since the patterns of association are far from strong and since such things as union restrictions are matters of degree and not all-or-nothing phenomena, three tendencies would be a more accurate characterization. First, there was the small minority of plants with significant labour-related constraints on efficiency; these were likely to have tried to change their industrial relations arrangements but not particularly likely to have changed their working practices. Second, another small minority had not changed working practices. These were not marked by high levels of union organization or by union restrictions. Instead, product market circumstances and an overall managerial view of the role of labour in the business tended to limit the desire to make changes. Finally, the majority of plants lacked union restrictions and had made changes in working arrangements. These changes reflected increasing levels of competition: there was a need to increase efficiency, but this was less to overcome specific problems of labour relations than to keep the business competitive.

Conclusions

The above results form part of a growing body of evidence that recent changes in labour relations have not involved a frontal attack on the institutional position of unions in the workplace. It would, however, be wrong to suppose that nothing has changed: new working practices, often of an all-embracing kind, have been widely introduced, and managements have made increasing use of consultative procedures to persuade workers and their representatives of the need for change. The picture is consistent with that from Chadwick's (1983) investigation of ten manufacturing firms in a Midlands town. Chadwick found that the firms had been strengthening their control of the shopfloor not by direct attacks on steward organizations but by using communication channels to inform workers of business realities and by using consultative arrangements to settle issues that had previously been dealt with through negotiation or custom and practice. The conduct of labour relations has changed even though the institutional structures of management–union relations remain in place.

Importance of, and Policy Towards, Labour Relations

Thus far, this chapter has considered some general developments in workplace industrial relations, treating the factory managers along with the other managers in the sample as reporters of the scene. With this background, attention may now turn to issues more centrally related to the focus of the study as a whole, namely, how far did factory managers feel that labour considerations were important in the overall running of the business and what policy did they adopt on labour matters?

Importance of Labour Relations

Respondents were asked to assess how the role of the personnel function had changed over the previous five years (Q. 97). At least two sets of factors might be expected to have reduced its importance: the weakening of unions' bargaining power in the recession, and changes of emphasis within management. With regard to the latter, the 1970s are widely seen as a decade of industrial relations reform, as a result of which process personnel departments grew in influence. With the completion of the process and with the increasing weight given to commercial matters, personnel issues might be expected to have declined in importance.[8]

As shown in table 5.2, the proportion of managers saying that the industrial relations function was much more important was lower than in the Warwick Survey: 19 per cent as against 56 per cent. Some of this is likely to be due to differences in respondents, although in the present survey there was no significant difference in replies between factory managers and other managers. And some may have reflected a genuine change betwen 1977 and 1984. Thus Batstone (1984: 198) reports that half his sample, as compared with 89 per cent in the comparable part of the Warwick Survey, saw the personnel function as more important than it had been previously. It appears that there has been a slowing down in the rise in the importance attributed to personnel matters, and not a reversal in the trends. In the present survey, the numbers seeing the personnel function as more important than in the past were much larger than those perceiving a decline (58 per cent against 14 per cent). And it was general managers and not personnel specialists who were giving this assessment.

Those perceiving a change in the role of personnel were asked why this had occurred. Of those seeing an increase, the majority (58 per cent) mentioned the effect of employment legislation, with a further 47 per cent mentioning the company's policy on employee involvement. Other reasons were comparatively unimportant, although 17 per cent mentioned the effects of the recession. The emphasis on employment legislation is consistent with the findings of the Warwick Survey (Brown, 1981: 33). It is, however, surprising at first sight, for has not the aim of recent legislation been to reduce trade union power and to limit the coverage of such things as the law of unfair dismissal? Two considerations explain the apparent anomaly. First, the sample contained only large plants, whereas the emphasis of some of the legal changes has been on very small firms (typically, those with fewer than 20 workers). Second, the law has not disappeared. It has tried to increase management's powers, but the exercise of those powers, for example, in altering closed shop arrangements or questioning the legality of a strike, depends on a knowledge of the law. As new laws have replaced old ones, factory managers are likely to have felt the need for expert guidance.

In addition to external influences in the shape of the law, internal matters concerning company policy were significant reasons for giving weight to personnel matters. As will be seen in detail below, factory managers gave considerable importance to labour relations issues. The nature of this importance may have changed, with procedural reform and unofficial strikes receding in significance to be replaced with wider questions of efficiency and employee involvement, but a shift in emphasis should not be confused with a decline in importance. There is, in short, little evidence that the recession has destroyed the importance of the personnel function.

The importance of labour matters was investigated further by asking respondents to rate the weight given to them in eight areas of decision-making (Q. 100). Since the interest is in the views of general manage-

ment, discussion will be limited to the factory managers; their replies
are classified in table 5.6. The importance given to labour issues was
plainly considerable. Even in an area such as fixed capital investment,
half the factory managers rated labour considerations as crucial or very
important. And the highest figure rating them as not very or not at all
important was 33 per cent, for decisions on the amount of overtime
worked.

'Importance' can mean at least two things: that labour relations were
seen as constraints on business decisions, or that they were viewed in
a more positive light (although the nature of that light would need
further elaboration). The evidence reviewed above makes the first
possibility unlikely. There were too few managers seeing labour
relations in terms of constraints for the role ascribed to labour consideration to be explicable in such terms. Cross-tabulations of answers
provide a similar picture. That by trade union status is shown in table
5.7, which shows the results of adding together the scores from the
eight areas to provide a composite measure of importance. Some slight
tendencies are observable, for example, a low overall importance of
industrial relations matters where there was no recognized trade union
(only 54 per cent coming into the two highest categories, as against 80
per cent where there was a full-time shop steward). But the differences
are far from dramatic (and they are not statistically significant). And
there is no clear gradient in the replies: if union status were important,
a steady rise in the proportion of respondents saying that labour matters
were crucial would be evident but there was no clear pattern of this
kind.

Comparison with earlier surveys is made difficult by differences in
respondents and in the coding schemes used. Thus the Warwick Survey
offered respondents the choice of 'plays the central role', 'heavily
involved', 'consulted', and 'not involved at all'. In addition to any
difference arising from the use of four, and not five, categories, the
differences in wording may have been significant. That used in the
Warwick Survey was not used here because it conflates two things:
playing the central role refers to the general importance of labour
considerations, whereas involvement and consultation relate to the
extent of participation by the personnel department in the relevant
decisions. Some comparison is, however, possible; the figures on the
three issues in the Warwick Survey which can be compared with the
present results are given in table 5.8. There has been, if anything, a
rise in the importance attributed to labour matters. The pattern of
replies on redundancy is similar, but on fixed capital investment and
changes in production methods the factory managers rated labour
considerations more highly than did personnel managers in 1977–8; on
the latter, for example, 83 per cent of factory managers said that they
were crucial or very important, whereas only 48 per cent of the Warwick

TABLE 5.6
Factory Managers' Views on Importance of Labour Relations in Decision-
Making (%)

	Crucial	Very Imp.	Fairly Imp.	Not very Imp.	Not Imp. At All
Decision area					
Fixed capital investment	14	36	24	17	10
Major changes in production methods	34	49	14	2	1
Redundancy	53	24	15	6	2
Manning levels	18	40	30	10	3
Overtime (amount worked)	3	19	44	26	7
Use of work study	11	32	28	17	12
Type of pay system	19	37	29	11	4
Flexibility of workers across tasks	31	47	16	5	1

Base: All factory managers (N = 177).

TABLE 5.7
Importance of Industrial Relations Considerations by Trade Union Status

	No. Recog. TU	Stewards	Senior Stewards	Full-time Steward
Overall importance of industrial relations[a]				
High	18	20	14	14
Medium/high	36	48	52	66
Medium	21	23	22	10
Medium/low	25	7	12	10
Low	0	2	0	0
	100	100	100	100

Note:
[a] Scores for the 8 decision areas added together and divided by 8. Scores thus run from 1 (low importance) to 5 (high importance). High scores are over 4.0; medium/high from 3.5 to 4.0; medium from 3.0 and less than 3.5; medium/low more than 2.0 and less than 3.0; low, 2.0 or less.

TABLE 5.8
Importance of Industrial Relations Considerations in 1977–1978 (%)

	Central Role	Heavily Involved	Consulted	Not Involved At All
Fixed capital investment	5	19	39	37
Major changes in production methods	9	39	37	15
Redundancy	38	47	11	3

Notes and *Source:* See table 5.2.

Survey's respondents said that they played the central role or were heavily involved. Batstone's (1984: 199) results point to a slight rise between 1977 and 1983 in the role played by personnel considerations in decisions on production methods, but a similar decline in decisions on redundancy.

In assessing these results, the importance attributed by managers to labour considerations should not be confused with widespread negotiation about them. Storey (1980: 129) found in a survey of 96 plants that negotiations on redundancy were reported in only half of them, while matters with no direct 'labour' component were rarely negotiated: production techniques were the subject of negotiation in 32 per cent of cases, while for investment policy and the purchasing of new plant the figures were, respectively, 6 per cent and 2 per cent. Similar results are reported by Cressey *et al.* (1981: 17–19) from their survey of 48 Scottish enterprises with more than 500 employees. Even in such large organizations negotiation was quite rare. On capital investment, no manager reported that there was negotiation, and only 25 per cent said that there was any degree of work-force involvement; on contraction and closure the figures were 4 per cent and 58 per cent, while it was only on the traditional issue of pay that negotiation was at all common. In short, 'importance' means that an issue is taken into account by managers in their own decision-making, and not necessarily that workers have any direct input to the process.

Perhaps the clearest indication of how respondents saw the matter comes from an open-ended question asking those who said that they were involved in the eight decision-making areas in what ways they felt labour relations matters to be important. This is admittedly a large question which can inspire vague answers, but it gave those who wished it the opportunity to specify union restrictions or other problems that they had to take into account. As the classification of replies in table 5.9 shows, however, such problems were mentioned only rarely. Those citing them tended to be concentrated in the paper, printing, and publishing industry. Two characteristic replies are given below.[9]

> We have very formal agreements with unions and we cannot make changes in any of these areas without making changes in agreements (024; PPP: 1,500 employees);

> Historically strong trade unions make necessary changes difficult (153; PPP; 720 employees).

Much more common were replies stressing the importance of labour relations in the overall operation of the business. Some of these were very general, for example:

> The whole efficiency of the factory depends on good labour relations (202; FDT; 250 employees);

> It is crucial to the efficient running of the business to have satisfactory labour relations (064; chems; 380 employees).

But even in a remark such as the last-quoted there is a recognition that labour relations are not just about disputes between management and workers and that workers are an important part of the business.

Several different emphases are evident in other responses. Thus some managers stressed the need for general co-operation;

> You cannot run a factory without the willing co-operation of the work force (018; other mfg; 325 employees);
> Labour relations are vital; there must be trust between employees and management (035; el. eng.; 540 employees).

TABLE 5.9
Factory Managers' Reasons for Seeing Industrial Relations Matters as Important in Business Policy (%)

For business ends/to increase efficiency	38
Important for own sake/need keep workers happy	25
Communication/participation	8
Trade union problems/agreements	3
Persuading people to accept change	6
Upset workers perform badly	3
Other	4
Don't know/vague/unclear	13

Base: Factory managers involved in decision-making areas listed at table 5.6 (*N* = 157).

Others were more concerned at the potential costs of industrial conflict if labour relations were not properly managed:

> The consequences of disruption are very serious (163; el. eng.; 1,500 employees);
> [labour relations are important in ensuring that] the ultimate decision can be implemented without frustrations due to labour difficulties (228; el. eng.; 500 employees).

But this last type of response was rare, as table 5.9 shows. And it reflects not a sense that industrial relations problems prevent change but that, although disruption is obviously always possible, appropriate managerial methods can minimize the risks. Other, and more common, replies saw labour relations in terms of releasing workers' creative potential, with words such as involvement, participation, and communication to the fore:

> If you haven't got a satisfied work force you have problems. By keeping them in the picture, they are happy about it (015; other mfg; 350 employees);

> We are introducing robots in the next few months. [We have] no labour problems because [the workers] can see the logic: a result of our good communications (022; el. eng.; 350 employees);

> [We employ] monthly discussion meetings: communication between management and work force ... To know is to understand; to be involved is to have corporate responsibility (028; FDT; 320 employees);

> The employees are the most important asset of the company and it is their capability, capacity and motivation which is the single most important ingredient in the success of the company (065; mech. eng.; 400 employees);

> [Labour relations are important in] keeping the labour force involved and knowing what is going on. We hold briefing groups with half the plant (166; el. eng.; 300 employees);

> Full consultation in order to get staff involved in the company, creating a company loyalty (216; chems; 960 employees).

These comments give some feeling for the way in which labour matters were viewed. At one level, it was obviously important to ensure that 'trouble' was avoided. But even here, the issue was not seen in the traditional industrial relations fashion of establishing appropriate procedures or reforming payment systems. It was more a matter of creating the broad conditions in which workers would see what management was doing and understand why. Thus, at a deeper level, there was a concern to promote a sense of identification with the company. A key means of doing this was to improve communication with the work force and to promote a sense of involvement in the firm. 'Involvement' and 'participation' are difficult words, for they can mean, in this context, that workers are encouraged to expect a say in decisions affecting them (together with the right to contest decisions that they dislike), or that workers are persuaded to accept the logics that management wishes to follow. It is plain that for the great majority of factory managers, the latter is what involvement is about. They did not argue that workers should be able to veto or even delay decision-making. If asked, they would probably have criticized forms of participation that give workers and their representatives the *de facto* right to challenge managerial assumptions or to delay change. They saw involvement in terms of telling workers what the needs of the business were, persuading them to accept these needs and the new technologies and new working practices that went with them, and creating a willingness to continue to accept, and indeed to look for, change.

In short, therefore, factory managers generally saw labour matters as important in their overall managerial decision-making. This is itself quite a significant result, for few surveys have looked at this stratum of management, and it is quite possible that they feel that labour relations are of very little importance as compared with their other responsibilities. Thus studies at higher levels in organizations (e.g. Winkler, 1974; Fidler, 1981) have shown that very senior managers tend to have little knowledge of or interest in labour relations within their firms. The present evidence suggests, perhaps not surprisingly, that those in charge of large manufacturing operations at establishment level are very conscious of the importance of labour. As shown in chapter 4, moreover, the factory managers were heavily involved in several areas of personnel policy. Their overall view of the importance of labour matters was not one of constraints on their ability to manage but one based on the need to take workers along with the rapid changes that were being implemented.

Labour Relations Policy
This point may be pursued further by considering managers' statements of their overall policies towards labour. They were asked (at Q. 98) whether their company had an overall policy or philosophy for the management of labour relations, with it being emphasized that the interest was not just in formal personnel policy but also in 'the place of workers in the organization of the enterprise as a whole'. This may, admittedly, have been a rather leading question in that it invited answers stressing the positive contribution of labour policy in business ends. But other questions had dealt with more basic factual matters, and it was considered important to examine broader issues of policy and style. Managers appear to have had few difficulties with the ques-

tion, and some answers were very full. Ninety per cent of the sample said that they had a policy in the sense indicated, and went on to describe it.

Categorizing the answers proved difficult, and the reasons for this need to be considered before the classification finally employed can be properly understood. The issues are not merely methodological, for some important substantive questions about the identification of types of managerial strategy for the control of labour also arise. Several recent contributions have pointed to the existence of differing strategies or styles for the management of labour. Among the best-known is Richard Edwards's (1979) view that American firms have moved from 'simple control' based on intense supervision and arbitrary managerial power, through the 'technical control' of mass production, to 'bureaucratic control' which relies on formal rules and gives workers rights as individuals. More specific is the attempt by Purcell and Sisson (1983: 112–18) to identify five 'styles' that characterize the labour policies of British private sector firms. At one end of the spectrum is the 'traditionalist' approach, which is based on forceful opposition to unions. Then comes the 'standard modern' pattern in which unions are recognized but in which there is little developed personnel policy, with decisions being based on the needs of the moment; this is the largest group in the classification. Third, there are the 'sophisticated moderns', who fall into two sub-groups: the 'constitutionalists', who operate with a clearly codified statement of managerial rights but who are very rare in Britain; and the 'consultors' who recognize unions but who resist codification and try to minimize the conflictual aspects of bargaining by developing detailed arrangements for communication and consultation. Finally, there are the 'sophisticated paternalists', most of whom refuse to recognize unions but who spend considerable time and resources in ensuring that their workers are satisfied; high wages, careful recruitment and training, and well-developed policies of communication are characteristic of this type of firm.

Each of these typologies has been subject to criticism. There is now a large literature on the work of Edwards and writers in the same tradition (see, for example, Thompson, 1983). For present purposes the main point is that a single type of control cannot capture either the range of variation in labour policies that exists across large firms or the various elements that any one firm uses. Many very diverse firms would come within the 'bureaucratic' category, and this category is unlikely to reflect the complex combination of negotiation, consultation, and communication that exists within each firm. Companies have many ways of managing labour relations, and these are not adequately taken into account in wide-ranging typologies.

Purcell and Sisson's approach is more useful. Companies such as Ford and IBM which are plainly very different, and yet which Edwards's categories are unable properly to distinguish, are analysed separately, as examples respectively of the consultative and the sophisticated paternalist styles. The analytical focus is also more specific: not the whole way in which workers are persuaded to work but the particular approaches to collective bargaining and collective representation adopted by large firms in Britain. Yet difficulties remain. The standard modern group embraces the overwhelming majority of the large manufacturing firms to which Purcell and Sisson devote most attention, and yet there are likely to be significant variations within this group. Indeed, this more or less follows from the definition of the group as comprising those employers without any developed company-wide personnel policy, for these employers are likely to devise their own arrangements in the face of their distinctive circumstances. It also appears that manufacturing plants cannot easily be assigned to one of the five categories. Deaton (1985) has derived a set of characteristics which members of each group should display; using data from the 1980 Workplace Industrial Relations Survey, he found that the expected clusterings did not occur and that many plants displayed characteristics associated with two or more of the ideal types of style. As Deaton admits, an assessment of formal arrangements may be unable to address the subtleties of a managerial style, which are about the climate and culture of a company. But he suggests that the marked lack of discrimination between plants raises questions about the applicability of the notion of style. Particularly notable is the absence of any demarcation between two groups which should stand in sharp contrast to each other, namely the standard moderns with their *ad hoc* approach and the sophisticated moderns who supposedly have a much more developed and coherent personnel policy.

The present argument develops from this point. It is useful to try to characterize the style of a particular firm. As Purcell and Sisson point out, in organizations such as ICI and Marks and Spencer there is a distinct and long-established culture which pervades the company. But such a style will reflect the general history and circumstances of the firm, and also the kind of workers' organization with which it has had to deal. A style is likely to be developed from several elements, sometimes as a matter of conscious policy and sometimes with no overall aim. But, although firms in similar conditions may develop broadly similar responses, there is no reason to suppose that styles will be shared between firms. There are thus two limitations to the applicability of the notion of style. First, there is the familiar point that ideal types are abstractions which are unlikely to occur in the real world. Second, they should be seen as characterizing tendencies and not as identifying mutually exclusive approaches: standard modern firms can have paternalist features, possibly because of their origins; sophisticated moderns will vary in the extent to which they have transcended the standard modern approach; and so on. This is not, to repeat, to deny the value of the concept of style. It is only to suggest that it applies best at the level of the individual firm, at which level several of the tendencies of each ideal-type may well coexist.[10]

It is thus not surprising that categorizing the present sample's statements of personnel policy proved difficult, for statements often contained several elements, suggesting that the classification would need to employ several dimensions to capture them all. An initial attempt produced no fewer than 55 different types of policy. It has been possible to reduce this number to 12 by concentrating on the main features and ignoring subtleties; the distribution of types is shown in Table 5.10. The list of types has some overlap with the notion of style. Thus the standard moderns would be expected to emphasize consistent procedures and working with trade unions. But the overlap is far from exact. This may be because a general question about policy may not really address the concept of style or because that concept does not work very well. No further speculation will be undertaken on this point; it will be left to users of the concept of style to explain how it ought to be applied.

As with replies on the importance of industrial relations, terms such as consultation, communication, and involvement loom large in the description of personnel policy: in 57 per cent of cases where a clear policy was stated (representing 46 per cent of all establishments), respondents used one of these terms, sometimes alone and sometimes in combination with others. The distinction between involvement and communication is often not very clear, as the following descriptions of policy indicate:

> Involvement and more complete communication with manual workers, e.g. Health and Safety Joint Council where unions and management participate in the whole business scene (003; el. eng.; 460 employees);

> We believe in having our own works council – the Japanese syndrome – where involvement is a joint thing. We meet once a month, each department elects a representative, and all matters are discussed through this (020; other mfg; 300 employees);

> Operative involvement is very much a growing thing ... We have a joint committee on quality control. Company results are discussed and passed on (055; text; 400 employees);

> We communicate to everyone the business situation as a whole ... Visiting clients are introduced to shopfloor workers to make them feel involved (075; PPP; 390 employees);

> Participation – everyone feels a part of the movement. A team approach is stressed (131; FDT; 450 employees).

Many other such accounts could be quoted. Two things stand out. One

TABLE 5.10
Labour Relations Policies by Trade Union Status

	No. Recog. TU (N = 26)	TU Recog. plus Stewards (N = 23)	Senior Stewards (N = 114)	Full-time Stewards (N = 38)	All
1. Consultation/information/communication	23	30	19	20	21
2. Involvement	4	14	13	16	12
3. Involvement plus ensuring workers know needs of business	13	13	17	16	16
4. Involvement plus other elements	0	16	2	0	3
5. Participation but controlled/limited	0	4	2	5	2
6. Managerial leadership/personal style/open door	9	5	6	9	7
7. Paternalistic/caring/worker based	22	10	17	10	15
8. Teamwork	6	0	5	6	5
9. Social responsibility	4	0	2	1	2
10. Fair and firm/consistent procedures	7	3	14	8	11
11. Work with TUs or stewards	0	4	3	5	4
12. Other	11	3	2	5	4
	100	100	100	100	100

Base: Respondents with a policy that was classifiable (N = 201). In 7 cases respondents said that they had a policy, but the answer was too vague to be classified.

is the stress on communicating with workers and generating a sense of commitment to the goals of the organization. The other is the detail and the specificity of the replies. It is not just managers picking up the currently fashionable language, for they were able to point to concrete arrangements such as works councils and quality circles which had been introduced or extended.

As argued above, involvement is not a matter of giving workers a veto power over decisions but rather one of persuading them of the reasons underlying these decisions. Some managers made close links between involvement and the needs of the business:

> To endeavour to involve them [workers] more in understanding the way business functions and to understand constraints and prospects facing the company (006; PPP; 450 employees);

> Aiming for an informed, effective, flexible, well-paid work force. From the management side, company is less tolerant of incompetence and bad behaviour (029; chems; 900 employees);

> Involvement, keeping them well informed. We believe in telling as much as is commercially viable about the business, so they can understand why things are decided (157; mech. eng.; 400 employees).

These replies, which, like those quoted above, come from a range of industries, stress that the purpose of involvement is to make workers aware of business realities. Other managers stressed the limits that they put on the participation process itself:

> Company have a policy of workers' involvement but want this to fall short of actual involvement and directorship (011; PPP; 270 employees);

> Worker involvement but not representation. I don't believe in worker directors but I believe in workers being involved in the things we do, e.g. investment plans, the way we run, job security (100; other mfg; 360 employees);

> We believe in a high level of consultation but not participation, participation being defined as part of the decision-making process (224; el. eng.) 7,800 employees).

These managers were making abundantly clear what seems to have been the implicit view of many others: that involvement was important but that it should stop short of being a large influence in decision-making. As the second manager quoted above puts it, he does not believe in worker directors.

These views have two, equally important, parts. First, there is the desire to create a sense of involvement. This indicates a shift from the traditional approach, at least of those approximating to the 'standard modern' model, wherein management negotiates pay and conditions but makes no attempt to tell workers about business plans or to involve them in a shared sense of purpose. Some managers spoke of breaking down the 'them and us' approach. Second, business needs, and in particular the need to introduce change and to raise productivity, were central to the process. Participation was not being introduced because managers believed that it was good for workers but because it had clear benefits in persuading workers that change had to come and that difficult decisions about job losses were necessary to the survival of the firm.

As writers such as Purcell and Sisson stress, there has always been a group of firms in which consultation has been important, but this group has been rather small and has been concentrated in the high technology and continuous process industries where firms have been able to afford a considerable investment of time and money in setting up consultative procedures. The above evidence, together with other material in the press on current trends in labour relations, suggests that the consultative approach has become much more widespread. There is less reliance on negotiation with the unions and an emphasis on dealing with the individual worker, aiming to engender a sense of commitment to company goals and to broaden the focus from wages and conditions of work. This has often been associated with alterations to traditional job demarcations and the introduction of simplified grading structures in which a worker in a particular grade does all the tasks for which he or she is trained. A good example is Lucas Industries, which until recently would presumably be classified as a 'standard modern' but which has made substantial changes in work organization and in the kind of commitment that it seeks from its workers (Turnbull, 1986; *Financial Times*, 5 September 1984).

If 'sophisticated' approaches are increasingly in evidence, they are far from universal. The style of being firm and fair and developing consistent procedures is still observable. One manager described his policy as being:

To deal quickly, fairly, and firmly with any matters arising, having made every effort to obtain all the relevant information (001; el. eng.; 260 employees).

And fire-fighting in the context of an entrenched shopfloor organization was also mentioned. Another manager had a policy that was

forced on us by the closed shop. We attempt to manage vigorously, which is constantly handicapped by the closed shop (175; PPP; 2,600 employees).

But these approaches were rare.

More interesting is the category labelled 'paternalistic/caring/worker based' in table 5.10. Purcell and Sisson, along with other writers, give little room for what might be called traditional paternalism, that is, a type of paternalism which rests not on a sophisticated and expensive personnel policy but on personal and familial connections. Deaton recognizes its importance by distinguishing within Purcell and Sisson's category of anti-union employers between those who are aggressively anti-union and resist giving workers any rights and those who, while also avoiding union recognition, promote a spirit of co-operation. The approach is less formalized and less carefully created and tended than is sophisticated paternalism, but it is equally concerned with treating the worker as an individual and caring for his or her welfare. How, though, does it differ from a participative style? Some of the 'paternalist' replies help to answer this question:

> This is a Quaker-founded organization, and the philosophy is based on Quaker ideals. Business is a partnership between labour and capital, and so everyone has a right to know and comment on company performance (023; el. eng.; 1,600 employees);

> We are paternalistic towards our workers and know them all and try to meet them frequently and listen to complaints to keep this a hard-working strike-free factory (053; texts; 250 employees);

> This company has a long history as a major employer and the welfare of the work force is of great importance. It is a cliche to speak of a company as a large family, but this one is (222; texts; 610 employees).

The first feature of traditional paternalism is its emphasis on the unbroken tradition of the firm; this is in contrast to the more short-term perspective in the consultative style described above. Second, there is the importance of personal ties and a sense of family spirit. A firm newly moving to communication and involvement is not particularly concerned with its workers as individuals. It certainly tries to deal with them at the individual level, as opposed to relying on negotiations through unions. But the individuals are important for their specific roles in the company and not because they are known personally to senior management. There is a sharp contrast between a formal, bureaucratized paternalism and one based on direct personal ties. And paternalism in general differs from a consultative approach in putting more weight on individual welfare and in developing an all-embracing company style in which the senior managers care for the interests of their subordinates.

These various policies are plainly not always sharply distinct. They reflect different tendencies and emphases. The overall pattern points to a growth in consultative approaches, at least in so far as it is possible to infer a trend from an examination of the survey evidence in the light of general perceptions of the past. There is no comparable evidence for, say, ten years ago, but the broad picture at that time was a predominance of the negotiatory approach of the standard modern firm. The frequency with which the present sample stressed involvement and cited such things as briefing groups, quality circles, and works councils is in contrast to the general pattern of the 1970s.

The classification of labour relations policy is an admittedly imprecise endeavour. The overlaps between categories and the ambiguity of some of the categories themselves make any detailed analysis of the sources of variation of policy unwise. It is, however, relevant to investigate a few such sources, less in order to develop causal arguments than to deal with possible criticisms of the exercise, such as that particular policies may be concentrated in particular types of firms.

One obvious test is the link with trade union status. It might be argued, for example, that traditional paternalism is the preserve of non-union firms. As table 5.10 shows, there was some tendency for such firms to have this type of policy more often than others, but the tendency was not large. Indeed, 10 per cent of those with full-time stewards fell into the 'paternalist' category. There were few substantial differences according to trade union status. This suggests that the key role played by union recognition in models of style, wherein the anti-union employers and the majority of the sophisticated paternalists are characterized above all by a refusal to recognize unions, may be exaggerated. There plainly is a group of firms in which union recognition is vigorously opposed. But not all non-union employers are hostile to giving workers the rights or representation that tend to go along with recognition. And unionized firms can develop employment policies which have many similarities with those adopted by their non-union counterparts.

There was, similarly, little variation between industries. Two features of this result warrant mention. The paper, printing, and publishing industry was as likely as any other to contain styles of 'involvement'. This may seem to contradict the previous evidence that labour restrictions were most common here and that changed working practices have been most widespread. But the restrictions were still rare enough in absolute terms to permit a place for a participative style, while the changes in working practices could well be a concomitant of such a style. Second, a paternalist approach was not particularly common where it might be expected to be most developed, that is in the traditional textiles industry, with its one-firm towns in which personal ties can grow. It was most common in food, drink, and tobacco; and the chemicals industry, perhaps even more surprisingly, also scored quite highly. Paternalism can flourish in some unexpected places.

This point also applies to a classification of firms by size. To the extent that traditional paternalism is given any attention, it tends to be equated with the practices of very small family businesses. But paternalistic methods and assumptions still exist among large firms. Lawson (1981) has described some of the practices of the Pye electronics firm, notably reliance on informal channels of recruitment and an attempt to develop a family atmosphere. As the classification in table 5.11 of an abbreviated form of the types of policy listed earlier shows, paternalistic approaches were certainly relatively rare in very large firms, but even there they were quite prominent, and in medium-sized firms they were as frequent as they were in small organizations. The only other notable size effect was for policies based on being firm and fair to be more common in small than in large firms. This presumably reflects the personal and particularistic basic of such policies. As the quotation above (from reference number 001 on p. 141) suggests, being firm and fair can rest on personal knowledge and authority, and not on the application of a set of rules.

It may be, of course, that managers in large organizations were taking for granted the existence of proper procedures and did not feel the need to specify them as part of their personnel policies. This possibility is, indeed, one reason why cross-classifications of the policy measure with other features of the firm should not be taken too seriously; a manager's statement of policy reflects what is at the front of his or her mind, and there may be many other aspects of corporate activity that have a significant bearing on labour issues but that do not enter statements of philosophy. What the analysis of policy can show is that factory managers have thought-out aims in their labour relations and that there are differing and sometimes surprising tendencies at work. The main tendency is reflected in the stress on involvement in business ends.

A final point is that managers seemed to have some considerable discretion in developing their own policies. Those who were part of a large group and who said that they had a policy were asked whether it was part of an overall company policy or approach and, if so, how uniform the policy was across all parts of the enterprise. Perceived local autonomy was surprisingly high: 29 per cent said that the policy was not part of an overall approach, 13 per cent that there was considerable local autonomy within an overall approach, 23 per cent that there was some autonomy, 16 per cent that it was largely uniform throughout the company, and only 18 per cent that it was completely uniform. Taken on its own, this finding might be written off as the result of exaggerated views of local independence. But it fits the evidence on managerial decision-making, presented in chapter 4, that local autonomy was quite high. It appears that factory managers not only take a close interest in labour matters and view them as very important but also have some considerable say, albeit no doubt within broad

TABLE 5.11
Labour Relations Policy by Company Size

		Total Company Employment			
		250–999 (N = 19)	1,000–4,999 (N = 43)	5,000–24,999 (N = 61)	25,000 and over (N = 60)
1 + 5	Participative	19	16	21	28
2 + 3 + 4	Involvement	24	28	38	35
6	Managerial leadership	6	4	10	7
7 + 8	Paternalist/teamwork	29	29	22	11
9	Social responsibility	0	0	2	3
10	Firm and fair	20	17	3	5
11	Work with TUs	3	1	2	8
12	Other	0	5	3	3
		100	100	100	100

Base:
Respondents with a classifiable policy, in firms where employment data were available (N = 183).
Note:
Categories have been merged from table 5.10, as indicated by the numbers in the headings; these relate to the categories of table 5.10.

expectations if not actual directives stemming from head office, in how they are managed.

Conclusions: The Macho Manager, Myth or Reality?

This chapter has given a broad overview of the institutional arrangements of labour relations and the importance that general managers gave to labour matters. It has not analysed in any detail patterns of variation observed in the sample, for the survey was not designed with the aim of studying, say, the links between the level of pay bargaining and strike activity. To have done so would have required a different sample design (in which, for example, small as well as large plants were included so that the effects of plant size could be taken into account), a different form of questioning (with many more questions than were in fact asked on the details of institutional arrangements), and a different respondent (a personnel specialist who knew the relevant details). The aim has been to look less at labour relations institutions than at the place of labour in the overall operation of the business.

There are three central conclusions. First, and in line with other survey evidence, there had been few direct attacks on the institutional position of shop stewards. The present survey has also produced some, perhaps less familiar, evidence suggesting that specific labour-related constraints on efficiency were rare. Second, however, substantial changes had been made in working arrangements, and the efficient utilization of labour was a pressing concern for the great majority of plants. The external threat of intensifying competition appeared to be a significant stimulus here. Third, labour relations were seen by the factory managers as important in the running of the business, with particular weight being placed on the need to secure workers' involvement in and commitment to the firm's goals. What are the implications of this evidence? This question may be assessed in two ways: first, by considering the dynamics of developments within the sorts of firm covered by the sample; and, second, by relating these trends to developments elsewhere in the economy.

One current interpretation is based on the concept of macho management. This has a number of strands which need to be distinguished. The main ones are the use of direct attacks on steward organizations; the reassertion of the right to manage; a refusal to treat workers with any consideration, with their being told to accept managerial decisions without question; and an aggressive policy in the event of industrial action, with the full weight of the law being used and with no compromise being tolerated. The present results plainly contradict a macho style in which all these elements are observable. Other evidence, of a survey and a more general kind, also brings the model into question. The extent to which employers have used their legal rights in areas such as the closed shop and industrial action has been variable. And a much-discussed feature of the recession, namely the fairly constant level of pay settlements (see Gregory *et al.*, 1985), suggests that firms have not simply been using their increased bargaining power to wrest concessions from the work force. An early summary of the present results appeared, indeed, under the title, 'myth of the macho manager' (P.K. Edwards, 1985).

But this is not to deny that some elements of a macho style have been present. Purcell (1982: 3) has produced a more subtle characterization of the style than the common-sense one given above: 'the spirit is almost of the divine right to manage, to broach [*sic*] no argument and get on with the job of directing, controlling and enforcing order over a demoralised workforce.' The emphasis here is less on attacking shop stewards head-on than on re-asserting managerial rights. Purcell identifies some possible concomitants of the approach, notably a decline in the role of the personnel function and in the use of joint consultation procedures. Neither of these appears to have taken place (although, as noted above, there is room for argument about the influence of personnel departments, as distinct from personnel considerations, in the formulation of company policy). But the evidence on the rise of consultation committees and on the weight placed by managers on 'involvement' is consistent with at least part of Purcell's argument: they have been among the means used by managers to by-pass traditional negotiating channels and to establish their own rights to make and implement key decisions. In short, the present findings do not deny that managements in large private sector establishments have been re-asserting the right, and indeed duty, of management to run the enterprise. But they have done so not by attacking negotiatory or consultative arrangements but by changing the way in which these are used. They have not ridden roughshod over workers' interests but have tried to persuade workers of the benefits of accepting and co-operating with the logic of the market as it is interpreted by management.[11]

The question is not whether or not there is a distinct phenomenon known as the macho manager but what aspects of a macho approach have been in evidence. The problem with the simple model of macho management, and indeed with some other interpretations, is the reduction of labour relations to bargaining power: when product and labour markets are tight, workers are powerful, but in recessions managers counter-attack. This view reduces the matter to a one-dimensional picture in which managers and workers are seen as being simply opposed and in which one side or the other wins according to the balance of bargaining advantage. In fact, there are several aspects of labour relations. Workers have certainly 'lost' in that their ability to *[margin note, top left, handwritten]* True, but OK my have been associated than the Tories that by pushing back the frontiers of control in their favour

resist such things as increases in the pace of work and the introduction of new technologies is being undermined. But such things as improved communications and quality circles can be taken as 'gains'. Labour relations do not shift according to the ebb and flow of bargaining power but change their character as firms use differing means to seek the compliance of their workers, and as workers evolve different forms of shopfloor organization.

Firms need to control their workers, but they also need to release their creative capacities (Cressey and MacInnes, 1980). The current fashion of involvement and participation, together with particular manifestations such as quality circles, reflects a stress on the latter aspect. But its implications need to be carefully considered. It is not a case of firms giving workers an increased say in the running of the business as a whole. Workers are certainly encouraged to take an interest in the firm's market position, to identify themselves with it, and to use their creative capacities to improve quality standards. They may well value the new importance that their contribution is given and the various attempts that are being made to break down the 'them and us' atmosphere of industry. At the same time, however, traditional means of opposing or altering managerial demands are being undermined. The right and the duty of management to manage the firm so as to increase productivity is being increasingly stressed. Although workers are informed of the reason for changes and are encouraged to participate in their implementation, it is made clear that the decisions have to be made in the interests of the business as a whole.

[margin note, handwritten] The illusion of participation (?!)

Richard Edwards (1979: 146–7) captures this point when he criticizes the common confusion of 'the lack of immediate external controls (self-direction) with the freedom to make decisions in one's own interest (autonomy). From the firm's perspective, all that is required is that workers perform according to the enterprise's criteria.' He goes on to note that workers, whether or not they internalize these criteria, are equally alienated in that they are forced to work according to the capitalist's rules. Although over-emphasizing the mere following of orders, as distinct from the willing pursuit of organizational goals (for which he has been widely criticized: see Burawoy, 1981), Edwards usefully distinguishes genuine autonomy from self-direction under the authority of management. As Grzyb (1981: 471–3) argues, managers have 're-collectivized' work with autonomous teams and so forth, but responsibility is a widely used part of this, with groups being expected to develop a culture that keeps workers in their place. 'Involvement' is a policy for the control of labour, and the aspects of power and authority must not be ignored.

[margin note, bottom left, handwritten] True, so this contradicts what you said further up.

A similar characterization is that of a 'hegemonic despotism' (Burawoy, 1985: 150). It is argued that arrangements until the 1970s were simply hegemonic: such things as collective bargaining gave workers

limited rights and induced acceptance of the system as a whole. As
long as firms were making adequate profits they were willing to tolerate
some constraints on their freedom to institute changes at shopfloor
level. With intensifying competition, they could no longer afford to do
so. They have made their regimes more despotic by making it clear to
workers that if they do not co-operate with changes then production
will be shifted elsewhere. Thus, although quality circles and the like
give workers some active involvement in their work, instead of their
being required to carry out precisely delimited tasks, the context in
which these operate reduces workers' independence of management
and introduces an element of despotism into the factory.

This characterization is useful in recognizing the range of ways in
which firms can seek control of their workers: the right to manage can
be secured through participatory methods as well as an aggressive
autocracy. But there are some problems. The concept of hegemony
may exaggerate the extent to which old systems of labour control were
able to generate an active consent among the work force. Such things
as disciplinary powers give management important punitive weapons,
and plant closures and rationalizations have been going on for many
years. Burawoy also makes an odd contrast between hegemonic despotism and participatory methods. Having defined the former as a system
in which workers are forced to make concessions to management to
keep their jobs he says, 'alternatively, management may bypass the
hegemonic regime. Recent fads such as Quality of Work Life and
Quality Circles signify management's attempt to invade the spaces
created by workers under the previous regime and to mobilize consent
to increased productivity' (p. 151). These things are surely not alterna-
tives to hegemony but are constitutive of it: the point is to establish
management as the source of authority and to persuade workers to
accept the legitimacy of this authority. If quality circles and the like
make workers feel involved in the enterprise without their in fact having
any substantial say in its policies, then hegemony has been reinforced.

There is, moreover, the danger in Burawoy's approach of exaggerating the success of 'hegemonic despotism'. It comes close to suggesting
that workers' power at the point of production has been destroyed.
Old forms of 'restrictive practices' may have been attacked, but workers
may be able to turn the new system to their own advantage. Precisely
because this system places such weight on workers' active involvement,
it is vulnerable in two ways: to a 'negative' withdrawal of involvement
and to a 'positive' attack wherein workers turn the language of participation against management by taking it at its face value in demands
for a larger say in company affairs. The idea of hegemonic despotism
tends to pre-judge the question of management's success and to neglect
the necessary uncertainty and instability of managerial authority.

The term suggested above for this new approach is enlightened managerialism: <u>managers assert not so much the right as the need to</u> <u>manage</u>; they stress 'business realities'; but they try to take workers along with them, and indeed must do so if they are to retain the flexibility that is increasingly necessary in new competitive conditions. The last point indicates the weakness of a simple macho approach. <u>Firms need to be able to adjust rapidly in order to introduce new</u> <u>products and to re-organize work to benefit from the latest techniques.</u> To treat workers as expendable instruments may work in the short-term, but is unlikely to have much success in the longer term.

If enlightened managerialism is the fashion, how successful is it? It is too early to make a thorough assessment of this question, since developments are still current, and it will be some time before their consequences are fully apparent. Yet some questions can be raised, about <u>how thorough-going the change in managerial style has been</u> and about whether managerial power is as substantial as might appear. On the former point, <u>it must be borne in mind that the forms of labour</u> <u>management</u> described above emerged in the context of the recession. <u>They owe at least part of their success in changing shopfloor attitudes</u> <u>to this context</u>, in particular a feeling among workers that it is necessary to accept some changes in order to keep the firm in business. As shown in chapter 2, the firms in the survey were just emerging from a period of job loss and falling profits. It would not be surprising if workers' acceptance of change had been heavily conditioned by this experience. Neither would it be surprising if the managers' views of their position, in terms of the management of the plant as a whole as well as just on labour issues, were affected. The factory managers had succeeded in keeping their plants in business during a very difficult period, and they naturally felt some sense of success in having done so. The question plainly remains, however, as to how long-lasting the resulting feeling of teamwork and commitment can be. Indeed, the birth of new approaches to labour management in the recession suggests that they have not been the product of long-term planning. <u>As responses to the</u> <u>crisis, they must involve a series of expedients and reactions to immedi-</u> <u>ate events.</u> This is not to suggest that the managers' belief in involve-ment was a pretence. It is to point out that their own and their workers' perceptions are likely to have been influenced by the context of the recession, and also that their philosophy of involvement is likely to have reflected short-term responses to events. That is, even if there has been a sharp change in managerial attitudes to the management of labour, the extent to which it has been possible for new attitudes to be embodied in clear, coherent, and long-term policies must be open to doubt.

The effectiveness of enlightened managerialism must also be ques-tioned. This is not to suggest that it is a purely temporary phenomenon or that, with an economic recovery, old forms of shopfloor bargaining will simply re-emerge. Just as recent changes should not be seen as no more than a result of a swing of power to management, so any future growth of workers' power is unlikely to be a replica of the past. Flexible ways of working across old lines of demarcation and other changes are plainly widespread and are unlikely to be reversed. But there are areas in which workers are able to exert an influence on management. Chadwick (1983: 11) points to two of them: to the extent that firms are stressing flexibility and the active role of workers, they are more dependent on workers than they were when job tasks were clearly defined and when only a minimal performance of specified duties was required; and as market pressures intensify they may feel it necessary to make concessions on the shopfloor, an example being allowing a good deal of 'unnecessary' overtime to be worked. As firms concentrate more on growth than on retrenchment they are likely to be increasingly worried about disruption to their operations. The ways in which workers make use of the opportunities presented to them may change, but managerial power is not total. And the fact that managers have chosen not to demolish shopfloor organizations gives workers some established means of developing their collective strength. It would be a mistake, for managers and analysts alike, to suppose that absolute managerial power has been instituted or that long-established ways of doing things, in particular the practice of negotiating the terms on which workers will work directly at the point of production, have been totally destroyed.

The trend towards enlightened managerialism is, moreover, one of several current tendencies, and it may not be the dominant one. At least three others may be identified. First, there is the tendency of many large firms to sub-contract parts of their operations and to use casual employees in place of permanent ones. The developments traced above thus relate only to the 'core' workers of the firms. Second, developments in the public sector appear to have had a more abrasive character than those among private firms such as those in the present sample. Some public sector managements have, under pressure from the government, moved away from the Whitley system of seeking consensus through long consultative procedures with the unions. Ferner and Terry (1985) demonstrate the power of a new aggressive style in the case study of the Post Office. Batstone and Gourlay (1986: 64) note in their survey of shop stewards that stewards in the public sector were more likely to perceive a tough line from management than were their counterparts in the private sector. The major examples of aggressive management in manufacturing come from public-sector firms such as British Steel and British Leyland. Third, in many parts of the economy outside the large-firm, manufacturing sector, developments are dominated by reductions in employment protection provisions, attempts to reduce wage levels, and an approach to labour relations based not on involvement and motivation but on the coercion of labour market pressures. Attempts to make labour markets work treat labour as a commodity to be bought for the lowest possible price and not as something which requires a sense of involvement in the enterprise if it is to function adequately.

The present sample thus represents one of several competing trends. It is, however, an important trend, for it represents what large and influential companies are doing. To the extent that commitment and involvement are being developed here while they have less and less significance elsewhere in the economy, it may also be a trend which diverges from other developments, with workers in these firms becoming increasingly differentiated from those elsewhere, in terms of wages, job security, and conditions of employment.

In this and the two previous chapters some of the main characteristics of the management of large manufacturing sites have been analysed. There has been some concern throughout for productivity, for example, in the consideration of what organizational barriers exist to increasing efficiency. The conclusion of this chapter is that labour relations constraints were not a significant barrier. It is, however, necessary to analyse the influences on productivity in their own right. This is the task of the following chapter.

Notes

1. It might be felt that a longer period, perhaps the five years going back to 1979, might provide a better reference point than two years. But there are problems of accurate recall if the period is so lengthened, which will be increased if the respondent was not in his or her present job five years previously.
2. A further problem is that the mean size of plant has been falling. Plants in the population in 1977 will not be in the population in 1984, either because they have fallen below the size threshold or because they have closed. There is little that can be done about this, for any adjustment of average plant sizes would be *ad hoc* and *ex post*: it is not possible with two snapshots to discover whether the surviving plant differed from those that left the population. But the main aim of the comparison is to compare the picture as it was in 1984 with that in 1977, and for this the snapshots are acceptable.
3. It is not very clear from Batstone's presentation how the re-weighting was carried out. But, according to David Deaton, who carried out the exercise, it involved weighting the Warwick Survey so that the industry and size distribution was the same as that in Batstone's sample. The result was thus an *ex post* weighting of the Warwick Survey in line with the non-representative character of Batstone's own sample. The reliability of the figures is thus somewhat hard to judge.
4. Thus a chi-square test for even quite a substantial difference, such as that on the presence of recognized senior stewards in electrical engineering,

points to a lack of statistical significance. The more marked changes in strike activity were, however, significant.

5. A possible reason for this is that, in the face of threatened plant closures, workers see the strike as a double-edged weapon and rely on other forms of pressure. This seems to have been the case here.

6. It must be recognized that new technology can be associated with many important changes in the use of labour, including manpower reductions and shifts in the balance of skills. The point here is that changes specifically directed at removing problems of a labour relations kind were rare.

7. A similar point emerges from an analysis of wage settlements included in the pay survey of the CBI Databank (Gregory *et al.*, 1985). External pressures were the main reason for making wage increases.

8. It is plainly necessary to distinguish between the personnel department and the personnel function. Factory managers could feel that labour relations were important while also seeing labour relations specialists as carrying out only routine functions: more generally, the present survey can provide no assessment of the importance of personnel departments within a corporation as a whole (for conflicting views on which see Purcell, 1985; Sisson and Scullion, 1985). But the distinction is unlikely to be clear-cut in practice: where labour considerations are important, the personnel department is unlikely to be relegated to a minor role. For present purposes, in any event, the function is more important: the aim was to assess how factory managers rated labour considerations and not to obtain their views of their personnel managers.

9. Here and with other quotations from verbatim answers, each reply is given together with the code number of the interview, the industrial location, and the size of the plant.

10. These arguments have been developed in more detail elsewhere: see P.K. Edwards (1986a: 39–42).

11. The argument about whether or not macho management exists seems to have created more confusion than illumination. Mackay (1986) has responded to the present writer's earlier argument (Edwards, 1985) by suggesting that the macho manager is no myth. Yet she misunderstands that argument in several ways and produces findings that are virtually identical to those she claims to refute. On a more substantial note, David Buckle, the Oxford District Secretary of the Transport and General Workers' Union is reported as saying that macho management exists, as evidenced by managements that break agreements with unions and attack 'mutuality', that is, the principle of setting conditions of work through agreements with shop stewards (*Personnel Management*, June 1985, p. 11). In fact, Buckle's views do not contradict those presented here. As a union official, he is likely to be involved only in the more extreme cases. And what to a unionist looks like an attack on mutuality may be seen by management as no more than the implementation of changes that are necessary to a firm's survival. It is not being denied that such changes may have raised problems for unions; as suggested below, they may have had a more profound impact than would a frontal assault. But it is being argued that firms have often tried to persuade workers that established traditions such as mutuality are no longer acceptable. One of the notable features of

the recent past has been workers' acquiescence in changes imposed on them, and their unwillingness to defend union principles. Managements have altered the conduct of workplace relations, but to characterize their style as 'macho' is to simplify and distort a complex series of developments.

6

Company Organization, Labour Relations, and Productivity

This chapter analyses the effects of the institutions and processes analysed above on the productivity of the companies in the sample. Productivity is, even in ideal conditions, difficult to measure, while explaining it is yet harder; and the present survey, not being purpose-built for the job, has some unavoidable weaknesses.[1] But it contains some rich data on the social relations of production in the survey plants. These relations comprise the ways in which people are brought together in the production process. They may be contrasted to the technical conditions of production such as the amount of capital equipment and the number of workers employed; these are merely quantities of factors of production, and how they are used in practice is a separate question. Studies of productivity have traditionally concentrated on the factors of production, but attention has recently been directed to the ways in which they are organized, and in particular how companies manage their human resources. The survey permits some of these new arguments to be assessed.

Introduction: The Analysis of Productivity

Competing Explanations
Within the plethora of writings analysing determinants of productivity and telling managers how to manage better, two schools of thought are of interest here, for both focus on human relations and company organization and provide hypotheses that can be tested against the

present evidence. The first is known as the Harvard school of economists, while the second may be termed the 'In Search of Excellence', or ISE, model, after the title of one of its leading works (Peters and Waterman, 1982).

The Harvard school (whose work is summarized by Freeman and Medoff, 1984a) focuses on trade union behaviour and argues that the conventional economists' model deals with only one of unionism's two faces. This is the 'monopoly' face, namely the tendency of unions to raise wages above their competitive level. In addition, unions have an effect on the operation of the enterprise: by channelling the views of workers they contribute to effective communication, and by challenging managerial authority they force managers to introduce improved methods. This is known as the 'collective voice' face of unionism. Drawing heavily on the work of Slichter (Slichter *et al.*, 1960; Slichter, 1941), Harvard writers argue that unions 'shock' management into more effective practices such as training supervision and replacing arbitary power with agreed rules. Their particular contribution has been a series of quantitative investigations in which productivity is related to the presence of a union. The results are that 'productivity is generally higher in unionized establishments than in otherwise comparable establishments that are non-union but that the relationship is far from immutable and has notable exceptions' (Freeman and Medoff, 1984b: 164).

As critics (for example, Addison and Barnett, 1982) have pointed out, however, several problems arise. It is one thing to suggest that unionization can be associated with improvements in the management of labour and another to show that the claimed consequences in fact follow. Even detailed case studies (for example, K. Clark, 1980) have difficulty in detecting specific effects of unionization. Such effects as exist, moreover, appear to be more indirect: the result of unions 'shocking' management into improving managerial methods and not something inherent in unions themselves. Once managers have learned the appropriate techniques of organization and recruitment they can presumably reap the benefits without depending on the shock of unionization. It may also be the case that the shock wears off. Thus Ichniowski (1984a, 1984b) argues that, although ten unionized paper mills were more productive than one non-unionized mill, among the former group there was a tendency for the extent of union activity, as measured by the grievance rate and the length of the collective bargaining contract, to be associated with low levels of productivity.

Some Harvard studies have found that unionism does not increase productivity, a finding also produced by other writers (for example, Hirsch and Link, 1984). Most of the evidence comes from America, and the main British study, Pencavel's (1977) investigation of coal mining, also finds an inverse link between unionization and productivity. This suggests that Freeman and Medoff's admission that the positive effects of unionism are far from universal needs to be taken rather further. Unions are likely to differ in their behaviour, and it is not satisfactory to treat unionization as a phenomenon with automatic consequences. Whether or not a plant has a union is, moreover, treated by the Harvard authors as a more or less self-contained feature of its operations. In fact, the decision by management to recognize a union may form part of a cluster of characteristics whose effects warrant study.

The Harvard model thus raises important questions about the impact of labour relations, although tending to reduce these relations to the one aspect of union presence. The present survey offers the chance to expand some of its concerns, and to investigate how it works in the British context.

The ISE approach shares with the Harvard school an origin in the United States but is otherwise very different. Its method is based not on formal econometric model-testing but on detailed investigations of particular firms. It is informal, indeed sometimes anecdotal, in style. Its focus is also different: while Harvard researchers examine one particular phenomenon, namely the productivity effects of unionism, writers in search of excellence are concerned with the culture and nature of a firm, aiming to identify the ingredients of success in the whole range of organizational activities. Labour relations are seen as part of the story. Peters and Waterman (1982) entitle one of their chapters 'productivity through people', in which they state: 'Treat people as adults. Treat them as partners; treat them with dignity; treat them with respect. Treat *them* – not capital spending and automation – as the primary source of productivity gains. These are fundamental lessons from the excellent companies research' (p. 238, emphasis in original). Successful companies have a deeply engrained concern for people, and go to great lengths to create a team spirit in which employees internalize the firm's goals; hierarchy and rules are shunned, and informality is prized. Kanter (1984) similarly stresses trust and decentralization. One piece of research, for example, compared 47 companies using progressive labour policies with firms that were otherwise similar but were less progressive; the former group out-performed the latter in terms of growth and profitability (p. 19). A British study in the same tradition (Goldsmith and Clutterbuck, 1984) comes to similar conclusions: the successful firms stressed decentralization and employee involvement and were not afraid to be called paternalistic.

The method employed in these studies is to identify several criteria of success such as the average rate of return on capital employed and the growth rate of assets. Companies which perform well on all the criteria are identified and their corporate cultures are investigated. The strength of the method is to go into some detail about a specific company and to assess how the various features of its operations cohere. Instead of the Harvard reliance on the sign of a coefficient in a regression equation, there is a picture of the operation of a real firm facing real problems. Yet there are also difficulties. One concerns the selection of the 'successful' firms. Although there is no doubt that the companies chosen were excellent performers on the relevant criteria, it is not clear whether there were other equally successful companies that were not studied. That is, it is not clear whether the characteristics of the firms chosen for special study were necessary in attaining success or whether other routes were possible. Similarly, there is very little detailed comparison of successful and unsuccessful firms, such as would be provided by a careful analysis of matched samples (Child, 1984: 213).

The informality of the method can also make it hard to identify the key characteristics which are being put forward as recipes for success. Consider, for example, the people orientation championed by Peters and Waterman. The authors warn against giving mere lip service to the importance of people, and they note that many managements ritually subscribe to the idea that human resources are important without really taking the notion seriously. The successful firms had a complete and thorough view of how they wanted to manage labour. The difficulty lies in identifying clear indices of the appropriate orientation. It is one thing to say that Hewlett-Packard or McDonald's has a developed people orientation and another to say exactly in what this consists and to specify how it can be measured in other firms. If a firm says that it has a policy of employee involvement, how are we to assess whether this is real or rhetoric?

One reply is that this question is misconceived; the analyst should not seek quantifiable indices but should assess each firm in its own right by looking in detail at its actual practices. There is nothing wrong with this answer as a general proposition, for it is a basic rationale for any form of qualitative, case-study research. But in the present context there remains the nagging doubt that the firms under scrutiny are said to have the required complete people orientation because they are successful: 'success' is being used to explain completeness, and an important element of circularity enters the argument.

Despite these and other difficulties with seeking recipes for success,[2] the 'in search of excellence' school provides some important hypotheses which can be assessed against the present data. These, together with those arising from the Harvard research, will be indicated before some methodological issues are addressed.

Research Hypotheses

The effects of a positive approach to people are testable: plants' performance can be related to various features of their labour relations, discussed in chapter 5, such as their use of consultative committees, the importance attributed to labour matters in their decision-making, and their overall policies or philosophies of labour management. As noted above, however, there may be problems with establishing how genuine and developed a people orientation is. The survey has data on less familiar matters which can also throw light on plants' performance. The 'excellent companies' literature places considerable weight on the development of a corporate culture and the acceptance of it at all levels of the organization. The information on the factory managers' careers provides a way of testing some aspects of the argument. The information on which managers had had experience of working at head office, for example, may indicate something about the sorts of firms that they worked for as well as about their own career mobility. That is, it may be that managers with such experience tend to be employed by the most progressive firms, which treat their managers as important company resources. Similarly, there is a good deal of information on the managers' perceptions of their firms; it is plausible to argue that 'successful' firms create a sense of loyalty and that there will be an association between a factory manager's perceptions of the ways in which his firm responds to his advice and needs and the success of the firm. In short, those without substantial criticisms of their firms (see above, p. 56) should work in the most successful companies. A third example is share ownership. It is possible that firms which encourage their factory managers to own shares have a view of the importance of developing a sense of company loyalty and that share ownership is thus associated with 'success'.

A further argument, developed in particular by Peters and Waterman (1982: 320), is that companies' procedures for monitoring their plants have an effect on performance. The writers talk of the 'simultaneous loose–tight properties' of successful firms, by which they mean that there is a combination of rigid adherence to basic values along with considerable autonomy for individual managers within the overall framework. The importance of the customer, and hence of quality, is one of the main values that is constantly reiterated and is made a major aspect of the self-discipline of everyone in the firm. Indeed, self-discipline and peer group expectations are more powerful means of motivation than formal rules and procedures. But local managers are given considerable autonomy as to how they operate in detail: the successful firms do not burden them with rules to follow but instead decentralize their operations and permit local managers considerable discretion. One test of this view from the present survey is the link

between performance and the extent of monitoring of plant performance analysed in chapter 4: very strict monitoring may stifle initiative
while a complete absence of measurement may mean that no proper
check is made to ensure that the basic aims of the firm are being met.
A moderate level of monitoring would then be associated with success.

The hypothesis of the Harvard school is more straightforward: unionization will encourage productivity. The present survey permits some
assessment of this in terms of the presence or absence of unions and
also the density of union organization. Given the very high level of
unionization in large manufacturing plants in Britain, however, the
number of non-union plants in the sample was small (11 per cent of
the total). This problem, together with some others discussed below,
can be reduced if not eliminated by using the Warwick Survey, which
had a much larger number of plants and which also included establishments with as few as 50 employees; the latter not only means that there
was a substantial number of non-union plants in the sample but also
helps to deal with one obvious point about the present survey, namely
that its concentration on large plants prevents a proper assessment of
the Harvard hypothesis because plant size is an important influence on
productivity. After the Warwick Survey was conducted, data were
collected on the companies whose plants were included in it. Some of
this material has been used by Marginson (1984) to assess the different effects of plant size and company size on labour relations, but
the present analysis is the first to use the information on company
performance.

Data and Methods
Both the present survey and the Warwick Survey contain information
that permits the 'union effect' to be assessed in more detail than the
Harvard analysis typically involves. The fact of being unionized is only
one among a set of features of a plant's shopfloor labour relations; it
is, for example, a commonplace that unions with similar levels of
membership density can operate in very different ways. Data on such
things as the presence of a full-time shop steward permit a closer
assessment of any union effect. The two surveys differ in their other
features. As noted above, the present one is relatively strong on aspects
of company organization, which were not investigated in the Warwick
Survey. But it is weaker on the details of industrial relations procedures
and manpower planning. The Warwick Survey included an important
series of questions about the skill composition of the work force, and
is thus able to take account systematically of one of the issues raised
in connection with the Harvard programme, namely the effects of work
force 'quality' on productivity. In the Harvard studies quality is usually
measured with some proxy such as the average number of years of
schooling that the work force had. Such proxies are plainly not very

direct measures of the extent to which skills are actually deployed in the production process. The survey questions, which asked respondents to classify their workers into the categories of skilled, semi-skilled, and unskilled, provide a closer assessment of the skill mix of the work force.

What variables should be used to measure productivity? As noted above, the ISE school treats success as a syndrome incorporating rapid growth, high profits, and a high rate of return on capital employed. It was not possible in the present research to consider all such features, or even particularly desirable to try to do so. Profitability, for example, is likely to be affected by many things such as the degree of monopoly enjoyed by a firm and other features of the market place. What is crucial is the efficiency with which inputs are transformed into outputs. The Harvard school uses two measures of productivity. One is the physical quantity of goods produced: so many tons of coal dug or so much cement produced. This has the benefit of being directly related to the productive process: if one factory produces more cement than another, using the same amount of inputs, it can be said to be more productive. But truly homogeneous goods are rare. For broader comparisons the usual dependent variable is therefore value-added per employee: the value of goods and services sold, less the costs of bought-in components, per worker. This permits comparisons of firms producing different goods but has two problems, as Addison and Barnett (1982: 151) note. First, estimates of value-added can be made only from the prices of goods bought and sold, and an apparent productivity effect may in fact simply reflect higher prices in one sector than another. Second, a 'union effect' may turn out to be no more than a reflection of a union–non-union wage differential, and not a genuine productivity effect of unionism. In an attempt to deal with this problem, two variables will be introduced where possible to act as controls. In so far as a price effect is likely to be associated with the degree of concentration in an industry (Cowling, 1982), the concentration ratio can be introduced to control for it. And possible wage effects can be assessed by including a measure of wages among the explanatory variables.

The following analysis will thus concentrate on productivity in the sense of net output per head, although some comments will be made about profitability (the rate of profit as a percentage of turnover) and growth (the rate of growth of sales). The key dependent variable is not, however, value-added per head but total turnover per head.[3] Turnover will be high in relation to value-added if, for example, a firm operates in an industry with a high level of bought-in components. Two corrections may be introduced to deal with such effects: industry dummies can be used to capture any general effects of being in a particular industry; and the specific effect of the relationship between turnover and value-added can be controlled by including the ratio of turnover to value-added in the industry in which a plant operates. Any differences between firms within an industry will not, however, be controlled for. The relevant data, and also data on the concentration ratio and the mean level of wages, were collected for each of the 115 Minimum List Headings of the Standard Industrial Classification. A plant was assigned the figure of the MLH in which it was located.[4]

Since turnover per head and value-added per head are highly correlated, and since two control variables are used to deal with any remaining discrepancy, the use of turnover per head as the dependent variable should not raise too many problems. A far more serious problem concerns the different levels of analysis at which the variables have been collected. The dependent variable is measured at the level of the company, a level also used for the collection of some other data. The most important of these is the amount of fixed capital employed by the firm. This is a key control variable, for it is obviously necessary to allow for the amount of capital employed before concluding that one firm is more productive than another. But other data refer to the individual plant while, as just noted, yet other information is at the level of the industry in which the plant was located. The assumptions necessary to employ variables used at different levels of aggregation depend on the type of the variable and its purpose in the analysis. Some are quite properly employed, as will shortly be indicated. Problems remain with others, and some means of minimizing these will then be discussed.

Since the dependent variable is at the level of the company, it is the use of industry- and plant-level independent variables that warrants comment. Of the three industry-level measures, one, the concentration ratio, is a phenomenon of a whole industry and plainly cannot be measured at any other level. It is used to control for possible price effects associated with different degrees of monopoly, and not primarily for its substantive importance. The problem is that the MLH in which one of its plants happens to be located may not be representative of all the industries in which a company operates. A conglomerate will have plants in several MLHs, and the concentration ratios of these may vary. But many firms are concentrated in a few industries, and for them the figure from one MLH should be a reasonable approximation. For others, a difficulty remains. All three industry-level variables are used, however, not for their substantive importance but solely to control for possible extraneous effects on the dependent variable. They are not ideal but their inclusion permits associations with the main variables of interest to be treated with more confidence than if they were ignored.

The plant-level variables also have differing characteristics. Some can be treated as characteristics of companies which happen to be measured at the level of the plant. Thus the closeness with which a plant's activities are monitored can be seen less as a feature internal to the plant than a characteristic of the company which is assessed by interviewing a manager at plant level. Other variables such as union density or the skill composition of the work force are plainly plant-level characteristics. The question then is how typical a plant's arrangements are of the firm as a whole. To the extent that a firm either operates in a small number of industries or has a clearly determined central policy on labour matters, any one plant is likely to be representative. That is, union density for example will not vary much between all the firm's plants, and density in any one of them can be used as a proxy for the overall company position. Little is known about this issue, but three considerations suggest that intra-company variation may not be too large a problem. First, the plants in the present sample were large, so that it is unlikely that practices within them were idiosyncratic or marginal to the firms owning them. Second, the evidence reviewed in chapter 4 points to the existence of broad company expectations even though plant managers may be given considerable discretion in carrying out their day-to-day tasks. Third, the Warwick Survey included, as would be expected, several cases in which more than one plant from a given company was included; in one case, 54 plants belonging to the same firm were in the sample. It is possible to look at these firms to assess the extent of variation in labour relations practices within them. The result of the analysis was that variations were not very great. Taking one plant from a company may thus be a reasonable procedure.[5]

Such points notwithstanding, it remains true that there is a large gap between the practices of a large multi-plant firm such as GEC or Thorn–EMI and arrangements at one of its plants. Further efforts to control for this gap were therefore made. The most significant involved selecting only those plants that constituted a substantial proportion of total company employment, on the argument that in such cases a plant will, because of its size relative to the rest of the firm, necessarily provide a fairly close indication of company characteristics. As shown in table 4.3, not many plants in the present survey accounted for more than a small part of company employment. The value of the exercise is thus somewhat limited. The Warwick Survey, however, with its wider representation of small firms, provides a reasonable basis for an analysis of this kind.[6]

Conclusions

In short, the data have some inevitable limitations in view of the aims of the survey as a whole. They have the advantage, however, of including information on matters not previously covered in studies of productivity, and they permit the extension of debates that have generally been based on American evidence to the British context.

Influences on Productivity: Bivariate Analysis

There is an enormous number of possible influences on productivity. This section looks at some of them, one at a time. This serves two purposes. It permits an initial assessment of the data, by showing which of the possible influences were in fact present within the sample. And it uses this demonstration to indicate why some variables were included in, and others excluded from, the more complex multi-variate analyses of the following section.

Trade Union Presence

The Harvard model expects an association between the presence of a trade union and productivity. An initial test is to classify four measures of performance (overall profitability, costs of production, wage costs per unit, and production per worker: see Qs 137–45) derived from interviews with respondents by trade union status.[7] This classification also takes the analysis further than the Harvard literature, by looking at the extent of union organization and not just its presence or absence.

The data are reported in table 6.1, which also includes a classification by one other obvious industrial relations variable, namely experience of strike action. There was an association between union status and reported profitability, with the absence of a union being associated with a high level of profit. Since there was little variation in reported profits by industry, this cannot be ascribed to an industry effect as distinct from a union effect. It is not clear whether a union effect was at work, however, for unions do not affect profits directly, but indirectly through the cost of production. There was no clear relationship between the presence of a union and the total costs of production; thus those without recognized unions reported below as well as above average costs less often than did other respondents, with more reporting on average level. There was also no strong relationship between experience of industrial action and profits or production costs. There is thus little evidence in support of the common-sense argument that unions and the things that they do, such as organizing strikes, interfere significantly with performance.

The Harvard view is more subtle. Having observed a tendency for unions to increase productivity, the Harvard analysts are faced with the linked questions of why unionized firms do not out-compete non-union ones and why firms do not rush to become unionized. The answer, which is based on general consideration of the issue and not on detailed research findings, is that it is widely noted that unions tend to be associated with wage levels that are higher than they are in comparable but non-union establishments. The wage effects and the productivity effects of unionism are supposed to cancel each other out.

TABLE 6.1
Revenues and Costs by Trade Union Status and Experience of Industrial Action

	Trade Union Presence				Industrial Action				All
	No Recog.	Recog., no Senior Stewards	Recog. Senior Stewards	Full-time Stewards	None	Other Only	Strike Only	Both	
Gross revenue									
Well in excess of costs	53	30	26	26	37	26	39	16	30
Enough for small profit	46	37	44	44	33	54	44	46	43
Break even	2	11	15	15	13	9	7	21	13
Insufficient to cover costs	0	10	9	12	11	3	9	12	9
Large losses	0	12	6	4	6	9	1	5	6
Costs of production									
Above average	18	30	23	37	30	21	13	30	26
Average	67	41	45	44	41	47	55	52	47
Below average	15	29	33	19	29	32	32	19	28
Wage costs per unit									
Above average	42	28	25	30	25	34	14	34	28
Average	28	44	48	50	46	44	58	39	45
Below average	31	29	27	20	29	22	27	27	26
Level of production per worker									
Above average	68	45	50	32	57	47	48	37	49
Average	32	56	38	57	37	41	38	57	43
Below average	0	0	12	11	7	11	14	6	9

Base : All establishments.

The expectation, therefore, is that unionization will be associated with levels of production and of wages that are higher than average; wage costs per unit of output would then be unrelated to union status. The data in table 6.1, do not fit this expectation. Levels of production per worker were higher the weaker the presence of the union in the factory. And there was also some tendency, albeit not a very strong one, for wage costs per unit to be above average. As against the Harvard expectation that non-union firms balance low productivity against low wages, such firms in the present survey appear to have had high productivity and high wages.[8]

A plausible explanation turns on the type of non-union firm included in the sample. As noted in chapter 5, writers such as Purcell and Sisson (1983) distinguish between anti-union employers and sophisticated paternalists. Given the size of the establishments and firms in the sample, it is likely that it is the latter and not the former who comprise the bulk of the non-union cases. Such firms have developed policies of paying high wages and providing good conditions of employment, not necessarily out of concern for their workers' well-being but because they believe that commitment, and thereby efficiency, is promoted. Improved productivity would at least balance the costs involved. The data to hand do not permit a detailed investigation of the non-union firms in the sample, and since there were only 17 of them not too much weight should be placed on statistical analysis (although it may also be said that the number of cases included in Harvard analyses is also small). But it is clear that the status of being non-union, and indeed that of being unionized, is not homogeneous. Sophisticated paternalists are unlikely to find productivity effects of the kind associated with the Harvard model, for their labour relations are already well developed and do not need 'shocking' into a concern with internal organization. The contrast between union and non-union plants is too crude to deal with such points.[9]

Corporate Organization and Practice
As already noted, 'in search of excellence' writers identify several corporate characteristics allegedly associated with success. Before this argument can be properly assessed, it is necessary to consider some other dimensions of corporate organization. An association between an ISE variable and productivity could be due not to a causal relationship but to separate links with a third factor. For example, a link between the presence of share-option schemes and productivity might be due to the fact that the former are found in large divisionalized firms (perhaps because such firms can afford them) which also tend to be highly efficient.

Measures of performance were correlated with the corporate status of a plant (that is, whether it was an independent establishment, part of a multi-plant group without distinct divisions, or part of a divisionalized corporation). There was little association. The managers of independent companies tended to report levels of profit that were lower than those reported in multi-plant firms, but there was no association when the costs of production or labour costs were investigated. Neither was the company-level measure of productivity, turnover per head, related to the corporate status of a plant. How much is made of this result depends on one's prior expectations. For anyone expecting that divisionalized firms will have the organizational structure to release economies of scale or otherwise to increase productivity, the results will be disappointing. But in the absence of any particular expectations on these lines, the main significance of the result is to strengthen the confidence with which other patterns of association can be treated, for they cannot be written off to the confounding effects of corporate status.

A variable of more substantive interest is the importance ascribed to labour relations matters in company decision-making. It will be recalled that managers were asked to rate the importance of these matters in eight different areas; an additive scale was created from these replies. It will be called IRIMP, with high scores representing a high importance of labour matters. The ISE literature expects a high score of IRIMP to be associated with high levels of productivity. There was in fact no association with respondents' assessments of their plants' profitability, total costs, or overall performance in relation to the average plants within the companies in which they were located. Neither was there a link with turnover per head or growth at the level of the company. There was a slight correlation ($r = 0.18$) with profitability, but further investigation showed this to be strongly affected by a few outlying observations, with there being no clear association across the sample as a whole.

One other plausible argument is that the use of joint consultation will provide a reasonably objective measure of the extent to which a co-operative style of labour relations is adopted in a plant; this may be more appropriate than an attitudinal measure such as the importance ascribed to labour relations. There was, however, no relationship between turnover per head and either the presence of committees or the time that they had been in existence.

Similar inconclusive results emerged with respect to a further index of labour relations arrangements, namely the overall policies or philosophies that managers said that they employed; there was no statistically significant relationship with measures of performance. Inspection of the categories suggested, however, that some influences may have been at work, albeit ones that were not strong. One pertinent tabulation is set out in table 6.2, showing mean profit rates and turnover per head for firms where managers said that they had different types of policy.

TABLE 6.2
Labour Relations Policy and Company Performance

		N	Mean Profit Rate[a]	Turnover per Head
(1)[b]	Consultation/information/ communication	40	1.75	39.5
(2)	Involvement	23	3.66	41.0
(3)	Involvement plus ensuring workers know needs of business	37	7.29	61.3
(7, 8, 9)	Paternalism/teamwork/social responsibility	46	5.54	44.8
(10)	Firm and fair/consistent procedures	21	2.04	45.5
(11)	Work with TUs or stewards	7	−1.32	32.9

Notes:
[a] Profit as % turnover in 1982.
[b] Numbers refer to the policy types listed in table 5.10. The present selection and amalgamation of categories is designed to capture reasonably homogeneous groupings for the purpose at hand.

The results are not consistent with what might be termed the vulgar model of labour relations, wherein any concern with consultation and communication is seen as leading to a breaking down of 'them and us' attitudes and a consequent increase in efficiency. Those describing their policies as being based on consultation and communication had levels of profit below the average. The data fit the more subtle views of Peters and Waterman who, as noted above, stress that policies of employee involvement must be thorough-going, and not merely ritual statements of the importance of human resources, if they are to work. Thus those who made clear links between involvement and meeting the overall needs of the business were in firms that returned the highest turnover per head and profit rates. Similarly, it will come as no surprise that the paternalists score highly. As Peters and Waterman again note, successful firms are not afraid of this label; and, as shown in chapter 5, paternalism is an aspect of the practice of quite large and sophisticated firms, and is not limited to small or marginal companies.

The absence of any statistical significance here reflects the large margin of error that must accompany classifications of labour relations policy, and also the effect of many other influences on productivity. The data are consistent with some expectations, but are not strong enough to provide any firm support for them.

Managerial Careers and Establishment Autonomy

In other areas some significant results emerged. There was, first, some association between factory managers' attitudes and experience and productivity. The managers who were most flexible in their approach to their jobs and who were least dissatisfied with the way in which their firms treated them might be expected to be found in the most successful firms. There were thus positive associations between turnover per head and the indices of personal flexibility and of attitudes in the company. The expectation that companies which promote share-holding among their managers will be rewarded with high levels of productivity was not, however, borne out: there was a significant tendency for firms where managers reported that they held shares to have low levels of productivity, a result considered further below. Finally, there was no tendency for firms in which managers reported either the presence of management development programmes or that they themselves had been involved in programmes that widened their experience of management (Qs 119 and 121) to have higher or lower levels of productivity than others. This is a mixed set of results for any expectation that there will be a clear pattern wherein share ownership, management development programmes, and developing a flexible approach among the work force are parts of an overall package of success. But they reveal that some parts of the pattern seem to have had an effect, while others have had an impact quite opposite to what would have been expected, which is something that requires further study using more complex statistical models.

The question of a manager's satisfaction and flexibility leads into an area where the most impressive results were obtained, namely the discretion given to, and the monitoring exercised over, subsidiary plants. The general expectation is that there needs to be a balance between stifling initiative and letting plants proceed in their own ways without any central leadership or control. One way to look at this is through the questions on the retention of revenues and the undertaking of investment programmes without special permission (Qs 130 to 133). There was no relationship with profitability or growth, but there were some clear links with turnover per head. Those plants which could not retain their own revenues were associated with high levels of turnover per head, as were those where there was an upper limit on the amount of capital expenditure that could be carried out without approval from a higher level of management. Productivity was highest where company management kept a tight rein on local spending.

Perhaps most revealing was the information on the extent of monitoring of plant performance. As noted in chapter 4, five areas of monitoring were investigated separately for the closeness of checking at the levels of the operating company and of the corporation as a whole.

Ten ordinal variables were thus available, and in every case the level of turnover per head was highest in the middle two categories and lowest in the two extreme ones: high productivity was associated with a moderate degree of monitoring. This is quite striking support for the views of Peters and Waterman.

As already suggested, variables of this sort can be treated as company-level and not plant-level measures: assuming that the experience of the plant in the sample is not out of line with company practice, and assuming also that factory managers' reports are reasonably accurate indices of the true picture,[10] they reflect company policy and can properly be used in the explanation of another company-level phenomenon, namely productivity. This suggests that there is some value in exploring the matter further, in particular by seeing whether the effect remains when that of other influences on productivity is controlled.

Determinants of Productivity: Multi-Variate Models

The Warwick Survey and the Union Effect

In applying multi-variate models to the data, it is convenient to begin with the effects of unionization. This is simply because the results turn out to be rather negative for the Harvard model, and it is preferable to cover them before turning to the more positive results for the ISE theory. For reasons noted above, the Warwick Survey provides the most appropriate set of data for examining unionization.

The dependent variable here, and in the other regression models reported, is turnover per head: growth and profitability proved, in a number of experiments, to be hard to predict and are, in any event, of less interest to the present analysis, which is focused on productivity and not other measures of performance. Several control variables are employed. Two are at company level: the amount of capital employed per employee (capital per head, CPH) and the mean level of wages and salaries paid. The latter (called REMUN) measures not the average per manual employee but is the total wage and salary bill divided by the total number of employees. It thus does not control directly for a union wage effect, which is likely to be most significant for manual workers. But in some ways it is particularly useful because it indexes the wage policy of the firm as a whole. The two industry-level variables are the five-firm concentration ratio in the industry in which the sampled plant was located (CONC, the proportion of total sales held by the largest firms), and ratio of value-added to turnover in this industry (called IGVAPC to stand for 'industry gross value added per cent'). The expected effects of three of these variables are clear. Turnover will obviously be expected to be higher the larger the amount of capital employed. Similarly, a high level of remuneration is likely to be associated with productivity; among the reasons is the familiar argument that high wages lead firms to use their labour as efficiently as possible. In so far as monopoly permits firms to increase their price, CONC should also be directly associated with turnover per head. Expectations for IGVAPC are less clear, but a possible argument is that as turnover per head becomes a worse proxy for value-added per head the effect of the variable will increase; this would mean that it would have a negative coefficient. To capture any other industry effects, dummy variables for each of 17 industry orders were created. Results for them are not reported separately; an indication is given in the tables as to whether they were included in an equation.

Three control variables at the level of the plant were used. It is important to try to allow for labour force 'quality' and the most appropriate index is the proportion of the manual work force that the respondent defined as being skilled (SKILL). The Harvard model expects a positive link with productivity. To allow for differing technical conditions, an admittedly crude measure of 'advanced' technology was introduced; this (called HITECH) took the value 1 when continuous process or mass production technologies were reported and zero otherwise. It is, in addition to CPH, a measure of technical, as distinct from labour-related, sources of productivity and is expected to have a positive sign. The proportion of non-manual employees in the total (NMPC) was included to measure the structure of the work force. Expectations as to its effect vary. The 'conventional' view is that white-collar and technical staff represent high-quality labour and that they tend to be concentrated in the advanced sectors; a large number of them will then be associated with high productivity. The 'radical' view, expressed by Gordon (1981), for example, is that a significant proportion of such staff is composed of supervisors and that a rise in the number of supervisors in the recent past reflects a problem in controlling shopfloor workers: such workers have become more recalcitrant, and more staff are needed to monitor and control them, the result being that the number of non-productive workers will be inversely associated with productivity.

Three variables indexing the presence and extent of union organization are reported here. NOTU indicates a case in which there was no union in the plant recognized for bargaining purposes. TUDENS measures the proportion of the work force who were members of unions. And HITU is a dummy taking the value of 1 where density was high (80 per cent or more), the aim being to assess whether there were any discontinuous effects of unionism; the Harvard argument that unions act to co-ordinate the preferences of their members, for example, requires that a union has a significant place in the running of the plant, and there may thus be specific effects arising where a union is well organized that are not captured by a continuous measure of unionization. The expected signs of these variables are clear.[11]

One other measure of shopfloor industrial relations that it was thought worth including was the use of payment-by-results schemes. These are often seen as part of a syndrome of wage drift, frequent disputes, and strikes; one possibility is thus that their presence will be associated with low levels of productivity. Alternatively, bonus systems might be felt to encourage effort and thus to stimulate productivity. A crude measure of the state of market demand was also included; this was a dummy (DEMANDUP) indicating that demand for the plant's products was said to have been increasing over the previous two years. This may help to control for possible effects associated with the extent of capacity utilization; for example, where demand has been falling it is unlikely that equipment will be fully used, and productivity may suffer as a result.

Finally, a measure of the discretion enjoyed by subsidiary plants was included. As reported above, the results of the present survey pointed to a high level of productivity where moderate levels of discretion were reported by factory managers. For the Warwick Survey, this effect was measured by setting up a dummy taking the value 1 when 'limited discretion within fairly detailed rules' was reported on industrial relations matters generally (see table 4.2 for details of the variable). This measure, of the six different areas in which perceptions of discretion were ascertained, was used because it acts as a summary measure for the general extent of discretion; since the pattern of replies was similar across all six areas, it would not, in practice, have made much difference which of the six was used.

The main results of the analysis are presented in table 6.3. The dependent variable, turnover per head, is expressed in logarithmic form, as are some of the independent variables (as indicated by the prefix 'L' to a variable name). This is done for theoretical and statistical reasons.[12] In view of the problem of linking plant-level and company-level data, it may be argued that the results for the whole sample provide little test of the Harvard thesis. Attention will thus be focused initially on the first column. This reports the results in cases where the sampled plant comprised at least 25 per cent of total company employment: the two levels of analysis will be fairly close together. The results for the four company-level and industry-level controls were as expected: high levels of turnover per head were associated with a large capital stock, high average wages, a high concentration ratio, and a low ratio of value-added to turnover in the relevant industry. (It should also be noted that taking this sub-sample also reduces the gap between industry and company levels of analysis because the industry in which the sampled plant is located will be characteristic of the environment of a substantial part of the firm's operations.) None of the other variables attained significant levels of association. The effects of SKILL, HITECH, and NMPC were small, and, as the results for the other equations reported show, the signs of the coefficients could vary.

In so far as the Harvard model sees these variables as controls for possible confounding effects, the results are of no particular interest, except that the lack of effect of the SKILL variable is somewhat surprising. Although the Harvard model itself makes no special prediction about this variable, the broader paradigm in which the model is located does make such a prediction. This paradigm is the conventional economists' approach, wherein productivity is seen as the outcome of the application of quantities of factors of production; more labour, or labour of a higher quality, will increase output. The production process itself is seen as a 'black box'. In a different view of production, in which social relations are seen as central, no clear predictions about the effects of SKILL need be made: the question becomes one of how creative capacities are used and not of the formal skill qualifications of the work force. Most obviously, a highly skilled work force, particularly one in a British context, where skill tends to mean craft-based knowledge and to be associated with craft unions, can have the ability to limit the deployment of its skills. In short, the negative result of SKILL should not be seen as surprising.

The results for the unionization variables are disappointing from a Harvard point of view. Most notably, the coefficient of NOTU was very close to zero, and not significantly negative as would be expected. The other two variables did not attain high levels of significance. HITU was in the expected direction, while LTUDENS was not. The explanation of the latter result seems to lie in the joint effects of these two measures. As a comparison of the second and third equations shows, when HITU was omitted the coefficient for LTUDENS was close to zero. The inclusion of HITU seems to have picked up the main positive effect of unionism on productivity, while LTUDENS pointed to a negative effect of any additional increase in membership density. There would be little value in speculating further about this result. There is some suggestion in the data that it is not so much the presence of a union but the existence of a well-established union organization which had the main effects on productivity. But the effect of the latter was not highly significant, and the safest conclusion about the Harvard effect is 'not proven'.

Two other results warrant comment. There was some tendency for PBR to be inversely related to productivity. Given the crude nature of the measure concerned, the result is fairly impressive: it seems that the use of payments-by-results schemes is associated with a poor productivity record. This is not, of course, to say that there is a direct or automatic link, but it is surely well established that many of the most

174

TABLE 6.3
Determinants of Turnover Per Head (Warwick Survey Results)

Sample N	Plant > 25% Company[a] 155	All Plants 650	All Plants 653	One Plant Per Company[b] 349	Plant Size > 250 Employees 543
Independent variables (t statistics in brackets)					
LCPH	0.55*** (9.28)	0.66*** (25.8)	0.66*** (26.4)	0.66*** (26.8)	0.62*** (21.5)
REMUN	0.27*** (4.10)	0.18*** (5.97)	0.17*** (5.86)	0.17*** (5.23)	0.18*** (5.56)
CONC	0.13** (2.09)	0.02 (0.65)	0.01 (0.49)		0.05 (1.29)
IGVAPC	-0.14** (2.10)	-0.13*** (4.50)	-0.13*** (4.71)		-0.15*** (4.55)
SKILL	-0.11* (1.74)	0.02 (0.60)		0.04 (0.49)	
HITECH	0.02 (0.34)	0.01 (0.23)	-0.01 (0.24)	-0.00 (0.20)	
NMPC	0.06 (1.09)	0.03 (0.97)			0.02 (0.62)
NOTU	-0.02 (0.29)	-0.02 (0.91)			0.00 (0.11)
HITU	0.14 (1.14)	0.10* (1.78)			-0.02 (0.76)

LTUDENS	-0.18 (1.35)	-0.13** (2.19)	-0.03 (1.19)	-0.03 (1.15)	-0.03 (1.15)
PBR			-0.07** (2.45)		-0.05 (1.62)
DISCR	0.03 (0.60)	0.05** (2.12)	0.05** (2.11)	0.03 (0.89)	0.03 (1.23)
DEMANDUP				0.01 (0.72)	
(Industry dummies included)	(Yes)	(Yes)	(No)	(Yes)	(Yes)
Summary statistics					
R^2	0.57	0.65	0.65	0.64	0.64
F	13.5***	76.4***	87.9***	62.2***	52.6***

[a] Cases where plant employment at least 25 per cent of company employment.

[b] In cases where more than one of a firm's plant were in the sample, the 'duplicates' were excluded by selecting at random one of the plants, thus avoiding cases where the dependent variable was the same for two or more observations.

*** = Significant at 1% level.   ** = Significant at 5% level.   * = Significant at 10% level.

Key: (Dependent variable: log of turnover per head)

LCPH — Log of capital employed per head (at level of company).
REMUN — Wage and salary bill divided by employment (company level).
CONC — 5-firm concentration ratio in industry (MLH) in which plant located.
IGVAPC — Gross value added as % 'turnover, in relevant MLH.
SKILL — % of work force defined as skilled by respondent.
HITECH — Dummy with value 1 when continuous process or mass production technology reported, and zero otherwise.
NMPC — % total work force who were non-manual.
NOTU — Dummy with value 1 when no recognized union present.
HITU — Dummy with value 1 when union density 80 per cent or more.
LTUDENS — Log of trade union density.
PBR — Dummy with value 1 when PBR in use for a significant proportion of work force.
DISCR — Dummy with value 1 when 'limited discretion within fairly detailed rules' reported on IR issues generally.
DEMANDUP — Dummy with value 1 when an increase in demand for the plant's products reported over previous two years.

progressive companies prefer not to link pay directly to performance on a particular job, concentrating instead on rewarding a more general commitment to the firm's goals and encouraging movement between jobs and not attachment to a particular narrow set of tasks. There was also a tendency for the discretion variable to achieve significant associations with productivity. Although neither strong nor present in all the equations, the effect was clear.

Finally, one methodological point may be noted. As discussed above, in several cases more than one plant from a company was included in the survey. There is the possible danger of taking cases where the dependent variable is the same. The fourth column reports the results where only one plant from each firm was taken; these are in line with those for the whole sample. The benefit, however, of using the whole sample is that it contains data from more than one of a firm's plants, so that the problem of typicality is reduced. That is, the likelihood that an unusual or unrepresentative plant had been chosen is much reduced, and the adequacy of linking plant-level and company-level data is further sustained.

Perceptions of Productivity: The Present Survey
Returning to the present survey, two sorts of dependent variable are available: managers' reports on each plant, and company data on turnover per head. The former may be briefly considered: do the effects noted above hold up when several variables are included in the analysis? It is difficult to be very sophisticated, since cross-classifications rapidly come up against a problem of numbers: a tabulation of two variables, each with four categories, produces 16 cells, and holding constant the effects of only one other four-category variable will produce 64 cells, so that numbers in each cell rapidly become very small. The approach adopted was to consider two independent variables at a time.

The main result was that non-union plants were reported by their managers to have high levels of production per worker. This tendency remained when various control variables, such as the level of demand for the plant's products and the extent of market competition, were introduced. The tendency was not very strong, but it is plainly inconsistent with Harvard expectations.

The Present Survey: The Basic Model
The basic regression model for the present survey is the same as that used in the Warwick Survey data, but there are some differences of detail due to differences in the variables included. No data on average remuneration were collected, and the average wage level in the industry in which the plant was located (IWAGE) has been used instead. In the absence of data on the skill distribution of the work force, the proportion of the work force who were women (FEMPC) has been used. A conventional expectation is that women tend to hold unskilled jobs, so

that a high proportion of women will indicate an unskilled work force; the result will be an inverse link between FEMPC and productivity. Some strong doubts could be entered about this view, but the variable is included for those who feel that some control for 'labour force quality' is needed.

Three variables not available in the Warwick Survey were also included. GROWTH measures the rate of change of turnover between 1978 and 1982; it is included to assess the possibility that productivity is affected by whether a firm is growing or stable. A reasonable expectation is that growth will be associated with a dynamic environment and will stimulate productivity. CAPAC is the level of capacity utilization at plant level: a high level is likely to allow economies of scale and to be associated with high productivity. COMP1 is a dummy taking the value 1 if competition was reported by the respondent to be severe or very severe: does being in such an environment stimulate productivity?

These three variables were used more as controls than for their importance in their own right. Two other variables assess company organization as such. SHARES is a dummy with value 1 when the respondent owned shares in the firm: as shown above, there was a (surprising) tendency for share ownership to be related to low levels of productivity. The current need is to see whether this holds up in a multi-variate model.

The second, CORPINT, is more complicated. As also noted above, there was a strong tendency for turnover per head to be highest in the middle ranges of both company and corporate monitoring of the plant. Since the pattern was the same for all five areas investigated, one, interest in pay settlements, was chosen for the multi-variate analysis. Significant associations were found between the dummies for the relevant categories of the company interest and corporate interest variables and the level of turnover per head. But in initial multi-variate tests the question arose as to whether these dummies were exerting an independent effect or were influenced by other variables. Examination of a correlation matrix showed that the levels of association with other independent variables were not unduly high. Thus the measure of capital employed, LCPH, had a correlation coefficient of 0.13 with the company dummy and 0.02 with the corporate dummy. The dummies were not simply reflecting the effects of other variables but had effects of their own. These effects were, however, influenced by the values of other variables. A test for the presence of interactions between the dummies and LCPH showed that the interaction terms were highly significant whereas the 'main effects' of the dummies, that is, their effects on their own, were not. The dummy with the larger effects was that measuring corporate interest. What this means is that corporations with a high level of capital per head also tended to be those taking a moderate degree of interest in plant performance, and that the effect of this interaction on turnover per head was highly significant. CORPINT

TABLE 6.4
Determinants of Turnover Per Head in the Present Survey

Sample N	All Plants 190	All Plants 190
Independent variables (t statistics in brackets)		
LCPH	0.51*** (9.16)	0.53*** (9.53)
GROWTH	0.32*** (5.07)	
CONC	−0.10 (1.33)	−0.10 (1.36)
IWAGE	0.07 (0.79)	0.14 (1.22)
IGVAPC	−0.03 (0.44)	−0.02 (0.40)
CAPAC	0.03 (0.42)	−0.04 (0.53)
DEMANDUP	0.04 (0.68)	0.08 (0.97)
FEMPC	0.12 (1.61)	0.13* (1.70)
NMPC		0.00 (0.21)
COMP1	0.12** (2.01)	0.13** (2.05)
NOTU	0.02 (0.35)	0.06 (0.58)
HITU	0.03 (0.47)	0.08 (0.72)
CORPINT	0.25*** (3.81)	0.25*** (3.83)
SHARES	−0.13** (2.02)	−0.12** (1.98)
PBR		0.10 (0.91)
PBRPC		0.00 (0.21)
(Industry dummies included)	(Yes)	(Yes)
Summary statistics		
$\bar{R}^2$	0.51	0.45
F	9.47***	8.72***

is the interaction term included in the regression model. It was, of course, correlated with LCPH, but the correlation coefficient was only 0.23, indicating that it was picking up a substantially different effect.

As in the Warwick Survey, LCPH was a powerful predictor of turnover per head. GROWTH also had a significant positive coefficient, but the model excluding it (the second equation of table 6.4) performed almost as well as the one including it. Unlike the Warwick Survey results, neither CONC nor IGVAPC attained significance, and the coefficient of IWAGE (in contrast to the results for REMUN in table 6.3) was also not significant. Of the plant-level variables, only COMP1, CORPINT, and SHARES were significant. The non-significance of the coefficients of NMPC and of the unionization measures was consistent with the earlier results (the result for union density, LTUDENS, is not given here, since earlier work had failed to establish any significant association with the measure of productivity).

The result for CORPINT is consistent with the previous evidence: internal company organization does seem to matter. That for SHARES is also in line with the bivariate analysis: even when the effects of other variables are taken into account, share ownership seems to depress productivity. The coefficient for COMP1 seems to support the view that being in a competitive industry stimulates productivity. The inconclusive results for the other variables require no special comment, although it is interesting that capacity utilization appears to have had such a limited effect. The result for PBR also contrasts to that for the comparable variable in the Warwick Survey.

The reasons for the contrasts to the Warwick Survey, for example the different results for the PBR variable, could be investigated further. This is not of major importance here, but one comparison between the surveys needs to be made. Since the Warwick Survey included small plants, the results are perhaps influenced by their inclusion. The equations for that survey were therefore re-run on plants with at least 250 workers, to put them on a comparable footing with the present survey. The key results, namely the non-significance of the unionization variables, remained (see the final column of table 6.3). The PBR variables also lost significance. In view of the different signs of the variable's coefficient in the two surveys, no firm conclusion can be drawn about its effect. Broadly, however, the results of the two surveys are consistent.

Key: (Dependent variable: log of turnover per head).
Variables are as defined in table 6.3, plus:
GROWTH % change in turnover, 1978–82.
IWAGE Average wage level in relevant MLH.
CAPAC % plant capacity utilized, on average, over previous year.
FEMPC % work force female.
COMP1 Dummy with value 1 when market competition severe or very severe.
CORPINT Interaction term between LCPH and dummy for moderate corporate interest in pay movements (see text for explanation).
SHARES Dummy with value 1 when manager reported owning shares in his firm.
PBRPC % work force covered by payments by results schemes.

Company Organization and Managerial Careers
In view of the encouraging results for measures of company organization, the matter was investigated further. As noted above, a manager's
personal flexibility seemed to be related to productivity, but this
relationship did not remain in multi-variate tests. This left, in addition
to share ownership and company interest in plant performance, four
variables. First, as also noted above, a manager's satisfaction with his
firm, as measured by the variable CRIT described in chapter 3 (p. 78),
was related to productivity; since a positive score on CRIT indicates
dissatisfaction, a negative sign for the coefficient is expected. Second,
experience of a planning role at company headquarters (HQ) is expected
to have a positive link with productivity since it reflects cases where
the factory manager is seen as a strategic resource. Third, OWNCAP
shows cases in which plants were given their own allocations of capital
by firms. As shown above (p. 169) there was a tendency for productivity
to be highest where there were limits on the capital expenditure undertaken at plant level. It has also been seen that moderate levels of
company monitoring seem to promote productivity. Cases taking a
value of zero on OWNCAP are either those where the plant can retain
its own revenues (and where, by hypothesis, company control is weak)
or those where no capital allocation is given to the plant (and thus
where company control is very tight). Cases taking a value of 1 fall
between these extremes, and OWNCAP is thus expected to have a positive
coefficient. Finally, CORPPROF indicates cases where a corporation took
a close interest in the profitability of the establishment; it is included
as a further measure of the links between a plant and the firm owning
it, looking at one of the extremes and not the middle range of company
interest, the aim being to see whether any effect in addition to those
captured by the other variables was present.
    In table 6.5 the results of looking at these six variables on their own
are presented; in addition, their effects once the company-level and
industry-level control variables are allowed for are assessed. There
could also be differences between divisionalized and non-divisionalized
firms in the operation of these models, for two reasons. First, variables
such as CRIT and HQ may differ according to the size and organizational
structure of a firm. Second, the measures of corporate interest in the
plant apply only to divisionalized firms. The category excluded from
the relevant dummy variables thus conflates cases where a corporate
structure existed but where the appropriate characteristic was absent
and cases without such a structure. To avoid these problems, the
analysis was carried out for all multi-plant firms and for divisionalized
ones.[13] The results were very similar. In particular, the interaction
variable CORPINT was highly significant in all equations, suggesting that
it was picking up a genuine effect and not an oddity of the way in
which it differentiated between plants.

TABLE 6.5
Turnover Per Head: Influence of Managerial Experience and Attitudes

Sample N Equation	All Multi-Plant Firms[a] 179 (1)	 (2)	All Divisionalized Firms[a] 136 (3)	 (4)
Independent variables				
SHARES	−0.08	−0.10*	−0.05	−0.11*
	(1.13)	(1.79)	(0.65)	(1.82)
CRIT	−0.12*	−0.05	−0.18**	−0.06
	(1.67)	(0.92)	(2.20)	(0.98)
HQ	0.05	0.03	0.04	0.03
	(0.70)	(0.55)	(0.49)	(0.53)
CORPINT	0.38***	0.24***	0.41***	0.24***
	(5.03)	(3.85)	(4.97)	(3.44)
OWNCAP	0.16***	0.09	0.09	0.06
	(2.25)	(1.58)	(1.10)	(0.92)
CORPPROF	0.08	0.02	−0.01	0.00
	(1.03)	(0.38)	(0.12)	(0.03)
CONC		−0.10*		−0.06
		(1.68)		(0.83)
IWAGE		0.02		−0.04
		(0.33)		(0.54)
GROWTH		0.24***		0.26***
		(4.33)		(4.06)
LCPH		0.55***		0.55***
		(9.03)		(7.51)
IGVAPC		0.02		0.06
		(0.30)		(0.97)
Summary statistics				
$\bar{R}^2$	0.15	0.50	0.17	0.50
F	6.08***	15.5***	5.69***	12.1***

Note:
[a] Including only those firms in which respondent was a factory manager.
Key: Variables are as defined in tables 6.3 and 6.4, plus
CRIT   Dummy with value 1 where manager had a critical attitude to company's approach of consulting him (see chapter 3, p. 78, for explanation).
H   Dummy (value 1) where experience at HQ level reported.
OWNCAP   Dummy (value 1) where plant given own allocation of capital.
CORPPROF Dummy (value 1) where great deal of interest in plant's profit performance, at corporate level, reported.

The results for measures of company organization were mixed. Headquarters experience for the factory manager and corporate interest in profits made no difference to productivity. OWNCAP also had a limited role, being significant in only one of the four equations. The coefficient for CRIT was of the expected sign, with critical attitudes being associated with low levels of productivity. When just the first six variables were considered, quite a high level of significance was achieved, but when the remaining five control variables were introduced this was lost. Given the nature of the variable, the latter outcome is not surprising. Indeed, the ability of a fairly simple measure of a manager's attitudes to attain any significant degree of association with the turnover per employee of the company employing him is notable.

The question of the direction of causality obviously arises: is it the case, as the model assumes, that managers' attitudes affect productivity, or is it, rather, that working for a successful firm leads to satisfaction?

Influences may run in both directions. The measure of the manager's attitude should not be seen as directly causing productivity. It is likely to form part of a set of managerial assumptions and forms of factory organization. Where managers feel out of touch with the corporate headquarters there may be a general lack of commitment and sense of direction which in turn affects productivity. The nature of the variable CRIT should also be borne in mind: it is not a general measure of job satisfaction but relates specifically to the manager's dealings with the firm. Cases in which there is dissatisfaction are likely to be those in which there are general problems of managerial organization. The variable can thus be taken as a reflection of the structure of the firm, and can reasonably be seen as affecting productivity. There may well also be influences in the opposite direction. A limitation of a regression model is its one-way and static quality, whereas in fact a high level of turnover per head is likely to promote a sense of self-confidence which further promotes satisfaction with company organization: success breeds success. The result should be taken as showing that firms which are able to create the conditions that make their factory managers satisfied with the way in which they are treated are also able to attain high levels of productivity, although over time these two things are likely to reinforce each other.

The result for SHARES is in line with those reported above, except that, surprisingly, the variable attains significance when the full set of variables is included but loses it when only the sub-set of organizational characteristics is considered. One possibility is that the variable is highly correlated with some of the company-level variables, the result being that the separate effects of each independent variable are hard to assess and that their significance levels are exaggerated (the problem of multicollinearity). In fact, the correlation coefficients between SHARES and the other independent variables suggested that this was not the case.

The answer seems to be that these other variables removed some of the confounding effects in the data, thus permitting the effect of SHARES to appear. It is difficult to describe this effect in words, but the analogy of cross-tabulated data may help. It is plain, as Upton (1978: 43), for example, notes, that when bivariate tables are produced no pattern of association may be present, but that when a third variable is introduced there is a clear pattern: collapsing the data into bivariate tables amalgamates into one cell cases of positive and negative association with the result that the 'average' picture is one of no association.[14] A similar effect may have been at work here.

These results can be no more than indicative. They would be stronger if a whole series of measures of company internal organization were related to productivity. In fact, a variable such as HQ failed to show any relationship. In addition, and not surprisingly, the effect of other variables, such as CRIT, was washed out when measures of capital employed were added. Given the nature of the variables involved, however, it would have been wrong to have expected too much from them. The fact that any significant associations emerged is quite notable. Taken together with the results for measures of company monitoring of plant performance, reported above, the data are consistent with the view that internal organization makes a difference to firms' productivity. Their wider implications must now be assessed.

Conclusions

The results reported above offer no support to the Harvard expectation that unionization promotes productivity, although there was equally no support for the common-sense obverse of this expectation, namely that unions interfere with efficiency: there was no measurable connection between turnover per head and several indices of union presence and organization. The evidence offers more encouragement to the 'in search of excellence' school. Aspects of company organization, in particular a moderate degree of monitoring of plant activity, had the expected positive effect on productivity.

The major exception was SHARES, for share ownership turned out to be associated with low levels of productivity, and not the high levels that would be expected from the theory that giving managers a stake in the firm encourages a high level of commitment and hence of performance. One possible explanation of this result is that share ownership is likely to be concentrated in small firms, particularly the owner-managed ones, and that these tend to have difficulty in achieving high levels of productivity. This account does not, however, work. First, the very small owner-managed firms are excluded from the analysis by the simple fact that there are no public data on their performance. Second, as table 6.5 shows, the negative sign of SHARES remains even when the analysis is restricted to divisionalized corporations. A more plausible argument returns to the question, raised in chapter 2, of whether share ownership encourages productivity, because it is a sign of commitment, or tends to be associated with low productivity because it reflects attempts by unsuccessful firms to turn themselves round. The present evidence is consistent with the latter interpretation: it may be that encouraging managers to own shares is part of a policy of establishing a sense of purpose but that the policy has yet to produce its expected advantages. This is, of course, only an interpretation. But the results show fairly convincingly that the effects of share ownership run in the opposite direction to what would be expected.

The most notable result, in the sense of being robust across several models and of having important substantive implications, is that high levels of productivity were associated with a moderate amount of checking of plant performance by the company or, where it existed, by the corporate group. The admittedly weaker results for CRIT, the measure of the factory manager's satisfaction with his treatment by higher levels of management, support this evidence. The practical conclusion for companies is that they may need to look at their methods of internal monitoring and control and, as suggested in chapter 3, at the ways in which they treat their factory managers.

No such clear results emerged for the several measures of labour relations that were employed. At first sight, this inconclusive evidence contradicts the arguments of the ISE writers that the management of people is crucial in corporate success; it also contrasts with the slightly different expectations of the Harvard economists concerning the impact of unionization. The evidence should, however, be seen neither as a refutation of the theories in question nor as showing that labour relations are unimportant. When appropriately developed, neither set of arguments should lead to the expectation that measures of industrial relations institutions will have a clear or consistent relationship with productivity.

The Harvard model, as stated, does contain such an expectation: having a union will tend to increase productivity. But there are at least two conceptual problems which are increasingly being recognized in the Harvard work: unionization is taken as having indirect effects on management organization, so that it is not the having of a union which is itself important; and the strength, and even the direction, of the union effect will vary. A further factor relating to the context in which the model is employed also has to be borne in mind. In the home of the model, the United States, whether or not a firm is unionized is often a very significant characteristic: an employer who recognizes a union is subject to numerous requirements about the way in which bargaining is carried out, and a union contract tends to be a long and detailed document specifying managerial rights and obligations. The possibility that unionization has a 'shock' effect is clear. In Britain, union recognition in manufacturing is more widespread than it is in American manufacturing industry, and unionization tends to have less fateful consequences. In the particular context of Britain the Harvard effect may be weaker than it is in the United States. But even in the latter country it is very unlikely that unionization always and everywhere encourages productivity. Much will depend on the nature of the industry, the character of the union, and the extent of union power on the shopfloor. To point out that unions can be associated with productivity gains is one thing. To suggest that all unions are the same or that their presence always has this desirable result is quite another.

The logical development of the Harvard approach is thus to try to identify the conditions under which unionization has a particular sort of effect. In addition to opening up the 'black box' of the production process it would be necessary to look inside the other box, namely trade union behaviour, that the Harvard economists show little interest in opening. That is, what do unions actually do at shopfloor level, and what implications does their behaviour have for productivity? The Harvard school is more interested in establishing a formal model of production than in assessing the day-to-day conduct of labour relations. As soon as the question is posed, it is apparent that a 'union effect' is neither simple nor one-dimensional. In some aspects of its operations a shopfloor organization can hinder management, for example by insisting on a particular level of manning. In others, it may assist management, a familiar example being the self-discipline exercised by some powerful work groups in parts of the engineering industry; in addition to the direct benefits of needing few supervisors, there were the indirect benefits for management of achieving the workers' compliance with production needs, a compliance that might well have been absent if more direct forms of managerial authority were to be imposed.

A union effect is, moreover, not independent of managerial behaviour or other aspects of the firm's situation. A shopfloor organization interacts with management in a particular context, and the effects of its behaviour have to be teased out by examining how it fits into the overall picture and not by assuming that its presence has discrete and independent effects. Thus the basic point made by the Harvard scholars, namely that unionization can, as against common-sense expectations, contribute to productivity, is of profound importance, but it does not lead to the expectation that there is a general and invariate relationship between the presence of a union and productivity. The inconclusive results from the present analysis, relating as they do to manufacturing industry as a whole, should not come as a surprise.

A similar point applies to the ISE model of people orientation. An institution such as a joint consultation committee can be associated with efforts to improve productivity, but an overall correlation between presence of a committee and productivity should not be expected. In warning against paying lip service to people management, Peters and Waterman underline this point. In view of this, and of their broader stress on cultures within companies, it may be asked whether applying quantitative techniques to their ideas is valid: if a corporate culture consists of strongly interlocking elements, one should surely not expect discrete features to operate independently, as a regression model requires. There is some truth in this, but the value of a cross-sectional analysis should not be neglected. It is useful to establish which variables operate across manufacturing plants as a whole, thus having general application, and which depend on corporate cultures for their effects. It is, more generally, helpful to try to develop precise tests of the rather vague ideas contained in the ISE literature. Thus if none of the variables tested had a significant link with productivity, it might be possible to conclude that the exercise has been a waste of time. In fact, some surprising results emerged. The inverse link between share ownership and productivity was not expected, and its existence has obvious policy implications.

The connections between company monitoring and productivity were expected. But it is none the less significant that they apply generally. That is, their effects are not dependent on corporate cultures of loose–tight properties but seem to exist across all firms, the great majority of which cannot, by definition, be 'successful'. It was also shown that, although general, the effects interacted with the capital intensity of firms. This again is an important result, demonstrating that ISE expectations can be extended through appropriate quantitative testing. In particular, the gains of a given type of monitoring seem to depend on being highly capital-intensive and do not exist independently. This result supports the observation made by Child (1984: 216) that the 'excellent' firms were in high technology sectors and that lessons relevant to them may not be more generally applicable.

The ISE model has two distinct emphases. One is the crucial importance of a total culture and the interconnected nature of the determinants of success. The other is that 'excellence' is possible for any firm. The present results speak to both the 'particularistic' arguments of the former and the 'universalistic' claims of the latter. The impact of monitoring is general, and not tied up with a whole culture. But it operates only in capital-intensive firms, suggesting that the lessons of 'excellence' apply differently in different types of firm.

Before turning to some wider conclusions, the argument that aspects of labour relations and company organization need have no direct effect on productivity may be related to some findings of previous chapters. It was shown in chapter 3 that managers with headquarters experience tended to put a high value on industrial relations matters in their decision-making. In chapter 4, this emphasis on the importance of labour matters was seen to be linked to the extent of company monitoring of plant performance. It has now been demonstrated that monitoring affected productivity. Although there was no direct association between approaches to labour relations and productivity, an indirect connection is evident in these patterns. There may be a culture comprising moderate company monitoring, a strategic view of the development of factory managers by giving them experience in other roles, and a concern for labour management that promotes productivity. This is no more than a possibility, and the data point only to a tendency for this kind of effect to exist and not a clear-cut model for 'success'. But it reflects some significant correlations within the survey data, and these 'objective' indications support the general argument that labour relations have effects on productivity, even though those effects may be hard to measure using conventional statistical techniques.

Two wider conclusions need brief comment. First, in everyday discussion as well as in the ISE literature, there is the implication that raising productivity will guarantee sucess and be in the interests of everyone in a firm. But the costs as well as the gains must be borne in mind: costs not only of job losses but also of the re-organization and possible intensification of work. Productivity as measured relates output to the number of workers employed. It does not indicate how hard workers are having to work. Productivity, however, does not guarantee commercial viability. The recent experience of Austin–Rover, formerly BL, illustrates this very sharply. There has been a widely heralded productivity miracle in the firm, and on some accounts output per worker is now as good as that in the leading European firms. But market share has continued to fall, reflecting intense competition from other firms and also commercial and marketing problems within the company itself.

Second, 'success' is a value-laden word. Even stripped of its overtones of moral superiority to mean merely achieving high profits, it can imply that firms denoted as 'successful' can and should be emulated by others. Yet success is by definition relative, and along with the winners there must be losers. The 'people management' methods of Peters and Waterman's firms, and of similar British firms, have, moreover, depended on histories of no redundancies, generous wages and conditions, and trust between managers and workers. In many cases they operate in sectors of the market where steady growth has permitted a high degree of job security and where profitability has allowed the substantial investment, in terms of training and managerial resources as well as in wage rates, in labour relations required by sophisticated personnel policies. IBM is an obvious example. In other cases, some personnel problems are externalized. Thus it is well known that one of Goldsmith and Clutterbuck's (1984) firms, Marks and Spencer, imposes very strict quality standards on its suppliers. Many of these firms operate in very competitive markets and cannot afford the costs of sophisticated personnel management methods. The benefits of a 'people orientation' may not be available to their workers.

This is not to criticize 'successful' firms but merely to point out that writers who laud their achievements can easily forget that these rest on particular conditions. Job security in these firms has to be set against the substantial and increasing insecurity in other parts of the economy. A competitive capitalist economy generates jobs with poor wages and little security. Workers in such jobs are unlikely, to say the least, to be offered the personnel management methods applied in the more 'successful' parts of the economy.

This chapter has looked at one of the key outcomes, productivity, associated with the patterns analysed in previous chapters. It remains to consider the implications of the analysis as a whole. This is the task of the final chapter.

Notes

1. A key weakness is the lack of hard data on sales, value-added, and capital employed at the level of the plant. It was decided not to seek such information because respondents might refuse co-operation and because the survey had several other aims which prevented detailed questioning on this one. The costs were felt to outweigh the possible benefits. It is worth noting that the most substantial comparison of productivity differences between plants (Ball and Skeoch, 1981) drew on data that firms were legally required to provide; it has the problem of excluding many of the variables, such as policy on labour relations, of interest here.

2. One obvious problem is the extent to which it is possible to control for non-managerial influences on productivity such as the amount of capital employed per worker. The ISE studies try to deal with this by comparing broadly similar firms, but methodological purists would question the extent to which adequate controls are included. More generally, there is an uncritical, indeed often laudatory, approach to the 'excellent' firms. One of these is IBM. As Cowling (1982: 21) notes, there is evidence that this firm has held back technical innovation to protect its dominant position in the market. Such use of monopoly power to attain success is skirted around by ISE writers.

3. This is because there are no data at the level of the individual firm that permit the value of bought-in components to be subtracted from total sales. It should also be noted that the dependent variables of turnover and profitability relate to 1982, while growth is measured over the period 1978–82. It might, on the first two, be desirable to use an average of a number of years. But this would take the dependent variable even further

away from the time of the survey, and it is doubtful whether the relative position of companies fluctuates much from one year to another.

4. Data relate to 1979. This year was chosen because the information is classified according to the 1968 SIC, which is the basis used by the fieldwork agency that carried out both the present and the Warwick Survey. The data are reported in 'Business Monitor, PA 1002, Report on the Census of Production, 1979', table 14 (HMSO). In the absence of evidence of substantial changes in the position of industries on the relevant measures between 1979 and 1984, the data are perfectly usable for present purposes.

5. Of particular interest here is the discretion allowed to subsidiary plants. If cases where a firm had at least six plants in the sample are taken as providing enough numbers from each firm for useful analysis, a total of 155 subsidiary plants emerges. The degree of discretion was recorded in four categories. The number of replies falling into the same cell in each company was recorded and this number summed across all firms. The proportion of identical replies ranged between 46 per cent (on redundancies and junior management pay) and 68 per cent (on dismissals). The proportion of replies falling into two adjacent categories ran from 74 per cent (redundancies) to 92 per cent (training policy). There is plainly a degree of variation here which might repay further study. But the general consistency of the replies was quite high.

6. Two further efforts in the present survey were: to use a manager's assessment of his plant's performance relative to the company average (Q. 145) to introduce an arbitrary correction factor in the recorded figure of turnover per head; and to employ data at the level of the operating company or division, in cases where it was clear that a plant belonged to a specific sub-unit of a firm. Neither effort produced results different from the simpler analysis reported below, and the data will not be discussed further. Their value is, however, to strengthen the claim that plant-level measures can be reasonable proxies for company-level variables.

7. These questions rely on respondents' assessments. How reliable are they? One indication is the link between respondents' reports and company data: for the 64 plants for which profit data were available at the level of the division, there was a strong tendency for reports of how the plant was doing to be related to recorded profits. There were also some associations between the replies, for example between wage costs per unit and total production costs, suggesting that respondents were giving internally consistent sets of replies.

8. It might be suggested that this result is of limited value: if, as seems likely, non-unionism is concentrated among the small, independent firms and if, moreover, these firms tend to have high productivity, it will be picking up not a union effect but a 'firm type' effect. In fact, there was no very strong tendency for a lack of unionization to be associated with single, independent establishments: 19 per cent of them had no recognized union, as against an average of 11 per cent, while, 12 per cent (compared with average of 17 per cent) reported full-time shop stewards. And such plants did not have levels of productivity different from the average.

9. Toner (1985) has recently provided some evidence that supports this view. He examined workers' opinions in four unionized and three non-union

firms. As against the Harvard expectation that unionized workers will display high morale, a low proneness to leave and so on, he found that the non-union workers had the higher morale and more opportunity to 'voice' their opinions. He explained this as the result of the stress on personnel management in some types of non-union firm, concluding that the neglect of such firms is a serious gap in the Harvard treatment.

10. It may be, of course, that factory managers tend to underestimate the true extent of monitoring. But this will not matter as long as the tendency to do so is constant: the ordering of companies across categories will be correct.

11. Some other indices of organization, such as the presence of a full-time shop steward, were included in preliminary work, but they failed to come close to statistical significance and the results including them are not reported here. Other measures, most obviously experience of industrial action, were also found to have no link with productivity.

12. The main statistical reasons are to reduce the dispersion of highly skewed distributions, and also to allow for non-linear effects. The theoretical one is that the relationship between output, Q, and input of capital, K, and labour, L, is usually given in the form $Q = ak^bL^c$, which implies an additive relationship of the form $\log Q = \log a + b (\log k) + c (\log L)$.

13. Divisionalized firms are those where one or more intermediate levels between the plant and the head office were identified by the plant manager.

14. Consider a hypothetical case in which yes/no replies to an attitude question were tabulated by sex (M or F) and race (black, B, or white, W). A complete table might be as shown. A tabulation of answers by either sex or race would show no association (50 cases in each cell). Yet there plainly is a pattern of association with black men differing from black women and from white men.

| | B | | W | |
	M	F	M	F
Y	40	10	10	40
N	10	40	40	10

7

Conclusions and Implications

The foregoing pages have described the rationale of the survey and analysed the main results. The concluding section of each of the four previous chapters has also considered some of the implications of the findings discussed in the body of the chapter. The details of these considerations will not be repeated here. The present aim is to relate the survey's findings to current trends in the management of the factory and to draw out some of the implications for future research and for practice.

Emergent Trends

The survey is part of a growing body of evidence that managements in large manufacturing firms have been making considerable efforts to improve labour productivity by introducing new equipment, increasing flexibility, communicating to workers the need to accept change, and creating a sense of loyalty and commitment. Publications such as the *Financial Times* and *Industrial Relations Review and Report* have carried numerous accounts of firms that have broken down job demarcations, introduced new and simplified grading structures, and otherwise tried to increase labour flexibility.[1]

Batstone and Gourlay (1986: 111–20) have recently questioned the extent of individualistic employment strategies. Their information comes from surveys of shop stewards, which makes it difficult for them to assess managerial motivations, but the broad facts, notably the slow spread of specific techniques such as quality circles and briefing groups, that they identify are impressive. The question, though, is whether this or that concrete device reflects the rationale of managerial policy: a firm need have made no change in its institutional arrangements whilst altering its ways of doing things. The fact that issues are still negotiated with shop stewards, for example, says little about the context or content of negotiation. The authors are certainly correct that wholesale attacks on workplace union organization have been rare. And their evidence on the limited and piecemeal nature of managerial changes is consistent with the argument sketched below that there has not been a well-developed and coherent plan to create a whole new system of labour relations. But they seem to underplay the extent of recent developments.

Before looking at these developments in detail, they need to be placed in context. As argued in chapter 5, they may apply to only a particular part of the economy, namely the relatively prosperous, large-firm, manufacturing sector. In other areas, efforts to increase productivity may be in evidence, but they are not necessarily based on ideas of involvement and participation. Flexibility may be the aim, but it can involve coercive measures as well as engendering a sense of co-operation. In large parts of the public sector and in the service sector managements do not appear to have made worker commitment a major priority.

The other key aspect of the context of change is, of course, the recession. Although its precise effects are hard to identify, it plainly put acute pressures on many firms, which often led to redundancies and to re-organizations of the remaining work force. But how long-lasting are the associated changes likely to be? It was thought at one time that as unemployment fell bargaining power would shift back to the shop floor (for example, Brown and Nolan, 1981). It is now plain that this was too simple a view: some plants with powerful shop steward organizations have disappeared, and changes that have occurred in others cannot be reversed. This is not the same as saying that shopfloor power has been wiped out. Permanent changes have certainly been made, but the problem of maintaining a high level of commitment remains.[2] It may even have increased, as firms rely more and more heavily on the willing co-operation of their workers, instead of seeking only a minimal agreement to carrying out some limited and precisely defined tasks. The recession's effects have been neither merely temporary nor so profound as totally to establish managerial power. Old problems remain, but they appear in new forms.

Respondents' Views of the Future
In assessing future developments, it is useful to know what respondents thought. They were asked (at Q. 152) what they saw as the key issues facing management in their plant over the next three years. Their replies have been classified in table 7.1. As would be expected, matters

TABLE 7.1
Future Issues for Management

	% of:	
	All Mentions	Respondents Mentioning
Internal and general management issues		
Secure new business	15	24
Increase efficiency	14	21
Introduce new technology	13	20
Introduce new products/processes	8	12
Control costs	10	15
Use capital for new investments	7	10
Secure sufficient investment funds	3	4
Managerial re-organization and training	4	6
Maintain quality	3	5
Maintain growth and profitability	5	8
External issues		
Adequate level of market demand	5	7
Conditions of supply of raw materials	2	3
Other external pressures	1	2
Labour management issues		
Maintain good industrial relations	4	6
Deal with trade union problems, cut wages	3	5
Rationalize wage systems, recruit new labour	2	3
Other issues	1	1
	100	

Base: Respondents identifying future problems or issues (*N* = 226).

to do with the general management of the plant, and not those relating either to external pressures or to specifically labour relations problems, received most attention. Only 12 per cent of managers mentioned external issues, of which the most important was whether demand for the firm's products would run at an acceptable level. Fourteen per cent mentioned labour issues, and there was considerable diversity here, with some respondents stressing the need to reduce wage costs and continue to deal with union problems, while others saw their main task as being to consolidate improvements that had already been made, with yet others feeling that there were new problems, notably a shortage of skilled labour, to be faced.

None of these replies was, however, as common as answers stressing general business needs. Of these, the single most common reply was that securing new business was the main priority. But more answers covered a range of issues concerned with the improvement of the performance of the plant: producing goods as distinct from selling them. The precise focus differed. For some managers it was the successful introduction of new technology or new manufacturing processes while for others it was the need to control costs. But the need to keep up the pressure for change and to reduce unit costs was one theme that repeatedly emerged. Indeed 15 per cent of respondents specifically mentioned controlling costs, and this often meant not just a general desire to be efficient but specific innovations in cost control. Cost consciousness was widespread. Similarly, the desire to increase efficiency was often reflected in specific innovations that were desired or planned.

Some of the respondents' replies indicate the position very clearly. A few managers felt that there were specific problems in the labour area still to be overcome. As would be expected, these problems were most common in the printing industry. One manager here saw the main issue as the:

reduction of manning levels on machinery, which are currently [made] artificially high by trade unions (178; PPP; 390 employees).

But such difficulties were not peculiar to this industry. Another manager included among his list of aims the need to:

improve labour productivity by more efficient manning. Removal of restrictive practices and control of overtime, together with technical improvements (212; FDT; 400 employees).

But more common than a need to deal with remaining problems on the labour front was a sense that achievements had been made and that it was both necessary and possible to consolidate them. Illustrative lists of aim included:

further improvements in productivity; investment in latest technologies ...; big improvements in quality standards needed; further develop consultative arrangements with unions (086; el. eng.; 2,100 employees);

improve productivity by persuading the trade unions to increase flexibility between grades and groups of workers, breaking down tradition ... single status between production and craft unions (135; metal mfg.; 2,000 employees);

investment in more efficient plant and obtaining full support of the labour force and [its] recognition of the need to be productive to stay in business (146; chems; 370 employees);

obtaining approval for wide-ranging capital investment to enable the recently made working practice to be translated into much higher levels of added value per employee (180; PPP; 520 employees).

Characteristic is the linking of labour matters to the introduction of new technologies or new products. Having an involved and flexible work force is of limited value if the latest technologies cannot be used to attain high levels of productivity; and the technology is unlikely to make an adequate return without the appropriate attitudes on the shopfloor. Also notable, as in the third quotation, is the stress on maintaining the workers' acceptance of high productivity as necessary to the survival of the business.

Most managers did not, however, make explicit mention of labour matters. Improving productivity and developing new products were key themes, and it was almost taken for granted that labour relations difficulties would not stand in the way. Of particular interest is the frequency with which new methods of cost control and quality control were mentioned, sometimes together with developments in new products:

increasing efficiency [on] current products: new product development; modern methods of quality control (038; PPP: 300 employees);

increasing productivity; tight control of fixed costs; increasing flexibility of manufacture to cope with changing market conditions; more new products (064; chems; 380 employees).

Significant here is the stress on flexibility, not just in the sense of reducing demarcations and increasing the range of tasks performed by any one worker, but also in terms of the operation of the factory as a whole: the whole system of manufacture must be flexible in order to respond rapidly to changing market demand and to the introduction of new products. It is not just a matter of having workers work on more tasks within the same old manufacturing system but of linking their flexibility to that of the hardware.

Flexibility and Involvement in Labour Relations
'Flexibility' is very much in fashion, both as a managerial objective and as a concept for identifying emergent tendencies. It is widely argued that firms are breaking down rigid job classifications and reforming their payment systems in order to release the skills of the work force. A related development is seen as the growth of sub-contracting and

the employment of temporary and casual workers: there is a widening gap between the core workers with reasonable wages and job security and the peripheral workers, with lower wages and who are hired and fired as market demand fluctuates (Thomas, 1985). The present survey was not designed to assess such arguments; it did not, for example, ask about the employment of temporary workers or go into the details of job re-grading. A few general observations may, however, be made before the links between the present findings and the debate about the future of industrial relations are addressed.

It is doubtful whether many employers have a fully developed employment strategy based on core and peripheral work forces. Thus a report by the Institute of Manpower Studies to the National Economic Development Council (NEDO), based on investigations of 72 firms, noted that few employers seemed to make a clear distinction between core and peripheral workers (*Industrial Relations Review and Report*, no. 359, January 1986, p. 14). It may also be asked how novel is the division between groups of employees in term of wages and conditions and security of employment: labour markets have for many years been split into differing elements. What might be newer is the differentiation of employees within firms. In the past, many of the divisions in the labour market were external to the firm, such that, for example, skilled male workers and semi-skilled female workers were in quite distinct situations. A change may be taking place if firms are no longer operating within such external markets and are instead dividing up their work forces as their own operating conditions dictate. But it follows from this argument that there cannot, by definition, be any one trend towards flexibility in anything other than the most general sense, for if firms are developing internal company-specific arrangements these will depend on product market circumstances, existing structures of labour relations, and managerial preferences that are peculiar to each firm.

The present findings should not, then, be seen as necessarily endorsing the stronger forms of the 'core and periphery' thesis. They are, however, consistent with some broader arguments that are common to it and some other interpretations. They suggest, in particular, that managements have increasingly been stressing the need to have employees involved in the aims of the enterprise. Underlying this, of course, is a clear statement of what those aims are and of the duty of management to try to attain them: 'involvement' means not co-determination but a willing endorsement by workers of the policies of the firm as these are defined by management. As argued in chapter 5, such developments are unlikely to be universal; it was suggested that management policy in large parts of the public sector and of the private service sector may have a much less participative character. In addition, within the large-firm manufacturing sector, a similarity of approach

may well lead to differences in practice because of differing circumstances. That is, respondents in the survey had a common concern to
increase the commitment of workers as individuals and to ensure that
change was accepted. But the precise ways in which they acted are
likely to have reflected past traditions and current conditions. Although
the climate is different from that of relatively relaxed negotiations,
there has not been a total destruction of existing procedures, as illus-
trated most clearly by the absence of any sustained attack on shop
steward organizations. The procedures are, it may be argued, being
altered but not destroyed, with the result that there will be important
elements of continuity with the past. The 'new industrial relations'
cannot be reduced to one model of managerial strategy that is applied
in all circumstances.

'Involvement', then, is a theme which may have several variations
and modifications. Some limitations in its progress are also evident, of
which two may be mentioned here. The future of market demand is
variable. As shown in chapter 2, reductions in demand over the previous
two years had occurred quite widely. Evans *et al.* (1985: 13) report
a similar picture in their study of 81 firms, of widely differing sizes,
carried out during 1983 and 1984. The involvement needs of firms with
growing markets may differ from those facing continuing declines and
redundancies. Some sense of this emerged in answers to the question
about the issues facing management in the next three years, with some
managers focusing on new products while others mentioned rationalizations and further labour shedding. The difference is revealed sharply
by two similarly sized establishments in the food, drink, and tobacco
industry, the respondent in one of which saw growing demand as the
main issue while the manager in the other cited falling demand. This
is not, it must be emphasized, to suggest that involvement is important
in one case and not the other; it is, instead, to argue that it may be
equally necessary but may take different forms.

The second limitation concerns the extent to which firms have radically altered workers' basic attitudes and assumptions. As argued in
chapter 5, questions must be raised about the two conditions necessary
for such an alteration to have been effected: that managements have
developed coherent and detailed programmes for employee involvement, and that workers have endorsed the aims of these. It was also
suggested that the emergence of new forms of motivation and control
in the recession made it highly likely that these were, to a greater or
lesser extent, responses to immediate crises and not well-developed
plans. Respondents to the NEDO survey, cited above, doubted whether
there had been a permanent shift in employee attitudes, and felt that
declining unemployment might lead to renewed problems. It should
not be inferred that these will be the same problems as those facing

firms in the 1970s for, as noted above, a great deal has changed. But the extent to which new forms of managerial authority have been established is likely to be variable and uncertain.

An editorial in the *Financial Times* (14 November 1985) makes some interestingly similar points. It asks how far flexibility agreements and managerial attempts to regain control have really progressed in the core areas of manufacturing. It also notes that 'union obstructiveness, even where present, is not an alibi any longer'. Management has to bear the responsibility directly, and can no longer shift the blame to alleged union power. It may be that 'too few companies have instituted genuine systems for involving, informing and motivating their workforces'. As argued above, managements have made significant changes in their labour relations arrangements, but questions remain as to how widespread and fundamental these have been: involvement is the watchword, and old-fashioned negotiation is disliked, but how thoroughly has a new system of managerial authority been implanted?

A final issue concerns the overall shape of the emerging system of industrial relations. In the short term, managements may be successful in establishing acceptance of their newly asserted authority. In the longer term new sources of challenge may emerge. Apart from a general tendency for workers to find ways of making the system acceptable to themselves, the system itself may encourage new demands. If workers are told that they are a key part of the enterprise, they may take this rhetoric seriously and start to demand a say in decision-making. The problems of shopfloor consent have not disappeared, and cannot do so, for in any system of work organization issues of motivation and control arise: total managerial control is impossible.

Analysts' attitudes to these trends also need comment. It is very easy to discuss 'involvement' and 'flexibility' as though they are either inevitable or desirable, or both. Analysts can easily slip into a quasi-managerialist endorsement of existing tendencies. An effort has been made here to stress the autocratic aspects of involvement, together with the clear limits that management put on it. This is not the place to speculate on alternative lines of development or the desirability of different policies. But the dangers of adopting an uncritical perspective are considerable. It is not just a matter of pointing out that coherent policies of involvement seem to be limited, as though more of them would be the answer. It is also necessary to underline the ways in which genuine freedoms for workers are being eroded. 'Skills' in the sense of technical abilities may remain, and quality circles may be valued. But the aim of firms is to tie workers to their own ends and to persuade them to work to policies laid down from above. It may be true that this is 'inevitable', and it is certainly true that it has some benefits for workers. But the re-imposition of managerial authority through participative means is also a managerially initiated strategy aimed at the better control of workers' behaviour. This should not be forgotten.

Decentralization
Labour relations have been the main focus in discussing change, for it is in this area that many of the most significant developments have taken place. These developments are also rather more public and readily discussed than are changes in, say, firms' systems of management appraisal. There is, however, one other set of changes that have implications for areas covered by the survey. These are trends towards the decentralization of operations.

There is some debate as to how common decentralization is, and how thorough-going it is in those firms that have adopted it. But it does not appear that there is any significant shift in the opposite direction. There is, if anything, a move by firms to reduce centralized direction. Indicative developments are the introduction of 'mini-factories', wherein a section of a plant is made autonomous from the rest of the establishment and is a profit centre, and the growth of flexible manufacturing systems, which permit firms to alter production runs rapidly in response to changing market demand.

Some observers see such changes as heralding a new form of industrialism, in which mass production by huge corporations is replaced by smaller-scale enterprises (for example, Piore and Sabel, 1984; for criticism, see Hyman, 1986). Although this is not the place to discuss such arguments, it is worth noting that they are not necessarily endorsed here and that they are quite distinct from more limited interpretations of decentralization. It is too early to say whether the system of mass production and huge firms is in terminal decline. And it is important to distinguish between a technical system of production and the way in which the system is controlled by units of capital. Flexible and small-scale operations can be co-ordinated by massive corporations, and co-ordination and control are facilitated by other technical advances in the areas of data collection and information transfer. Large firms are not necessarily on the decline, and the present concern is changes within them.

To the extent that the current drift is in favour of decentralization, the role of the factory manager will grow. Decisions will be left more in the hand of these managers, although the outcomes of these decisions may be monitored higher in the organization. In this event, the issues of corporate decision-making and the company monitoring of plant performance discussed in chapter 4 will assume increasing importance. It will become more important to firms that they develop appropriate systems of monitoring and control and that they achieve a balance between central direction and local discretion. One of the themes of chapter 6, namely the association between moderate levels of company monitoring and productivity, may also become more important. If the balance between centralization and decentralization becomes more critical as firms try to exploit the benefits of flexible manufacturing systems, then the influence of this balance on overall productivity may also rise. In technical terms, the size of the coefficient of the monitoring variable in an equation predicting productivity will increase.

The personal role of factory managers may also grow. For researchers, the conclusion would then be that the kind of analysis carried out in chapter 3 of factory managers' careers and attitudes should be developed and refined. For companies, systems to recruit, develop, and reward these managers, together with means of integrating them into the management of enterprise as a whole, will become more salient.

In short, if the fashion for increasing flexibility and local autonomy has any permanence, the importance of many of the issues discussed in this study will increase. Factory managers, far from becoming mere functionaries carrying out orders from above, will have new responsibilities and new opportunities to develop their plants. This does not mean that they are likely to have total freedom to do as they like. Indeed, the pressure to produce results is likely to grow. The responsibilities of achieving continued success are as important in shaping the working lives of factory managers as are the opportunities to take their own decisions. This developing role for factory managers carries some important implications for companies, as suggested below.

Implications for Research and Practice

Research

Previous chapters have mentioned several areas that need further elucidation. Some of the key areas may be briefly indicated. But methodology is as important as specific substantive areas; it is not just a matter of saying that information is needed in certain fields but also of indicating what kind of information is required and what sorts of research are likely to produce useful results.

One key area, mentioned in chapter 4, is managerial decision-making: what are the systems of power and influence within firms, how are factory managers monitored and controlled, who is involved in making decisions about new investment or a pay award, and so on? Surveys such as the present one and that of senior company-level managers carried out by Hill and Pickering (1986) can indicate some of the overall patterns in terms of levels of decision-making. But more detailed qualitative work is also needed to explore the actual processes involved. What does it mean to say, for example, that factory managers tend to take the final decision on pay awards for manual workers? What kinds of constraint are imposed on the decision from elsewhere in an organization, who else is involved in the decision, and how are possible disagreements resolved? To raise these questions is not to imply that factory managers are powerless or that they simply operate within constraints imposed from above, for they may be able to avoid or amend these constraints, arguing perhaps that they need to alter the structure of their pay systems in order to accommodate more flexible methods of working and that they must have the authority to fit pay awards to local needs. But more needs to be known about the processes involved, and plainly case-study work is needed to develop the picture derived from surveys.

A related area is the work experience of factory managers and similar groups of employees. Types of managerial career, systems of training and development, and roles performed within management all warrant closer investigation than has been possible here. An appropriate method would be to analyse factory managers and other general managers within different types of firm. It has been shown above, for example, that factory managers saw labour relations matters as very important and reported a high degree of personal involvement in decisions on these matters. Such a broad picture requires elaboration and development, and this can be provided through detailed analysis within individual firms.[3]

A third issue for study is productivity, and in particular the influence on it of the social relations of production. As discussed in chapter 6, managers, consultants, and academic researchers have been increasingly interested in these human factors in productivity, that is, in such things as the different levels of productivity that can be observed in firms with very similar technical systems of production. Two related lines of inquiry suggest themselves. As explained in chapter 1, the present survey was not focused specifically on productivity, and the questions relating to it were necessarily general in character. Future surveys could try to develop more adequate measures of plant-level productivity. Establishments already have to make returns for various official statistics and there is in principle no reason why private researchers should not seek these data on sales, the value of bought-in components, and capital employed to develop quantitative indices of productivity. These indices could then be related to evidence obtained by interviews on managerial organization, labour relations arrangements, and so forth. Detailed work would be required on defining and measuring the independent as well as the dependent variables, but the outlines of what is needed seem reasonably clear.

A second approach is more qualitative. As argued in chapter 6, a major recent approach relating trade union behaviour to productivity, that of the Harvard school of economists, has run into difficulty. Its view that unions can contribute to productivity is an important reversal of conventional views, and the difficulty lies not in the theoretical approach but in the way in which it is tested. To treat unionization as a phenomenon which is universal in its effects and unrelated to other aspects of firms' behaviour is unsatisfactory. It should not come as a surprise to find that measures of unionization were not related to productivity in the present sample. As also argued in chapter 6, however, this does not mean that labour relations are unimportant. But their effects are more complex and subtle than can be revealed through regression techniques. One valuable service performed by these techniques is the demonstration of which influences have a universal effect on productivity and which do not. Common-sense expectations might be that unions interfere with productivity while having personnel policies based on 'involvement' stimulates it. The evidence is that such effects do not operate: there is no general tendency across firms as a whole in line with them, although each could be true in specific circumstances.

The implication for methodology is that, in moving beyond this form of analysis, methods are needed which can capture the multi-faceted nature of labour relations and draw out the connections with productivity. This implies some case-study form of investigation, although one that is rigorous in its efforts to link processes to concrete outcomes. Comparisons between high and low productivity firms in the same industry and historical investigations of long-term processes of change appear to be among the most promising lines of inquiry.

One other research-related issue may be mentioned. It was argued in chapter 1 that there are good reasons to link analysis of changes in labour relations to more specifically management-oriented issues. When defined broadly labour relations includes not just the institutions of collective bargaining but all the ways in which firms recruit, reward, control, and motivate their employees. These issues spill over into the area of general management and cannot be confined within the personnel department. A parallel argument was that, in looking at factory managers, there were good reasons not to assess their position in society as a whole but to concentrate on the employment relations aspects of their position: their relations with their superiors and subordinates. It was also suggested that it remains valid to conduct analysis at the level of the individual factory. If this programme is convincing, the implication is that traditional barriers between industrial relations, management studies, and organizational behaviour may be less and less apppropriate, as research comes to connect things hitherto seen as separate.

Practice

The survey did not set out to provide direct lessons to practitioners of industrial relations, and it would have been presumptuous to have done so. Instead, it identifies some issues and trends that practitioners will need to consider: providing information and comment that may form the basis of decision-making but without offering specific lessons. The previous section discussed some emergent trends in the management of labour. How these relate to firms' and trade unions' policies may now be addressed.

A major issue for management is how to build on schemes for involvement. It is one thing to communicate the bad news in the hope that workers will accept plans for change, and another to announce increasing profits. How genuine and thorough-going is a policy of involvement to be, and how does it fit in with other business aims? There may be benefits but there will also be costs. These will not only include direct costs but such indirect ones as the need to improve training at many levels of the organization, possible heightened expectations of further involvement that might be created, and possible resentment among managerial staff who may feel that shopfloor workers are being treated with more consideration than they themselves are. How would a significant rise in production affect the firm's ability to absorb it? If, for example, there are no developed plans to capture available markets, more production could be an embarrassment. It could even be a positive disadvantage if workers had to be told that, after all their efforts to work harder, they were going to be laid off. This has happened in some firms, and it plainly makes talk of involvement sound rather hollow. (It also raises questions about the more glib prognostications that industrial relations are being 'Japanized'. Of course, no one suggests any more that all Japan's workers enjoy lifetime employment, for the evidence is that this is the privilege of a minority. What is really being talked about is the division between core and peripheral workers. But for those Japanese workers with life-time employment there is a substantial expectation of continued security. This does not seem to have been established in Britain: even core workers' rights to continue employment are, in most firms, limited and conditional.)[4]

Some more specific labour issues also arise. Schemes for joint consultation appear to be popular at present. Yet there is also evidence that such schemes decay as well as grow and that their impact can be rather limited (MacInnes, 1985). What does management want of them, and is managerial commitment to them more substantial than it would appear to have been in the past? And what of traditional collective bargaining? To the extent that management seeks a largely non-negotiatory approach to labour relations, it will have to devise means to handle the issues formerly settled by bargaining. Alternatively, if bargaining retains a role, what is the desired level and scope of bargaining? Managements that are seriously concerned to re-structure their labour relations will have to address such questions. Since these issues also affect unions, it will be convenient to address the implications for unions before looking at some of the wider managerial issues arising from the survey.

This survey, together with some others (for example, Mackay, 1986), has suggested that union organization in the factory is in danger of being by-passed, with firms going direct to the shopfloor and with compliance being sought not by negotiating agreements but by involving workers directly in the aims of the firm. The position for unions is thus more secure than might have been expected a few years ago, when predictions of a managerial onslaught on the basis of union organization were commonplace. But the question remains of what role union workplace organizations are to play. Some observers (for example, Brown, 1983) foresee the growth of 'enterprise unionism', wherein workers are increasingly dependent on particular firms as skills become firm-specific and as internal labour markets with few ports of entry develop; the union movement is then seen as adopting a similar focus, with national and even industrial solidarity being weakened. As with arguments about the core and periphery, one may ask how new such a development is, for the rise of shop steward organizations during the 1960s is generally seen as something independent of, and often in opposition to, national organizations. The depth of feelings of solidarity should also not be overlooked; as the national engineering strike of 1979 showed, workers could be mobilized behind a national dispute even when they stood to gain little directly from it and even though local leaders were sometimes sceptical about the tactics being employed at national level (see Edwards and Scullion, 1982a).

Much will depend on how thorough-going managerial reforms turn out to be. A rough distinction may be made between firms where work re-organization is wide-ranging in scope, such that workers' traditional bargaining leverage is greatly weakened, and those in which only more limited changes have been made, with the opportunity of the recession to introduce new work practices being grasped but without the basic parameters of the effort bargain being shifted. Try (1985) has made such a distinction and has suggested cautiously that it could be applied to the place of the unions of craft workers in Lucas and BL respectively. At Lucas, the traditional power of craft groups, notably toolmakers, has been weakened by new systems of manufacturing. At BL, the direct onslaught on union organization has of course been much stronger, but the organization of work and the ability of workers to influence the effort bargain has been less radically altered. The implication is that union organizafion is more likely to retain a specific role in the latter type of firm than it is in the former.[5]

A distinction also need to be drawn between types of enterprise unionism. Two organizations can be equally enterprise-oriented but can adopt different tactics, based on the different nature of the effort bargain. In one type, workers accept enlightened managerialism, and in particular the fact that traditional ways of bargaining about wages and effort are no longer open. In the other, shopfloor bargaining retains a place. The implications for unions may be less stark than appears at first sight. Batstone's (1984: 274) evidence, that the number of issues about which managements bargain has not declined, should also be borne in mind. Unions retain a place in formal structures. The question is what concrete role this permits them to play. In addition to the danger of being by-passed there are some clear opportunities. To the extent that firms stress consultation and communication, the union can present itself as the natural channel for these processes. And if firms begin to disseminate more information of business plans they may well be giving to the unions something that has often been desired, namely the data on profits and investment plans that have hitherto often been kept out of the bargaining arena. Whether such opportunities are grasped is an open question, and there are substantial problems to be faced. But it should not be concluded that shopfloor unionism has no future. Having said that, it is not enough to point to the resilience of workplace organization in the past, as though this will be sufficient for the future. There are new problems to be faced, and new approaches will be necessary if they are to be overcome.

British unions are far from being dead. It has to be remembered, moreover, that the above comments, like those of several other writers, relate only to the traditional union heartlands and to the workplace level of union activity. Other developments such as efforts to develop a framework of legal rights for all workers would also have to be taken into account in any overall assessment of British unionism. Suffice it to say here that such developments strengthen the argument that unionism as a whole retains considerable vitality, although the problems faced are large.

Turning to the wider implications for management, the first point concerns the role of factory managers. The survey has shown widespread satisfaction about the ways in which they were treated by their firms. But such satisfaction cannot be taken for granted, and in one area, the interchange of personnel between head office and operating units, quite a high level of dissatisfaction was noted. Systems of appraisal and reward and development were also considered, and it was suggested that firms may need to look at these systems: how formal or informal do they want their salary structures to be, how far do they want to treat factory managers as corporate resources and what are the implications for career development, and what types of performance appraisal are appropriate? These questions take on an added importance in those firms adopting a policy of decentralization. As suggested above, such a policy puts the factory manager in an increasingly important position, and training for the role and the package of rewards that goes with it may need some careful attention.

Company managers will need to try to develop a balance between too much monitoring and too little. In this context, one of this study's main findings takes on a particular significance. This is that companies exerting moderate levels of control of their plants tended to be those where productivity levels were the highest. There are, in short, some very specific gains to be made by developing an appropriate form of control which neither stifles initiative nor allows plants to go their own way without any clear control being exercised over their performance. It must also be noted, though, that in the detailed analysis of productivity in chapter 6 it was shown that company monitoring was not independent of the amount of capital employed per head of the work force: the interaction between the two was important in explaining productivity. One important implication is that it may not be sufficient for firms to alter their monitoring arrangements if they want to increase productivity. As against pundits who offer recipes for instant success, it appears that only some types of firms are able to reap the benefits, and it would be a mistake to suppose that there are formulae for success which can be applied automatically to all types of firm.

Attention would also need to be paid to the most appropriate forms of monitoring: just what is a 'moderate' level of monitoring? The present data come, of course, from factory managers, and their views of what is moderate need not coincide with the views of higher company personnel. An obvious first step is to investigate what use, if any, is made of data collected from establishments, and to concentrate on only the important measures. A further step is to involve factory managers in defining what is an appropriate system of control and monitoring. This may appear to imply that such managers should be given control of the procedures used to monitor their own performance. But it would be only the system of monitoring, and not the detailed targets set within it, that would be the subject of discussion. Companies should not, moreover, be frightened of treating their factory managers as responsible members of the managerial team. There is some evidence in the survey that dissatisfied managers tended to be found in the less productive firms. And if firms are keen on ideas of employee involvement it would be sensible to extend the principle to managers as well as shopfloor workers. The evidence of chapter 3 suggests that the factory managers saw themselves as important members of management, and developing appropriate means to build on their commitment may be one of the most effective ways in which firms can deploy and develop their 'human resources'. There are, in short, several aspects of the survey which point to the importance of factory managers and to the need to assess systems for motivating and controlling them.

Several other surveys have focused on 'communication' as a means of raising productivity. One by the Institute of Directors and the Bolton Dickinson communications firm (reported in *Financial Times*, 30 August 1984) found that companies believed communications to have improved productivity and lowered absenteeism. A second, based on 72 executives in 'successful' firms, and published by the CBI, found that decentralization of decision-making and the use of communication to promote a company culture were among the concomitants of success (*Financial Times*, 13 November 1985). The present results suggest the need for caution in assessing such arguments. There is a difference between beliefs that communications are important and hard evidence as to their effect. And they may be difficult to disentangle from other influences. This is not to deny their role. And of course the present cross-sectional data do not bear directly on questions of changes over time in specific firms. But the data permit the issue of the general impact of personnel policy to be raised. It plainly can affect productivity, but as Peters and Waterman (1982) were at pains to point out, it needs to be thorough and determined. The present results also suggest that a firm may need to have a high level of capital intensity before some gains such as decentralization can be realized. The determinants of productivity change, and are complex and interconnected. An implication, although not a direct outcome, of the analysis is that one somewhat neglected feature of the whole picture, namely the integration of factory managers into the firm, may warrant attention.

The survey on which this book is based has looked backwards to previous surveys in order to assess trends in the management of labour and to compare factory managers with other managerial groups. This chapter has looked forward to possible future developments. It has argued that factory managers may have an increasing role to play, both in the formulation and implementation of labour relations policy and in more general managerial matters. Their jobs may warrant close scrutiny from researchers and practitioners alike.

Notes

1. Illustrative case studies of changes in which flexibility was important include the following from *Industrial Relations Review and Report*: Cadbury (no. 328, September 1984); Lyons-Tetley (no. 334, December 1984); Perkins (no. 340, March 1985); Govan Shipbuilders (no. 364, March 1986); and Babcock Power (no. 367, May 1986). As discussed below, decentralization has also been a significant, if less widely discussed, trend: see the account

of the decentralization of bargaining to plant level at Pilkington (no. 341, April 1985).

2. This point came out in a discussion of current trends among senior industrial relations practitioners held at Warwick University in March 1986. Some participants noted that management's ability to institute changes rested on the recession, while others stressed that developments had been such that the clock could not be turned back. For a summary, see P. K. Edwards (1986b).

3. Research projects recently initiated in the Industrial Relations Research Unit aim to take up some of these issues by investigating the role of general managers in the handling of labour-related issues.

4. It is hard to convince workers that the firm is a partnership if they stand the risk of being laid off or made redundant at short notice. Some managers recognize this. Paul Roots, the Director of Industrial Relations at Ford, has recently argued (at the conference mentioned in n. 2 above: see P.K. Edwards, 1986b: 3; for a development of these views, see Roots, 1986), that lay-offs generate mistrust, and has contrasted the position in Britain with that in West Germany, where they are virtually unknown. For the more general argument that limits on firms' ability to dismiss or lay-off workers in West Germany has encouraged better manpower utilization, which has in turn contributed to work force acceptance of change and to higher productivity see Streeck (1986): apparent constraints can in fact lead to better systems of management and encourage firms to adopt new production and marketing strategies, which help secure an established position in the market, and this in turn contributes to manpower planning and to a further strengthening of the labour relations system.

5. This argument may seem surprising in view of the extensive changes made at BL's Longbridge factory (Willman and Winch, 1985). But many of these have involved management in using its new-found power in a bargaining context which is largely unchanged. Other firms have arguably gone much further in removing the basis of shopfloor union organization.

Appendix A

Data and Methods

The Sample

This section gives brief details of the nature of the sample, response rates, and possible sources of bias. The sample was drawn from the IFF Master File, which is based on local authority valuation lists and contains details on more than 45,000 establishments; it is regularly updated, and has a comprehensive coverage of the large manufacturing sites which were the target of the study. The sample is, with appropriate weighting, representative of plants employing at least 250 full-time workers in manufacturing industry. The unweighted distribution of achieved interviews is given in table A.1. As will be seen, the aim of obtaining at least 30 interviews in each of the five sectors chosen for special study was achieved, with the exception of textiles (27 interviews); the remaining 69 plants were chosen from the rest of manufacturing. As explained in the text, weights were divided by a constant so that the weighted number of cases was close to the unweighted number (235 as against 229); the largest weight was 2.35, for large plants in other manufacturing, and the smallest was 0.44, for small plants in chemicals.

The aim of interviewing the senior manager of the plant was generally met. As table A.2 shows, 77 per cent of respondents had job titles which enabled them to be categorized as factory managers. All the other respondents appear to have been fairly senior managers, who can be taken as having a thorough knowledge of managerial practice in their plants. They can thus be used as respondents where the plant is the unit of analysis although not, of course, where the factory manager himself is the focus. This argument is strengthened by the

TABLE A.1
Distribution of Interviews (Unweighted) by Industry and Plant Size

	Plant Size 250–499	(No. Full-Time Employees) 500 and over	Total
Food, drink, tobacco	23	9	32
Chemicals	17	18	35
Electrical engineering	15	18	33
Textiles	15	12	27
Paper, printing, publishing	20	13	33
Other manufacturing	46	23	69
Total	136	93	229

TABLE A.2
Respondents by Job Title (Unweighted)

	Number	Per Cent
All factory managers	177	77
Managing director/chief executive	89	39
Works, plant, factory director or manager	84	37
Operations director or manager	4	2
Deputy managing director	14	6
Production/manufacturing director or manager	16	7
Personnel director or manager	16	7
Financial director	4	2
Company secretary	1	(..)
Not known	1	(..)
	229	100

absence of a significant difference between factory managers' and other managers' replies to some key questions. Two of these are mentioned in chapter 1. The evidence in chapter 3, on age, careers, and length of service is also pertinent. There were some small differences on other matters. Thus factory managers were somewhat less likely than other managers to feel that the personnel function had increased in importance (55 per cent as against 65 per cent). And, as would be expected, the factory managers displayed a relatively high degree of discontent with the degree to which personnel were interchanged between the plant and the headquarters of the firm, and with the extent to which local managers were kept abreast of the firm's strategic plans (Q. 124). But there was no significant difference on other attitudes to the firm. Neither were there any differences in the importance attributed to labour matters in the eight areas of decision-making listed at Q. 100. In short, amalgamating the replies from the different types of respondent are unlikely to have introduced any biases into the data.

Overall response rates are a potentially more serious problem. The details of attempted interviews are shown in table A.3, where the last category given is simply the result of the need for interviewers to screen establishments selected from the Master File to ensure that they fell within the industries and size bounds set up for the survey. Excluding this category and the 'unavailable within deadline' group gives a ratio of interviews to total contacts with qualifying establishments of 229 to 435, giving a response rate of 53 per cent. This is lower than in some other surveys. Daniel and Millward (1983: 326), for example, report an overall response rate of 75 per cent, while the figure in the Warwick Survey was 68 per cent (Brown, 1981: 125). Part of the reason for the low figure in the present sample may lie in the time constraints of the survey: there was simply not the time to send follow-up letters or to pursue questions of access at higher levels in the organization. Thus Daniel and Millward report considerable efforts to secure co-operation at the headquarters of organizations in which plant-level respondents felt that they could not participate without permission from above. Similarly, there was little time available in the present survey to persuade respondents of the value of the exercise or to arrange alternative times for interview. In some cases managers agreed to be interviewed but had pressing demands which forced them to cancel appointments,

TABLE A.3
Response Rates

	Number	Per Cent
Interview achieved	229	26
Outright refusal	185	21
Qualified for interview but refused	20	2
Breakdown during interview	1	(..)
Unavailable within deadline	64	7
Did not qualify, out of interviewer's quota, duplicate address, closed down	370	43
	869	100

and it was not always possible to arrange another time. Alongside these time pressures has to be set the nature of the respondent's job. It may be that the personnel managers who were the respondents to the surveys mentioned above had more time in which to accommodate an interview lasting an hour or more than did factory managers, who have many immediate demands on their time. In short, the relatively high refusal rate here may reflect genuine problems of obtaining an interview of the required type in the time available.

There were no substantial variations between respondents and refusals in terms of industry location or plant size. The main reason given for non-participation was that the respondent was too busy, did not co-operate with any market research studies, or saw no value to the company in participating. Taken together with the evidence of few significant differences between factory managers and other respondents, these facts suggest that there are unlikely to have been any large sources of bias in the results. That is, response rates become worrying if it seems likely that respondents differ in material respects from non-respondents. It remains possible, of course, that factory managers who are interested in labour matters were more likely to find time to co-operate with a survey about the management of labour than were those displaying little interest in these things. The comparison between factory managers and other managers goes some way towards dealing with this problem. The other information discussed here indicates that it is unlikely that there were any obvious sources of bias. But the possibility has to be recognized that here, as in any research requiring the co-operation of informants, whether these be case-study subjects or respondents to structured questionnaires, those who are willing to help may differ from those who are not.

Statistical Methods

Most of the statistical techniques used in this study are standard. Where variables are purely nominal in form, for example the industry sector in which a plant was located, chi-square tests are appropriate. Where there is a clear ordering of categories, such that one category scores higher than another but without the extent of the difference being ascertainable (for example, increasing, static, and decreasing demand for the product), other tests are available. These include lambda and gamma. Except where formal models are reported, the text has not been burdened with discussions of statistical significance. Where a 'significant' difference is reported, this generally means significance at the 5 per cent level (that is, there are five chances in 100 that the difference is in fact due to chance). In addition, such differences are reported only where they appear to have some substantive importance.

Consider, for example, two three-category ordinal variables. A 'significant' difference might emerge wherein the middle category of the dependent variable was higher on the independent variable than the two extreme categories. Unless a theoretical explanation of this can be produced, statistical significance is substantively meaningless, and reporting a significant association would not be warranted.

Where data of a continuous nature are available, for example in years of service or company profits, more powerful tests are available. The simplest is to correlate two such ratio level variables and report the significance of the correlation coefficient; similarly, the values of such a variable may be calculated for each value of a categorical or ordinal variable, with significance being tested with an F test. (The breakdown of turnover per head across categories of company monitoring is an example: see above, p. 17).

More complex multi-variate models are used in chapters 3 and 6. The regression techniques used in the latter are generally well known and will not be discussed in detail. The models all use the Ordinary Least Squares method; t tests measure the significance of each independent variable and R^2 estimates the proportion of the variance in the dependent variable accounted for by the independent variables. Correlation matrices of the latter have also been inspected to ensure that no two variables are so highly correlated with each other that estimates of their independent effects are unreliable. In addition, the 'residuals' of regression equations have been examined. An equation predicts a value on the dependent variable for each case, and the residual is the difference between this value and the actual value. If residuals are very large on a few observations, these are sometimes seen as 'mavericks' and excluded from further analysis. If there is a clear pattern in the residuals, for example a tendency for them to be larger as plant size increases, it is likely that an omitted variable is having an effect. This could mean that the effects of the included variables are mis-specified. If, however, residuals are randomly distributed, it can be concluded that all the necessary variables have been included. This does not, of course, mean that everything about the dependent variable has been explained; it shows only that the measured effects of the model are not contaminated by other unmeasured effects. In the models reported here, the residuals did not point to any severe problems.

Discriminant analysis, used in chapter 3, is less familiar. The technique takes two or more groups, for example managers who had worked at headquarters and those who had not, and uses a set of independent variables to form a function which maximizes the discrimination between the groups. With more than two groups it is possible to have more than one discriminating function, but for simplicity here only two groups will be employed. Several methods for forming discriminating functions are available, but perhaps the most usual is that which aims to minimize a statistic known as Wilks's lambda. The greater the degree of separation between the two groups, the lower will be lambda. One model can be compared with another according to the size of lambda, with a smaller figure indicating a better result. A second summary statistic is the canonical correlation coefficient, which measures the correlation between the discriminating variables, treated as a set, and the groups being distinguished. The square of this measure gives an indication of the proportion of variance explained, analogous to the familiar R^2 of regression analysis. The influence of each independent variable can be assessed in several ways. In stepwise models, variables are entered according to their role in minimizing lambda: those which are entered first can be seen as being more influential than those entered subsequently. A second criterion is the significance of the change in lambda that their inclusion induces. The test statistic, p, is similar to a chi-square statistic; a p of 0.010 indicates significance at the 1 per cent level. Finally, coefficients indicating the loading of each variable on the discriminating function are produced. When expressed in standardized form these are analogous to the standardized beta coefficients of regression analysis. They thus indicate the relative strengths of the effects of the independent variables.

Appendix B

The Questionnaire

This appendix reproduces the whole of the questionnaire with the exception of some obvious routing instructions, for example an instruction to ask certain questions about trade union organization only in estabishments with recognized unions. Items in capitals are interviewer instructions. Hence the reader can ascertain whether a list of responses was read out to interviewees (for example, at Q. 12) or whether the interviewees were left to give their own answers, with the interviewers fitting answers into appropriate categories (for example, Q. 13). In all cases where an answer was coded as 'other' the full reply was recorded. In several instances these answers have either been assigned to an existing category or made into a new category. Items in square brackets are interpolations indicating for reasons of brevity that the wording follows wording used in other questions; on the actual questionnaire all these were typed in full. Copies of the questionnaire, together with a technical report that describes the sample and reproduces all the verbatim comments recorded, have been lodged at the ESRC Data Archive at the University of Essex. The basic data tape is also at the Archive.

A Company and Establishment Background

Firstly, I'd like to pick up some factual details about this establishment.
1   What is the main business activity of this establishment? PROBE FOR
    FULL DETAILS OF PRODUCTS MADE/HANDLED. DO NOT ACCEPT ANSWERS
    SUCH AS ENGINEERING.
2   (a) How many *full-time* employees work here? By full-time I mean
        employees working at least 21 hours a week.

    (b) How many of these are *manual* workers?

    (c) And non-manual? CHECK 2c + 2b = 2a.

    (d) What proportion of the manual employees are female?

    (e) How many *part-time* workers do you have?

3   Are several types of product produced at this establishment or only one?

4   (Thinking of the type of product that involves the most workers), is it in practice possible to vary the sequence of the operations used in making the product?

    IF NO AT 4.

5   Does a breakdown or stoppage in one part of the production process bring the whole operation to a standstill?

    ASK ALL

6   Apart from normal seasonal variations, has the demand for the products produced by this establishment been rising, falling or generally remained static over the past two years?

7   Is there a company registered at this site?

8   Is this establishment a single independent establishment with no others in the UK, or is it one of several establishments in the UK belonging to the same organization or group?

    IF PART OF A GROUP.

9   Is this establishment part of a *division or subsidiary company* which is in turn owned by a larger corporation group or holding company?

    IF YES.

10   Roughly how many intermediate levels are there *between* this establishment and the overall headquarters of the corporate group or holding company?

    IF 2 OR MORE AT Q, 10.

    Throughout the interview, could you think of the intermediate level that most influence on this establishment's business operation.)

11   From now on I will refer to this intermediate level in which ever way is most convenient to you – division, operating company, subsidiary company or whatever. Which would you prefer?

    INTERVIEWER: Use this phrase from now on when company is used on questionnaire.

12   What is the basis of this intermediate level?

    READ OUT AND CODE ALL MENTIONED.

    Product group

    Geographical

    Historical ownership pattern

    Other (DESCRIBE)

    ASK Q. 13 IF PART OF A GROUP (OTHERS GO TO Q. 19a).

13   How many employees does the *company* have in total in the UK (including this establishment)?

    250–499

500–999
1,000–1,999
2,000–4,999
5,000–9,999
10,000 or more
14 How many establishments does the *company* have in the UK?
2–3
4–5
6–10
11–20
More than 20
ASK ALL WHO ARE PART OF A GROUP (FROM Q. 8).
15 (a) Is this establishment a *profit centre* (i.e. the lowest level at which operating profit is calculated)?
IF NO.
(b) At what level is the profit centre?
READ OUT AND CODE ALL MENTIONED.
Intermediate level
Whole company
Several levels within the establishment
ASK ALL WHO ARE PART OF A GROUP.
16 (a) Is this establishment owned by a UK company or by a foreign organization?
ASK Q. 16b IF FOREIGN (OTHERS GO TO Q. 18a).
(b) Where is the headquarters of this organization?
United States/Canada
European
Other (SPECIFY)
17 In approximately how many other countries does this organization have operating facilities?
1–2
3–5
6 or more
ASK ALL WHO ARE UK OWNED (OTHERS GO TO Q. 19a).
18 (a) Does this company have operating facilities outside the UK?
IF YES.
(b) In approximately how many countries?
1–2
3–5
6 or more
ASK ALL.
19 (a) Is this establishment directly or indirectly affiliated to any employers' organization that carries out collective bargaining. I am not referring to pure trade associations here.
IF YES.

(b) Which ones(s):

ASK ALL.

20   (a) Are there any TRADE UNION members employed here?

IF YES.

(b) What proportion *manual* workers belong to a trade union?
——%

(c) Are any manual workers' unions recognized by management
for negotiating pay and conditions?

IF YES.

(d) What proportion of the manual employees here are covered
by these negotiations?

(e) Do the manual unions have stewards or representatives here,
apart from those concerned exclusively with health and safety
matters?

IF YES.

(f) Do any of these stewards act as *senior stewards or conveners*?

IF YES.

(g) Are they recognized or acknowledged by management as such?

(h) Do any of these senior stewards or conveners in practice spend
all or most of their time on workplace union affairs:

ASK IF PART OF A GROUP (OTHERS GO TO Q. 22).

SHOW CARD A.

21   At which of the levels on the card is pay bargaining for manual
workers carried out?

CODE ALL MENTIONED.

This establishment *only*

This establishment together with *some* other estabs in the co.

This establishment together with *all* other estabs in the co.

This establishment together with *some* other estabs in the organization

This establishment together with *all* other estabs in the organization

This establishment together with estabs from other cos in the
UK, e.g. through an industry agreement.

ASK Q. 22 IF NOT PART OF A GROUP (OTHERS GO TO Q. 23).

22   At which of the following levels is pay bargaining for manual
workers carried out? READ OUT.

If both, please relate your answer to the more important level at
the last pay settlement.

This establishment *only*

This establishment together with establishments from other companies in the UK e.g. through an industry agreement

ASK ALL.

SHOW CARD B.

23   Which, if any, of the forms of industrial action shown on the card

have taken place within this establishment over the last two years?
    Strike of one day or shift or less
    Strike of more than one day or shift
    Ban or restriction on overtime
    Work to rule or go slow
    Blacking of work
    Work in/sit in
    Other (SPECIFY)
    None
ASK ALL.

24 (a) Is any substantial group of manual employees paid by results (PBR) i.e. does their pay vary according to the amount of work done or its value?
IF YES.
(b) Roughly what proportion of manual workers are covered by PBR?
(c) Which of the following forms does the PBR scheme take?
READ OUT AND CODE ONLY ONE.
    Straight piecework.
    Piecework with a high fall-back rate (over 75% average earnings)
    Group bonus
    Bonus scheme related to output of whole factory
ASK ALL.

25 (a) Do you have any form of shift working in this establishment that affects a significant proportion of your operation? i.e. excluding small groups such as cleaners.
IF YES.
SHOW CARD C.
(b) Which of the forms shown on the card does shift working take? If more than one system, please answer for the one affecting the largest group of manual workers.
    Day and night shift (rotating)
    Permanent night shift
    Double-day
    Double-day plus night shift
    3-shifts 5 days a week
    Continental shift/3-shift, 7 days a week
    Twilight shifts only
    Twilight plus one of above (SPECIFY)
  Other (SPECIFY)
IF 3-SHIFT, 7 DAYS A WEEK/CONTINENTAL SHIFT GO TO Q. 27a. ASK ALL OTHERS Q. 26a.

26 (a) Would it be technically feasible to increase the utilization of existing equipment with a different shift system?

IF YES.
SHOW CARD C.
(b) With which of the sorts of system on the card?
(c) Have you considered using such a system?
IF YES.
SHOW CARD D.
(d) Which of the reasons on the card have prevented its introduction?
CODE ALL MENTIONED.
And which of these is most important?

	Prevented	Most important
Lack of product demand		
Lack of capital for investment		
Workers would not like it		
Trade union resistance		
Lack of skilled labour		
Extra costs of shift premia, etc.		
Other (SPECIFY)		

ASK ALL WITH SHIFT WORKING.
27 (a) Does shift working create any special problems for management?
IF YES.
SHOW CARD E.
(b) Which of the problems on the card does it create?
CODE ALL MENTIONED.
Which is the greatest problem?

Creates	Greatest
Increased labour turnover	
Increased absenteeism	
Poor quality of work	
Extra supervision needed	
Difficulties of management communication	
Costs of shift premia	
Shifts are socially undesirable	
Other (SPECIFY)	

ASK ALL WITH SHIFT WORKING.
28 (a) In the past three years, have you made any changes in your shift working arrangements at this establishment?
IF YES.
(b) What changes have you made?
CODE ALL MENTIONED.
Elimination of night shift
Reduction of number of shifts worked
Introduction of new shifts
Other (SPECIFY)

(c) What reasons prompted the changes?

CODE ALL MENTIONED.

Lack of product demand

Costs of shift system

Increase in market demand

Other (SPECIFY)

ASK ALL WITH NO SHIFT WORKING.

29 Have you operated any form of shift system in the past three years?

IF YES.

SHOW CARD C.

30 What sort of system was it? If more than one system, please answer for the one affecting the largest group of manual workers? [List as at Q. 25b]

SHOW CARD F.

31 For which of the reasons on the card did you stop using this shift system?

CODE ALL MENTIONED.

Lack of product demand

Trade union resistance

Excessive labour turnover

Excessive absenteeism

Poor quality of work

Excessive amount of supervision needed

Difficulties of management communication

Costs of shift premia

Social undesirability of shifts

Other (SPECIFY)

(b) Would you consider re-introducing the system you had or introducing another system if conditions changed?

32 (a) ASK ALL WHO HAVE NOT OPERATED SHIFT WORKING IN LAST THREE YEARS.

[Qs 32a to 32d identical to Qs 26a to 26d]

B The Manager's Career

I would now like to establish some details about your career in management to date.

33 In which of the industrial sectors on the card was your first full-time job? [Card listed 20 categories based on the SIC]

34 How many employees did the whole organization have in the UK?

Less than 25

25–99

100–499

500–999
1,000 or more

35 Which of the departments on the card did you work in initially?
CODE ONLY ONE.
Production
Maintenance
Quality control
Stock control, distribution, warehousing etc.
Industrial engineering
Personnel
Finance
Sales, marketing
Purchasing
Research and development
General administration
Planning
General trainee
Other (SPECIFY)

36 And at which of the levels in the card did you start off?
CODE ONLY ONE.
Plant manager, chief executive of a distinct site or operation
Director
Departmental manager
Superintendent of shift or section
Assistant to a staff manager
Supervisor of *non-manual* workers
General foreman or supervisor of *manual* workers (2nd line of supervision)
Foreman or supervisor of *manual* workers (1st line of supervision)
Routine white-collar worker
Skilled manual
Semi-skilled manual
Unskilled manual
Apprentice
General management trainee
Other (SPECIFY)

37 At what age did you take up your first full-time job?
38 Was it within this organization?
IF NO ASK Q. 39; IF YES GO TO Q. 49.
39 Roughly how many firms did you work for before joining this one?
40 Did you have any significant changes of functional responsibility, e.g. moving from finance to production, before joining this firm?
41 At what age did you join your present firm?
42 Did you take up your present post?
IF YES TO SECTION C; IF NO ASK Q. 43.

43 In which of the departments on the card was your first post in this firm?
    [List as at Q. 35]
44 Roughly how many separate posts have you held for a significant amount of time between your first job in this firm and your present post?
45 Have you had any significant changes of functional responsibility, e.g. moving from finance to production, during your career with this firm?
    ASK Q. 46 IF PART OF A GROUP (OTHERS GO TO SECTION C).
46 Has your career in this firm been in this plant only or in other parts of the organization as well.
47 How many *other* distinct establishments of the organization have you worked in?
48 Has this involved any time at headquarters dealing with strategy or overall planning? GO TO SECTION C.
    IF FIRST JOB IN PRESENT ORGANIZATION.
49 Have you ever worked for any other firm?
    IF NO ASK Q. 50; OTHERS GO TO Q. 55.
    [Qs 50–4 reproduce Qs 44–8]
55 How long did you stay with your present firm after you first joined it?
56 Roughly how many firms did you work for before returning here?
57 [Reproduces Q. 40]
58 At what age did you return to this firm?
59 [Qs 59–65 follow Qs 42–8]

C The Manager's Job

I'd now like to ask a few personal details about your own job.
66 (a) At what age did you take up your present post?
    (b) How long have you held it?
    (c) What is your job title?
    ASK IF PART OF A GROUP (OTHERS GO TO Q. 73a).
67 (a) Are you paid according to a formal salary structure, i.e. within a specific band or grade?
    IF YES.
    (b) What range of managerial posts is covered by the salary structure?
    READ OUT AND CODE ONLY ONLY.
       All management personnel from supervisors upwards
       All middle managers and upwards
       Plant/factory managers only
       Plant/factory managers plus senior staff at company HQ

Plant/factory managers plus some other senior managers on site and some corporate personnel
Other (SPECIFY)

68 (a) What determines which grade of the structure a particular post goes into?
CODE ALL MENTIONED [IN LIST BELOW Q. 68b].
ASK IF MORE THAN ONE MENTIONED (OTHERS GO TO Q. 69a IF PERSONAL MERIT MENTIONED AND ASK Q. 68c IF NOT).
(b) Which of these is the most important determinant?
Mentioned   Most important
CODE ONE ONLY.
Length of service in the post
Overall level of responsibility
Size of the plant
Personal merit
Other (SPECIFY)
ASK IF PERSONAL MERIT NOT MENTIONED AT Q. 68a (OTHER GO TO Q. 69a).
(c) Does the company's evaluation of the *personal merit* of a manager influence what band he or she is placed in?
ASK ALL PAID WITHIN SALARY STRUCTURE.

69 (a) Are you subject to any regular system of *management appraisal*?
ASK IF YES.
(b) Does the outcome of the appraisal affect your overall level of remuneration?
(c) Are any *other* managers in this establishment given performance appraisals?
ASK IF YES.
(d) What is the *lowest level* at which an appraisal system operates?
READ OUT AND CODE ONLY ONE.
Senior functional/departmental managers
Middle management
Supervisors
Other (SPECIFY)
ASK ALL WHO ARE PART OF A GROUP AND PAID WITHIN SALARY STRUCTURE.
SHOW CARD J.

70 (a) Which of the phrases on this card best describes the way increases in your general level of remuneration are arrived at?
CODE ONE ONLY.
Company discretion
Annual award, amount at company discretion
Annual award tied to profitability or other measure of performance

Annual award tied to negotiations with trade unions of *non-manual* workers
Annual award tied to negotiations with trade unions of *manual* workers
Same award as other groups of workers, not tied to negotiated agreements
Other (SPECIFY)

(b) Apart from your basic salary and any fringe benefits and pension arrangements that are part of your overall package of benefits, does your total income vary according to *bonuses or profit-sharing* schemes? Please exclude any income derived only from personal holdings of company shares.
ASK IF YES.

(c) What sorts of schemes are involved?
READ OUT AND CODE ALL MENTIONED.
Bonuses related to performance of *plant*
Bonuses related to *overall company performance*
Other (SPECIFY)

(d) Do the same or similar schemes operate for *non-managerial* employees?

(e) If you think of your basic pay as 100%, what percentage is added, on average, by variable elements?
PROBE FOR BEST ESTIMATE.
ASK IF PART OF A GROUP BUT NO SALARY STRUCTURE.

71 What principles govern the way in which you are paid:
READ OUT AND CODE ALL MENTIONED.
Pay tied to that of non-manual staff
Direct bargaining between manager and company
Other (SPECIFY)
[Qs 71b to 72d follow as 70a to 70c]
ASK IF NOT PART OF A GROUP (OTHERS GO TO Q. 74).

73 (a) Are there any general principles governing how your pay is determined, or does it simply depend on what the company can afford at the time?
General principles
Depend on what can afford at the time
[Qs 73b to 73d follow Qs 70b to 70d)
ASK ALL.

74 Do you own any *shares* in your company?
ASK IF YES.

75 Have you purchased them under a company scheme offering special terms to employees, or have you acquired them by other means?
ASK IF ACQUIRED BY OTHER MEANS.

76 By what means did you acquire them?

READ OUT AND CODE ALL MENTIONED.
   Family holding in the business
   Normal market purchases
   Other (SPECIFY)
ASK ALL OWNING SHARES.

77 If you think of your normal basic salary at 100%, approximately what figure would you put on the *capital value* of your shares?
PROBE FOR BEST ESTIMATE.

ASK ALL

78 Are you covered by a *company pension scheme*?
ASK IF YES.

79 Is the scheme *contributory*?

80 Are your pension rights transferable to other employments?
ASK IF TRANSFERABLE.

81 Does your company pension scheme allow transfer of accumulated rights?
READ OUT AND CODE ONE ONLY.
   Within your *operating company* only
   Within your *corporate group* only
   To some other companies also, OR
   Are they totally transferable?
ASK ALL.

82 Would you say that your pay has generally kept in line with the cost of living in recent years?

83 And what about your position in relation to other groups employed by this company ... do you think your pay has generally *increased*, *decreased*, or stayed about the same in relation to the pay of ...
READ OUT
   (a) *Non-Manual* workers
   Managers pay *increased*
   Managers pay *decreased*
   Stayed the same
   (b) *Manual* workers
   Managers pay *increased*
   Managers pay *decreased*
   Stayed the same
SHOW CARD K.

84 On this card are a number of statements about a person's job. Please say how far each of them applies to yourself, using the scale on the card.

CARD K

Statement	Definitely true	Fairly true	True to some extent	Not very true	Definitely false
(a) I prefer a job which is always changing	1	2	3	4	5
(b) I enjoy finding myself in new and unusual circumstances	1	2	3	4	5
(c) I like to have a regular pattern in my working day	1	2	3	4	5
(d) I would generally prefer to do someting that I am used to rather than something different	1	2	3	4	5
(e) I enjoy taking on new problems	1	2	3	4	5

D The Manager and His/Her Plant

88 I would now like to ask you about the organization of managerial tasks relating to *productivity* and *labour relations matters* in this plant. Does this establishment have a manager whose primary responsibility is personnel or industrial relations?
ASK IF NO (OTHERS GO TO Q. 91).

89 Are personnel and industrial relations matters *your* responsibility or that of another manager?
Respondent's responsibility
Another manager's responsibility
ASK IF ANOTHER MANAGER RESPONSIBLE.

90 What are the *other* responsibilities of this manager?
CODE ALL MENTIONED.
Production
Other (SPECIFY)

91 And roughly how often does he or she *seek your advice* or *consult* you about personnel matters?
At least once a day
2 or 3 times a week
Once a week
Less often than once a week
ASK ALL.

92   Do you have a manager whose primary responsibility is *production*
     ASK IF NO (OTHERS GO TO Q. 94).
93   Are production matters *your* responsibility or that of another
     manager?
        Respondent's responsibility
        Another manager's responsibility
     ASK IF ANOTHER MANAGER RESPONSIBLE.
94   Roughly how often does this manager seek your advice or consult
     you about production matters?
        At least once a day
        2 or 3 times a week
        Once a week
        Less often than once a week
     ASK ALL.
95   I'd now like to discuss areas of managerial decision-making.
     SHOW CARD L.
     I am now going to read out a list of areas of managerial decision-
     making, please tell me which code on the card comes closest to
     the situation in this plant.
     IF PART OF A GROUP ADD: Answers are classified according to *your
     own direct* personal involvement and the degree of involvement of
     management at a higher level within the organization.
     IF NOT PART OF A GROUP ADD. In your case obviously only the first
     column will apply.
        (a) Keeping to overall production schedules
        (b) Monitoring and maintaining quality control standards
        (c) Dealing with production bottlenecks or plant breakdown
        (d) Selection and promotion of supervisors
        (e) Pay negotiations for manual workers
        (f) Recruitment, that is, the total number of workers to be
             employed
        (g) Re-deployment of workers within the establishment
        (h) Setting overtime requirements
        (i) Dismissing workers for disciplinary reasons
        (j) Applying discipline short of the sack
        (k) Amount of overtime to be worked
        (l) Use of short-time working or layoffs
        (m) Redundancy of substantial number of manual workers
     ASK ALL.
     SHOW CARD M.
96   Here is a list of statements about the organization of management
     within your organization. As you can see, each statement is pre-
     sented with its opposite. If you *totally* agree with the left-hand
     statement please give a score of 1. If you *totally* agree with right-
     hand statement, give a score of 7. In between scores indicate a
     leaning towards one or other extreme.

CARD L

Direct personal involvement	Decision can be taken in this plant	Higher level consulted	Decision rests with higher level
Always/usually involved directly, and take final decision	1	2	n.a.
Always/usually involved, final decision taken by other manager(s)	4	5	6
Involved only in difficult cases, and take final decision	7	8	n.a.
Involved only in difficult cases, give advice to manager(s) responsible	10	11	12
Not directly involved but kept informed on progress	13	14	15
Not generally involved at all	16	17	18

(a) The general manager has been superseded by the specialist
Generalists remain crucial in keeping an overall view of the business as a whole

(b) Managers from different functions tend to see the business through the narrow perspective of their own specialisms
Functional managers are able to take the broader view of the business as a whole

(c) Junior managers need to be given discretion and the scope to develop their own abilities
Junior managers need to be kept aware of company policy and the need to operate within it

(d) Supervisors are important members of line management
Supervisors today have few responsibilities left

97   (a) Thinking of the *personnel* function within management at this plant, would you say that its importance over the last 5 years has ...

READ OUT AND CODE ONE ONLY
Greatly increased
Increased
Stayed about the same

Declined somewhat
Declined a great deal?
ASK IF CHANGED – IF STAYED SAME GO TO TO Q.98.
(b) Why do you think this has happened?
CODE ALL MENTIONED.
Effect of employment legislation
Company policy on employee involvement
Growing trade union power
Recession
Declining trade union power
Fewer personnel/industrial relations problems than in past
Other (SPECIFY)
ASK ALL.
98 Would you say that your company has, in this establishment, an overall policy or philosophy for the management of labour relations? By labour relations I mean not just matters of formal personnel policy or institutional arrangements but also a policy regarding the place of workers in the organization of the enterprise as a whole.
ASK IF HAS LABOUR RELATIONS POLICY.
99 (a) How would you describe the philosophy?
PROBE FULLY AND WRITE IN.
ASK IF PART OF A GROUP.
(b) Is this policy part of an overall *company* policy or approach?
ASK IF YES.
(c) To what extent is the approach the same across all parts of the company?
Completely uniform
Largely uniform
Some local variation/autonomy
Considerable local autonomy
ASK ALL.
SHOW CARD N.
100 How important are *labour relations matters* in each of the following areas of managerial decision-making? Please use the scale on the card.
101 (a) Generally speaking, how involved are *you* in these areas? Are you ...
READ OUT
Very involved
Involved to some extent
Not really involved?
IF SOME INVOLVEMENT.
(b) In what ways are labour relations issues important? [OPEN-ENDED Q]

CARD N

		Crucial	Very impt	Fairly impt	Not very impt	Not at all impt
(a)	Fixed capital investment decisions	5	4	3	2	1
(b)	Major changes in production methods	5	4	3	2	1
(c)	Redundancy decisions	5	4	3	2	1
(d)	Manning levels	5	4	3	2	1
(e)	Amount of overtime worked	5	4	3	2	1
(f)	Use of work study techniques	5	4	3	2	1
(g)	Type of payment system employed	5	4	3	2	1
(h)	Flexibility of workers across different tasks	5	4	3	2	1

    (c) Have labour relations matters prevented you implementing changes in these areas?
    IF YES.
    (d) What changes?
    ASK ALL.

102 Approximately, what percentage of the technical capacity of this plant has been utilized over the past year?
PROBE FOR BEST ESTIMATE.

103 Are there any *internal* constraints which would prevent this plant from operating at its technical capacity, assuming that all *external* constraints on your level of output, such as the state of market demand for your product, were removed?
ASK IF THERE ARE INTERNAL CONSTRAINTS.
SHOW CARD Q.

104 (a) Which of the constraints on the card exist?
ASK IF MORE THAN ONE MENTIONED.
And which of these would you say is the most important?
(a) Important at all   (b) Most important
    Age/unreliability of machinery
    Balancing production on different operations
    Quality of management
    Lack of adequate maintenance arrangements
    Trade union restrictions in *maintenance* areas

Trade union restrictions in *production* areas
Overmanning
Lack of worker effort in general
Absenteeism
Other (SPECIFY)

ASK ALL WHERE INTERNAL CONSTRAINTS.

105 You estimated that ——% (AS IN Q. 102) of the technical capacity of this plant was utilized last year. Roughly what percentage of the gap between this figure and full capacity working is accounted for by *internal* factors, and what percentage of *external* factors?
Internal factors ——%
External factors ——%

CHECK ADDS TO 100%.

ASK ALL.

106 Over the past two years, have you made any changes in working arrangements, or introduced any schemes to *increase the efficiency of labour utilization* in this plant?

ASK IF YES.

107 What did the system(s) involve?
CODE ALL MENTIONED.
Introducing new technologies
Improving labour efficiency with existing equipment
Cutting excess overtime
Increasing flexibility of working
Ending/reducing demarcation lines
Removing other restrictive TU practices
Other (SPECIFY)

108 Were they broadly successful?

109 Did they meet any significant resistance from the work force?
ASK IF MET RESISTANCE.
SHOW CARD P.

110 Which of the forms on the card did the resistance take?
CODE ONE ONLY.
A strike or other industrial action which successfully frustrated management
A strike and/or other industrial action which failed to prevent the change
Bargaining, followed by acceptance
A refusal to accept change, followed by management backing down

111 What effect do you think that the changes have had on the overall climate of industrial relations in this plant? Do you think they have ...
READ OUT
Improved

Remained much the same
Worsened?
ASK IF MANUAL TRADE UNIONS RECOGNIZED (YES AT Q. 20c) (OTHERS
GO TO Q. 114).

112   Have you made any changes in the way in which you *bargain
with your trade union representatives* in the past two years?
ASK IF YES.

113   What have been the most important changes?
CODE ALL MENTIONED.
Reducing number of shop stewards
Reducing number/influence of senior stewards
Removing facilities for stewards
Ending closed shop arrangements
Generally encouraging awareness of the need for change
ASK ALL.

114   Do you have any *joint consultation committees*?
ASK IF YES.

115   Have any of them been introduced in the last three years?
ASK IF NO.

116   Would you say that their importance over the last three years has
. . .
READ OUT AND CODE ONE ONLY
Greatly increased
Increased
Stayed about the same
Decreased?

117   How would you compare the importance which you place on *joint*
consultation, with *negotiations with trade unions*?
Joint consultations more important
TU negotiations more important
Both equally important
ASK IF JOINT CONSULTATIONS MORE IMPORTANT.

118   Why do you think this is so?
PROBE FULLY AND WRITE IN.

E   The Manager and His/Her Firm

I would now like to ask you some questions about relationship with
your employing organization as a whole.
ASK ALL WHO ARE PART OF A GROUP (OTHERS GO TO Q. 134).

119   Does the corporation employ *management development programmes* to widen the experience of managers at your level?
ASK IF YES.

120   Have *you yourself* been involved in any programmes?
      ASK IF YES.
121   Which of the following have they involved?
      READ OUT AND CODE ALL MENTIONED.
        Training courses: in house
        Training courses: outside company
        New experience in other functions or parts of the firm
      ASK ALL EMPLOYING MANAGEMENT DEVELOPMENT PROGRAMMES.
122   How valuable have you found the experience?
        Very valuable
        Fairly valuable
        Not at all valuable
123   Are similar programmes in operation for *other* managers at this establishment?
      ASK ALL WHO ARE PART OF GROUP.
      SHOW CARD Q.
124   Here are some statements about the ways in which a company can respond at intermediate or corporate level to the advice of managers such as yourself. Could you tell me how each is true in this firm, using the scale on the card?
      SHOW CARD R AND LEAVE WITH RESPONDENT TILL AFTER Q. 128.
125   And how close a check does the company level of management keep on the following areas within your establishment? Please use the scale on the card.
      ASK Q. 126 FOR EACH AREA WHERE A VERY CLOSE/CLOSE CHECK IS KEPT.
126   Is there a regular system of monitoring plant performance in terms of ——————— (NAME AREA) against formal criteria or targets?
      ASK ALL WHO ARE PART OF CORPORATE GROUP (YES AT Q. 9) (OTHERS GO TO Q. 130).
127   And does management at the *corporate* level take an interest in any of these matters on the card or are they dealt with solely at an *intermediate level*?
      ASK IF CORPORATE LEVEL TAKES INTEREST.
128   Which ones does corporate management take an interest in?
      CODE ALL MENTIONED IN GRID BELOW (LIST AS AT Q. 125; GRID RECORDED ANSWERS TO Qs 128 AND 129 FOR EACH ITEM).
      ASK FOR EACH MENTIONED.
129   *How much* interest does corporate management take in this area – a great deal, some, or a little?
      ASK ALL WHO ARE PART OF A GROUP (FROM Q. 8).
130   Can this establishment retain the revenue that it generates for financing its own capital expenditure?
      ASK IF NO.

CARD Q

		Com-pletely true	True most of time	True some of time	Rarely true	Never true
(a)	In implementing a pay award, company managers pay attention to the advice of the man on the spot	1	2	3	4	5
(b)	In developing financial accounting systems, company managers ignore the needs of individual plants	1	2	3	4	5
(c)	Company managers tend to be bureaucratic and out of touch with the realities of day-to-day operations	1	2	3	4	5
(d)	The allocation of funds for investment involves full consultation with local managers	1	2	3	4	5
(e)	Local managements tend to be kept in the dark about long-term strategic planning at company headquarters	1	2	3	4	5
(f)	There is an adequate degree of interchange of personnel between operational management and company strategic management	1	2	3	4	5

131 Is it given its own allocation of capital by the company?
ASK ALL WHO ARE PART OF A GROUP.
132 Is there an upper limit on items of capital expenditure that can be undertaken here without the approval of a higher level in the organization?
ASK IF YES.
133 What is the limit?
WRITE IN £——.

CARD R

		Very close	Close	Not very close	Not at all close
(a)	Movement of pay outside negotiated settlements	1	2	3	4
(b)	Industrial disputes	1	2	3	4
(c)	Production schedules	1	2	3	4
(d)	Quality standards	1	2	3	4
(e)	Profit targets	1	2	3	4

ASK IF SINGLE ESTABLISHMENT (IF PART OF GROUP GO TO SECTION F).

134 Do you sit on the Board of Directors of your company?

135 Is it a *publicly quoted* company?

136 In achieving the profitability of your company, how important are matters *concerned with efficient production* and *labour utilization*, compared with such things as securing capital for investment and marketing your product?
READ OUT.
The most important influence
One of the most important
Fairly important
Not very important
Not important at all

F Outcomes Data

Finally, I would like to ask you a few questions about the overall performance of this establishment.

137 In assessing its overall performance, would you say the *gross revenue* earned over the past two years has been
READ OUT AND CIRCLE code
Well in excess of costs
Sufficient to make a small profit
Enough to break even
Insufficient to cover costs
So low as to produce large losses?
SHOW CARD S

138 How would you compare the *costs of production* at this establishment with the rest of the competition in the country? Please use the scale on the card.

> Well above average
> Above average
> Average
> Below average
> Well below average

IF WELL ABOVE AVERAGE/ABOVE AVERAGE ASK Q. 139 (OTHERS GO TO Q. 141/143).

139 Do you feel that the obstacles to improving plant performance in this respect are mainly external or internal?

IF INTERNAL INFLUENCES.

140 Which of the following internal influences have you found to be detrimental to plant performance?

READ OUT AND CODE ALL MENTIONED.

> Capital equipment
> Wages levels
> Labour productivity
> Other (SPECIFY)

IF BELOW AVERAGE/WELL BELOW AVERAGE AT Q. 138.

141 Do you feel that this level of plant performance has been influenced more by external or by internal factors?

IF INTERNAL INFLUENCES.

142 Which of the following internal factors have influenced the level of performance?

READ OUT AND CODE ALL MENTIONED.

> Capital equipment
> Wage levels
> Labour production
> Other (SPECIFY)

ASK ALL.

SHOW CARD S.

143 How would you compare *wage costs per unit of output* at this establishment with the rest of the competition in this industry? Please use the scale on the card.

[Scale for Qs 143–5 same as for Q. 138]

144 How would you compare the *average level of production per worker* at this establishment with the rest of the competition in this country? Please use the same scale as before.

IF PART OF A GROUP ASK Q. 145.

145 How does this establishment's performance rate generally compared with other plants in the company? Please use the same scale.

ASK ALL.

146 How would you assess the severity of the competition in the markets in which you operate *throughout the world*?
READ OUT.
Very severe
Severe
Of average severity
Not severe
Not very severe
ASK ALL.

147 Over the last three years, would you say that the level of competition has ...
READ OUT
Increased
Decreased
Stayed the same?

148 Do you face any significant amount of competition from *foreign* firms in these markets?
IF YES.

149 Would you say that the foreign competition is
Very strong
Strong
Neither strong nor weak
Weak
Very weak?
IF STRONG OR VERY STRONG.

150 Why do you think this is? [OPEN-ENDED Q]
ASK ALL.

151 Compared with foreign competitors, would you rate your *labour productivity* as
READ OUT
Much better
Better
Neither better nor worse
Worse
Much worse?

152 What do you see as the main issues facing management in this plant over the next three years?

153 Do you have any other comments about any of the issues we have discussed?

154 Many thanks for your help. We will be preparing a summary report of the study. Would you like a copy when it is ready?
CODE SEX OF RESPONDENT ———————

References

Addison, J. T., and A. H. Barnett. 1982. 'The Impact of Unions on Productivity', *British Journal of Industrial Relations*. Vol. 20, July, 145–62.

Bain, George Sayers, and Robert Price. 1972. 'Who Is a White-Collar Employee?', *British Journal of Industrial Relations*, Vol. 10, November, 325–39.

—— 1980. *Profiles of Union Growth: A Comparative Statistical Portrait of Eight Countries*. Oxford: Blackwell.

Ball, John M., and N. K. Skeoch. 1981. *Inter-Plant Comparisons of Productivity and Earnings*. Government Economic Service Working Paper 38. London: HMSO.

Batstone, Eric. 1984. *Working Order: Workplace Industrial Relations over Two Decades*. Oxford: Blackwell.

—— Ian Boraston, and Stephen Frenkel. 1977. *Shop Stewards in Action: The Organization of Workplace Conflict and Accommodation*. Oxford: Blackwell.

—— and Stephen Gourlay. 1986. *Unions, Unemployment and Innovation*. Oxford: Blackwell.

Birch, S., and B. Macmillan. 1971. *Managers on the Move: A Study of British Managerial Mobility*. London: British Institute of Management.

Brown, William (ed.). 1981. *The Changing Contours of British Industrial Relations: A Survey of Manufacturing Industry*. Oxford: Blackwell.

—— 1983. 'Britain's Unions: New Pressures and Shifting Loyalties', *Personnel Management*, October, 48–51.

—— and Peter Nolan. 1981. 'The Context of the Next Incomes Policy', *Policy Studies*, Vol. 1, February, 138–45.

Buckley, Peter J., and Peter Enderwick. 1985. *The Industrial Relations Practices of Foreign-Owned Firms in Britain*. London: Macmillan.

Burawoy, Michael. 1979. *Manufacturing Consent: Changes in the Labor Process Under Monopoly Capitalism*. Chicago: University of Chicago Press.

—— 1981. 'Terrains of Contest: Factory and State under Capitalism and Socialism', *Socialist Review*, no. 58, 83–124.

Burawoy, Michael. 1985. *The Politics of Production*. London: Verso.

Chadwick, M. G. 1983. 'The Recession and Industrial Relations: A Factory Approach', *Employee Relations*, vol. 5, no. 5, 5–12.

Child, John. 1984. *Organization: A Guide to Problems and Practice*. 2nd edn. London: Harper and Row.

—— and Bruce Partridge. 1982. *Lost Managers: Supervisors in Industry and Society*. Cambridge: Cambridge University Press.

Clark, D. G. 1966. *The Industrial Manager: His Background and Career Pattern*. London: Business Publications.

Clark, Kim B. 1980. 'The Impact of Unionization on Productivity: A Case Study', *Industrial and Labor Relations Review*, Vol. 33, July, 451–69.

Clegg, Hugh Armstrong. 1979. *The Changing System of Industrial Relations in Great Britain*. Oxford: Blackwell.

Clements, R. V. 1958. *Managers: A Study of Their Careers in Industry*. London: Allen and Unwin.

Cowling, Keith. 1982. *Monopoly Capitalism*. London: Macmillan.

Cressey, Peter, and John MacInnes. 1980. 'Voting for Ford: Industrial Democracy and the Control of Labour', *Capital and Class*, no. 11, 5–33.

Cressey, Peter, John Eldridge, John MacInnes, and Geoffrey Norris. 1981. *Industrial Democracy and Participation: A Scottish Survey*. Department of Employment Research Paper 28. London: HMSO.

Crockett, Geoffrey, and Peter Elias. 1981. 'British Managers: A Study of Their Education, Training, Mobility and Earnings', Discussion Paper 13, June, Manpower Research Group, University of Warwick.

—— 1984. 'British Managers: A Study of Their Education, Training, Mobility and Earnings', *British Journal of Industrial Relations*, Vol. 22, March, 34–46.

Daniel, W. W., and Neil Millward. 1983. *Workplace Industrial Relations in Britain*. London: Heinemann.

Dawkins, Peter, and Derek Bosworth. 1980. 'Shiftworking and Unsocial Hours', *Industrial Relations Journal*. Vol. 11, March, 32–40.

Deaton, David. 1985. 'Management Style and Large-Scale Survey Evidence', *Industrial Relations Journal*, Vol. 16, Summer, 67–71.

Deeks, John. 1972. 'Educational and Occupational Histories of Owner-Managers and Managers', *Journal of Management Studies*, Vol. 9, May, 123–49.

Edwards, P. K. 1985. 'Myth of the Macho Manager', *Personnel Management*, April, 32–5.

—— 1986a. *Conflict at Work: A Materialist Analysis of Workplace Relations*. Oxford: Blackwell.

—— 1986b. 'Industrial Relations: Challenges and Prospects. A Report on the Warwick Conference of March 1986', Warwick Papers in Industrial Relations, no. 6, May. Coventry: Industrial Relations Research Unit.

—— and Hugh Scullion. 1982a. 'The Local Organisation of a National Dispute: The British 1979 Engineering Strike', *Industrial Relations Journal*, Vol. 13, Spring, 57–63.

—— and Hugh Scullion. 1982b. *The Social Organization of Industrial Conflict: Control and Resistance in the Workplace*. Oxford: Blackwell.

Edwards, Richard. 1979. *Contested Terrain: The Transformation of the Workplace in the Twentieth Century*. London: Heinemann.

Ellis, Tony, and John Child. 1973. 'Placing Stereotypes of the Manager into

Perspective', *Journal of Management Studies*, Vol. 10, October, 233–55.

Evans, Stephen, John Goodman, and Leslie Hargreaves. 1985. *Unfair Dismissal Law and Employment Practice in the 1980s*. Department of Employment Research Paper 53. London: HMSO.

Ferner, Anthony, and Michael Terry. 1985. ' "The Crunch had Come": A Case Study of Changing Industrial Relations in the Post Office', Warwick Papers in Industrial Relations, no. 1, November. Coventry: Industrial Relations Research Unit.

Fidler, John. 1981. *The British Business Elite: Its Attitudes to Class, Status and Power*. London: Routledge and Kegan Paul.

Freeman, Richard B., and James L. Medoff. 1984a. *What Do Unions Do?* New York: Basic.

—— 1984b. 'Trade Unions and Productivity: Some New Evidence on an Old Issue', *Annals* of the American Academy of Political and Economic Science, Vol. 473, May, 149–64.

Gill, R. W. T., and K. G. Lockyer, n.d. (1978?) *The Career Development of the Production Manager in British Industry*. London: British Institute of Management Foundation.

Goldsmith, Walter, and David Clutterbuck. 1984. *The Winning Streak: Britain's Top Companies Reveal their Formulas for Success*. London: Weidenfeld and Nicolson.

Goldthorpe, John H. 1980. *Social Mobility and Class Structure in Modern Britain*. Oxford: Clarendon.

—— and Keith Hope. 1974. *The Social Grading of Occupations: A New Approach and Scale*. Oxford: Clarendon.

Gordon, David M. 1981. 'Capital–Labor Conflict and the Productivity Slowdown', *American Economic Review Papers and Proceedings*, Vol. 71, May, 30–5.

Gregory, Mary, Peter Lobban, and Andrew Thomson. 1985. 'Wage Settlements in Manufacturing, 1979–84: Evidence from the CBI Pay Databank', *British Journal of Industrial Relations*, Vol. 23, November, 339–58.

Grzyb, Gerard J. 1981. 'Decollectivization and Recollectivization in the Workplace: The Impact of Technology on Informal Work Groups and Work Culture', *Economic and Industrial Democracy*, Vol. 2, November, 483–520.

Guerrier, Yvonne, and Nigel Philpott. 1978. *The British Manager: Careers and Mobility*. London: British Institute of Management.

Hill, C. W. L., and J. F. Pickering, 1986. 'Divisionalization, Decentralization and Performance of Large United Kingdom Companies', *Journal of Management Studies*, Vol. 23, January, 26–50.

Hirsch, Barry T., and Albert N. Link. 1984. 'Unions, Productivity, and Productivity Growth', *Journal of Labor Research*, Vol. 5, Winter, 29–37.

Horne, J. H., and Tom Lupton. 1965. 'The Work Activities of "Middle" Managers: An Exploratory Study', *Journal of Management Studies*, Vol. 2, February, 14–33.

Hyman, Richard. 1986. 'Flexible Specialisation: Miracle or Myth?', paper to EGOS Colloquium on 'Trade Unions, New Technology, and Industrial Democracy', University of Warwick, June.

Ichniowski, Casey. 1984a. 'Ruling out Productivity? Labor Contract Pages and Plant Performance', National Bureau of Economic Research, Working Paper 1368.

Ichniowski, Casey. 1984b. 'Industrial Relations and Economic Performance: Grievances and productivity', Alfred P. Sloan School of Management Working Paper 1567–84.

Institute of Personnel Management. 1979. *Disciplinary Procedures and Practice*. London: IPM.

Joyce, Paul, and Adrian Woods. 1984. 'Joint Consultation in Britain: Results of a Survey During the Recession', *Employee Relations*, Vol. 6, no. 3, 2–7.

Kanter, Rosabeth Moss. 1984. *The Change Masters: Corporate Entrepreneurs at Work*. London: Allen and Unwin.

Kinnie, Nicholas. 1985. 'Local Managers' Control over Industrial Relations: Myth and Reality', *Personnel Review*, Vol. 14, no. 2, 2–10.

Lawson, Tony. 1981. 'Paternalism and Labour Market Segmentation Theory'. *The Dynamics of Labour Market Segmentation*. Ed. Frank Wilkinson. London: Academic Press, 47–66.

Lee, Gloria L. 1981. *Who Gets to the Top? A Sociological Study of Business Executives*. Aldershot: Gower.

Leggatt, Timothy, 1978. 'Managers in Industry: Their Background and Education', *Sociological Review*, Vol. 26, November, 807–25.

Littler, Craig R., and Graeme Salaman. 1982. 'Bravermania and Beyond: Recent Theories of the Labour Process', *Sociology*, Vol. 16, May, 251–69.

MacInnes, John. 1985. 'Conjuring up Consultation: The Role and Extent of Joint Consultation in Postwar Private Manufacturing Industry', *British Journal of Industrial Relations*, Vol. 23, March, 93–113.

Mackay, Lesley. 1986. 'The Macho Manager: It's No Myth', *Personnel Management*, January, 25–7.

Marginson, Paul M., 1984. 'The Distinctive Effects of Plant and Company Size on Workplace Industrial Relations', *British Journal of Industrial Relations*, Vol. 22, March, 1–14.

Marples, D. L. 1967. 'Studies of Managers: A Fresh Start?', *Journal of Management Studies*, Vol. 4, October, 282–99.

Marsh, Arthur. 1982. *Employee Relations Policy and Decision-Making: A Survey of Manufacturing Companies Carried out for the Confederation of British Industry*. Aldershot: Gower.

Melrose-Woodman, J. 1978. *Profile of the British Manager*. London: British Institute of Management, Management Survey Report 38.

Mintzberg, Henry. 1970. 'Structured Observation as a Method to Study Managerial Work', *Journal of Management Studies*, Vol. 7, February, 87–104.

Nichols, Theo, and Huw Beynon. 1977. *Living with Capitalism*. London: Routledge and Kegan Paul.

Pencavel, John H. 1977. 'The Distributional and Efficiency Effects of Trade Unions in Britain', *British Journal of Industrial Relations*, Vol. 15, July, 137–56.

Peters, Thomas J., and Robert H. Waterman. 1982. *In Search of Excellence: Lessons from America's Best-Run Companies*. New York: Harper and Row.

Piore, Michael, and Charles Sabel. 1984. *The Second Industrial Divide*. New York: Basic.

Poole, Michael, Roger Mansfield, Paul Blyton, and Paul Frost. 1981. *Managers in Focus: The British Manager in the Early 1980s*. Aldershot: Gower.

Purcell, John. 1982. 'Macho Managers and the New Industrial Relations', *Employee Relations*, Vol. 4, no. 1, 3–5.

—— 1983. 'The Management of Industrial Relations in the Modern Corporation: An Agenda for Research', *British Journal of Industrial Relations*, Vol. 21, March, 1–16.

—— 1985. 'Is Anybody Listening to the Corporate Personnel Department?', *Personnel Management*, September, 28–32.

—— and Keith Sisson. 1983. 'Strategies and Practice in the Management of Industrial Relations', *Industrial Relations in Britain*, ed. George Sayers Bain. Oxford: Blackwell, 95–120.

Roots, Paul. 1986. 'Collective Bargaining: Opportunities for a New Approach', Warwick Papers in Industrial Relations, no. 5, April. Coventry: Industrial Relations Research Unit.

Sisson, Keith, and Hugh Scullion. 1985. 'Putting the Corporate Personnel Department in Its Place', *Personnel Management*, December, 36–9.

Slichter, Sumner H. 1941. *Union Policies and Industrial Management*. Washington, DC: Brookings Institution.

—— James J. Healy, and E. Robert Livernash. 1960. *The Impact of Collective Bargaining on Management*. Washington DC: Brookings Institution.

Sofer, Cyril. 1970. *Men in Mid-career: A Study of British Managers and Technical Specialists*. Cambridge: Cambridge University Press.

Stanworth, Philip, and Anthony Giddens (ed). 1974a. *Elites and Power in British Society*. Cambridge: Cambridge University Press.

—— 1974b. 'An Economic Elite: A Demographic Profile of Company Chairmen', in Stanworth and Giddens, 1974a, 81–101.

Steer, Peter, and John Cable. 1978. 'Internal Organization and Profit: An Empirical Analysis of Large UK Companies', *Journal of Industrial Economics*, Vol. 27, September, 13–30.

Storey, John. 1980. *The Challenge to Management Control*. London: Kogan Page.

Streeck, Wolfgang, 1986. 'Industrial Relations and Industrial Change in the Motor Industry: An International View', text of a Public Lecture at the University of Warwick. Coventry: Industrial Relations Research Unit.

Thomas, David. 1985. 'New Ways of Working', *New Society*, 30 August.

Thompson, Paul. 1983. *The Nature of Work: An Introduction to Debates on the Labour Process*. London: Macmillan.

Toner, Bill. 1985. 'The Unionisation and Productivity Debate: An Employee Opinion Survey in Ireland', *British Journal of Industrial Relations*, Vol. 23, July, 179–202.

Try, Peter. 1985. 'The Changing Role of the Mechanical Engineering Craftsman', MA Thesis (Industrial Relations), University of Warwick.

Turnbull, Peter. 1986. 'The "Japanisation" of Production and Industrial Relations at Lucas Electrical', *Industrial Relations Journal*, Vol. 17, no. 3, forthcoming.

Upton, Graham J. G. 1978. *The Analysis of Cross-tabulated Data*. Chichester: Wiley.

Watson, Tony J. 1977. *The Personnel Managers: A Study in the Sociology of Work and Employment*. London: Routledge and Kegan Paul.

Whitley, Richard. 1974. 'The City and Industry: The Directors of Large Companies: Their Characteristics and Connections', in Stanworth and Giddens, 1974a, 65–80.

244   *References*

Williamson, Oliver E. 1970. *Corporate Control and Business Behavior*. Engle-
wood Cliffs: Prentice-Hall.
—— 1975. *Markets and Hierarchies: Analysis and Antitrust Implications*. New
York: Free Press.
Willman, Paul, and Graham Winch. 1985. *Innovation and Management Control:
Labour Relations at BL Cars*. Cambridge: Cambridge University Press.
Winkler, J. T. 1974. 'The Ghost at the Bargaining Table: Directors and Industrial Relations', *British Journal of Industrial Relations*, Vol. 12, July,
191–212.

Index

monitoring of plant performance
policy or philosophy applied to labour
relations, 135–52
and productivity, 167–8, 202
stress on involvement and commitment
of, 5, 86–7, 138–46
Poole, M., 6, 36, 43
Post Office, 151
posts held in present firm, number of
career path(s) and, 45, 46, 61, 65
and corporate status of plant(s), 45
and factory managers' attitudes to
company management, 76, 77
and movement between firms, 45, 46
and personal flexibility, 69, 71
Price, R., 6, 21n.7
product demand
falling, 28
increase in, 27–8, 29
and shift working, 31–3
see also market demand
product market
competition, *see* competition
and factory managers' attitudes to
company management, 76
and personal flexibility, 69, 70, 74, 75
production costs, factory managers'
attitudes to company management
and, 79, 82
production manager, presence of, 34
productivity
and changes in working practices, 126,
127
and company control(s), 103, 104–5
definition of, 103, 161–2, 170
factory managers' attitudes to
company management and, 169,
180, 182, 183, 184
'hard' data on, 13, 14, 188n.1
Harvard school model of, 14, 156–7,
160–1, 164, 166, 170–6, 183,
184–5, 189–90n.9, 190n.11, 201–2
'In Search of Excellence' model of,
13–14, 157–8, 159–60, 161,
166–70, 183, 184
and labour relations, 187
and level of decision-making, 103, 104,
169
and 'loose–tight' link between plants
and head office, 110
and monitoring of plant performance,
103, 104, 169–70, 177–8, 180, 184,
186, 199–200, 206
need for further research on, 201–2
payment-by-results schemes and, 172,
173, 176, 178
and perceived importance of labour

matters in overall decision-
making, 110, 167
possible costs of, 187–8
and share ownership, 52, 169, 177,
178, 180, 182–4
structure of work force and, 171, 178
and unionization, 14, 156–7, 164, 166,
170–6, 178, 184–5, 189–90n.9,
190n.11, 201–2
use of industry-level measures to
explain, 162
use of plant-level measures to explain,
162–3, 170, 172, 176, 189n.5,
189n.6
Warwick Survey data on, 160–1, 163,
170–6, 189n.5
profit centre(s)
and company performance
company size and level of, 26
definition of, 26, 107
as indication of plants' place within
firms, 26
proportion of plants treated as, 26,
107
profit targets, monitoring of, 105, 107
profit-sharing schemes, factory managers'
attitudes to company management
and, 82
profitability, company
changes in, 27, 29
definition of, 161
and factory managers' attitudes to
company management, 76, 79, 82,
84
and personal flexibility, 69, 75, 82, 83
see also company performance;
productivity
profitability, plant, 5
and 'critical' stance towards company
management, 82
diversity in, 29
and personal flexibility, 70
see also financial performance of
plant(s)
'progressive' firms, 83
Purcell, J., 2, 3, 4, 10, 91, 99, 100, 115,
136–7, 141, 142, 147, 153n.8, 166
Pye electronics firm, 144

recession
diversity of effects of, 28–9
impact on firms' bargaining power of,
4, 147, 192
and strike action, 120
relationship between plant(s) and
firm(s), 9–12, 90–3
discussed in previous studies, 9–10, 11,